The Handwriting of God

Sacred Mysteries of the Bible

Grant R. Jeffrey

Frontier Research Publications, Inc.
P.O. Box 129, Station "U", Toronto, Ontario M8Z 5M4

The Handwriting of God

Library of Congress Cataloging in Publication Data:
Jeffrey, Grant R.
The Handwriting of God
1. Apologetics   2. Eschatology   3. Bible and Science
4. Witnessing
1. Title

October 1997, Frontier Research Publications, Inc.

ISBN 0-921714-38-6

Unless otherwise indicated, Scripture quotations are from the Authorized King James Version.

Cover design: The Riordan Design Group
Printed in Canada: Harmony Printing Limited

COMMENTS ON GRANT JEFFREY'S
SEVEN BEST SELLING BOOKS

ARMAGEDDON   MESSIAH
APOCALYPSE   THE PRINCE OF DARKNESS
FINAL WARNING   THE SIGNATURE OF GOD
HEAVEN

"Grant Jeffrey has written an extraordinary new book, *The Signature of God*, that provides astonishing proof that the Bible was inspired by God. Grant is recognized as the leading researcher in Bible Prophecy today."
Hal Lindsey, Hal Lindsey Ministries

"*Prince of Darkness* was written by acclaimed Bible Prophecy teacher Grant R. Jeffrey. This unequaled masterpiece is the result of 30 years of intense research. It will stir you and inspire you as few books have. . . . It is extremely well written — extraordinarily researched and fascinatingly presented . . . this is the best book I have ever read on this subject."

"Grant's book *Messiah* is one of the finest fact-jammed prophecy books I've ever read. . . . It is well written, solidly scriptural, fully documented and extremely easy to read and understand . . . this astounding book will enlighten and inspire you and your friends."
Jack Van Impe, Jack Van Impe Ministries

"Grant Jeffrey . . . is now a bestselling author throughout North America. . . . His breakthrough book was his first, *Armageddon: Appointment With Destiny*. . . . Bantam Books later picked it up, and it turned out to be their No. 1 religious best seller in 1990."
Philip Marchand, Book Review Editor, Toronto Star, Aug. 1, 1992

"We need to have a biblically-based outlook on Bible prophecy. That's why we are featuring Grant Jeffrey in our magazine. His book *Armageddon: Appointment With Destiny* explores the amazingly accurate fulfillment of past prophecies, and examines the prophecies that relate to this time period leading to the Second Coming of Christ."
Jerry Rose: Past President, National Religious Broadcasters

"*Armageddon: Appointment With Destiny* has been our hottest single religious title. . . . We took it on with tremendous enthusiasm because there was something very exciting about the way Grant wrote, and it was something that we thought might go beyond the traditional religious audience."
Lou Arnonica, Vice Pres. Bantam Books, New York Times, Oct. 22, 1990

Table of Contents

Acknowledgements

The Handwriting of God is the result of countless hours of research involving thousands of books, articles, and commentaries, plus countless hours of Bible study over the last thirty-five years. Although almost one hundred volumes are referred to in the footnotes and selected bibliography, these books represent a fraction of the authors who have influenced and challenged my thinking. However, the inspired Word of God is the major source and continual guide to my studies.

The Bible is under relentless attack today in the universities, the seminaries, and the media. Yet everything we believe as Christians, our hope for salvation and heaven itself, depends upon the total truthfulness and trustworthiness of the sacred Scriptures. I believe it is time for Christians to stand up and launch a vigorous defence of the inspiration and authority of the Word of God. *The Handwriting of God* is a small contribution to that defence of the authority of Scripture. This book continues the theme established in my last book, *The Signature of God*, that the Lord has clearly placed within the sacred pages of the Holy Bible evidence that should convince any inquiring mind that the Bible is the true and inspired Word of God.

My parents, Lyle and Florence Jeffrey, have inspired within me a profound love for Jesus Christ and His holy Word. Their encouragement over the years means so much to me.

A very special thanks to Adrienne Jeffrey, my niece, who has worked very closely with me through this entire project in the research and editing.

My heartfelt appreciation to Nancy Phillips, whose superb editorial skills have made this manuscript complete.

I dedicate*The Handwriting of God* to my lovely wife, Kaye, who is my inspiration, my faithful partner in ministry, and the manager of our publishing company.

I trust that the information revealed in the following pages will encourage you to personally study the Word of God and come to know Jesus of Nazareth in a deeper way.

Grant R. Jeffrey,
Toronto, Ontario
October 1997

Introduction

Can we trust the Bible? Does Scripture present the truth about God, mankind, and eternity? Is Christianity credible? Can we rationally believe that Jesus of Nazareth actually rose from the dead two thousand years ago? Is Jesus Christ truly the only way of salvation for mankind? Is it possible, as we approach the year 2000, for an intelligent person to still believe that the ancient Scriptures are truly the inspired Word of God? Is the Bible truly "without error" and trustworthy, despite the growing attacks on its authority in our generation? The answers to these questions are vital if we are to arrive at any meaningful conclusions about the Bible's claim that it alone is the genuine written revelation of God.

The Bible is certainly the most fascinating and controversial book ever written. The Word of God is unique among religious and philosophical literature. No other book in history has boldly and repeatedly made the absolute claim that it alone is the unique and authoritative revelation of God to humanity. The Bible declares in over three thousand verses that it is the Word of God. Both the Old and New Testaments abound with statements such as "saith the Lord." (Exodus 4:22; Hebrews 8:8).

The Bible is under relentless attack today both in the universities, the seminaries, and the media. Yet everything we believe as Christians, our hope for salvation and heaven itself depends upon the total truthfulness and trustworthiness of the sacred Scriptures.

In the first few centuries of this era Christianity suffered greatly from its outward enemy, pagan Rome. However, in the final generation as we look for Christ's return the greatest attacks on the fundamental beliefs of the Church come from those who profess to be Christians while abandoning every one of the tenets of the orthodox faith that have been defended by believers for two thousand years. I believe it is time for orthodox Christians to stand up and launch a vigorous defence of the inspiration and authority of the Word of God. *The Handwriting of God* is a small contribution to that defence of the authority of Scripture. This book continues the theme established in my last book *The Signature of God* that the Lord has clearly placed within the sacred pages of the holy Bible evidence that should convince any inquiring mind that the Bible is the true and inspired Word of God. I hope to provide you with the evidence from the words of Scripture together with the evidence from science, history, and the Bible Codes that proves that the Bible is truly the Word of God.

The issue that must be addressed by every inquirer is the question of the literal truthfulness and spiritual authority of the written revelation of God as it appears in the Bible. Is every passage in the Bible equally inspired, or are there statements that are purely human or passages that reflect an inaccurate knowledge of science? This is a fundamental question. Its resolution is vital for every human who desires to know the truth about God and eternity. For two thousand years, hundreds of millions of Christians have accepted without question that the Bible is an absolute "rule of faith."

In the strongest terms the apostle Paul declared that the Scriptures were written under the direction and authority of Almighty God. Paul wrote the following words to his disciple Timothy: "All scripture is given by inspiration of God, and is profitable for doctrine, for reproof, for correction, for instruction in righteousness" (2 Timothy 3:16). It is clear that the doctrine of the infallible Scripture is directly related to the divine sovereignty of God. If God is truly the supernatural Creator of the universe, then His written revelation would display the same characteristics of His sovereign, supernatural nature. The sovereignty of God's nature guarantees the accuracy of His written record.

Both Christianity and Judaism are historical religions whose faith and doctrines are based directly on historical events that were recorded by human authors in the Holy Scriptures. Christianity is based directly on the facts of the death and resurrection of Jesus of Nazareth, as prophesied in the Old Testament and fulfilled in the historical accounts of the Gospels. These remarkable events were observed by hundreds of living witnesses who were still alive when the written accounts were first distributed throughout the Roman Empire. This fact alone establishes their truthfulness to anyone who carefully considers the issue. Christianity would have died stillborn had the eyewitnesses to the miracles of Jesus and the events of his crucifixion and resurrection denied the accuracy of these supernatural accounts in the written Gospel accounts. Christianity could never have survived, let alone have flourished, in the first century if the Gospel accounts had been untrue.

The Bible declares that the whole of God's creation reveals His majesty and glory. The Psalmist David wrote these words three thousand years ago: "The heavens declare the glory of God; and the firmament showeth his handiwork. Day unto day uttereth speech, and night unto night showeth knowledge. There is no speech nor language, where their voice is not heard. Their line is gone out through all the earth, and their words to the end of the world. In them hath he set a tabernacle for the sun" (Psalms 19:1–4). However, while the glory of creation reveals, to any unbiased observer, that there must be a supernatural Creator, humanity needed a written revelation from God to confirm our relationship to Him and His plan to redeem us.

Despite the overwhelming evidence of God displayed by the wonders of creation, there are many people in our generation who still reject His existence and deny His divine revelation, the Bible. In this book we will explore astonishing scientific discoveries that provide overwhelming evidence that the Bible could not have been written by men alone. We will also examine fascinating new discoveries that will convince any impartial reader that the Scriptures were created thousands of years ago under the direction of a supernatural mind.

Despite the claims of the critics that the Scriptures are not historically accurate, the science of archeology discovers new evidence every month throughout the Middle East that establishes the absolute trustworthiness of scriptural accounts. We are living in the first time of human history that archeology is fulfilling the age-old prophecy of Habakkuk — the stones are speaking and revealing the knowledge of the Lord. This prophecy of Habakkuk was made over twenty-seven centuries ago. "For the stone shall cry out of the wall, and the beam out of the timber shall answer it. . . . For the earth shall be filled with the knowledge of the glory of the Lord, as the waters cover the sea" (Habakkuk 2:11, 14).

Some have responded that they personally feel no need to examine proof of the authority of the Scriptures. However, there are millions of people in our society that have heard so many attacks on the credibility of the Bible that they find it hard to believe any statements found in the Word of God. Those in honest pursuit of truth deserve to have their questions answered. As Christians, we are commanded by God to be able to give people a reason for our faith in Jesus Christ. The apostle Peter advised us as follows: "But sanctify the Lord God in your hearts: and be ready always to give an answer to every man that asketh you a reason of the hope that is in you with meekness and fear" (1 Peter 3:15).

The Bible declares that every one of its words is inspired by Almighty God. The word "inspired" means that God over-shadowed the mind and spirit of the human writers of the Scriptures, motivating them to write the precise words as recorded in the Word of God. The apostle Paul declared that all of the Scriptures, from Genesis to Revelation, was inspired by God: "All scripture is given by inspiration of God, and is profitable for doctrine, for reproof, for correction, for instruction in righteous-ness" (2 Timothy 3:16). Jesus Christ declared that this inspiration included much more than simply the thoughts of the sentences or even the words used to express those thoughts. He boldly affirmed that the very grammar and the spelling of the words found in the original biblical manuscripts as written by its human authors were under the control of the supernatural inspiration of the Holy Spirit of God. The gospel writer Matthew recorded His declaration about the inspiration of the Word of God: "For verily I say unto you, Till heaven and earth pass, one jot or one tittle shall in no wise pass from the law, till all be fulfilled" (Matthew 5:18).

The Handwriting of God will examine a number of the sacred mysteries of the Bible, including the astonishing Bible Codes. It will provide fascinating insights into the nature of God's revelation to humanity. It is significant that the apostle Paul wrote, "Behold, I show you a mystery . . ." as he introduced the wonderful doctrine of the future resurrection of our bodies from the dead, when each Christian will receive a new body like the body Jesus Christ had after He arose from the grave. Part of the mystery surrounding the Holy Scriptures arises from the great chasm that stands between the time of its composition and the modern generation in which we now live. The huge gulf between the world of the human writers of the Bible and our world consists of two thousand years of time, language, history, and culture. Although the Scriptures were written thousands of years ago, they still communicate to us the timeless wisdom of God with fresh truth regarding our life and purpose as God's precious creation.

The Bible has often been referred to as "the greatest book ever written." It has captured the imagination and love of countless generations of readers who have found within its pages the truth about God and a hope of resurrection from death that awaits us all. The Scriptures have captivated people throughout the centuries with its fascinating stories about biblical heros and heroines who have succeeded against great odds through the supernatural power of God.

Naturally, the other major world religions reverence various written books that also claim to be the revelation of God. The religious books of other religions include the Koran of the Islamic peoples, the Veda and Upanishads of the Hindus, the Tripitaka, acknowledged by the Buddhists, and the Zend-Avesta of Zoroastrianism. It is fascinating to note that none of these other religious books claim divine inspiration (except for the Koran, as written by Mohammed). Interestingly, Mohammed acknowledged that the Bible is inspired by God. He called both Jews and Christians the "people of the Book," referring to our acceptance of the authority of the Bible as the written revelation of God. John Calvin, one of the greatest of the reformers leading the Protestant Reformation in Europe, spoke of the unique ability of this ancient Book to speak to Christians with the living voice of God. Calvin wrote, "It is only in the Scriptures that the Lord hath been pleased to preserve his truth in perpetual remembrance; it obtains the same complete credit and authority with believers, where they are satisfied of its divine origin, as if they heard the very words pronounced by God Himself" (John Calvin, *Institutes*, Vol. 1, 1536).

The word "Bible" is derived from the Greek word *biblios*,

meaning "book," which comes from the word *byblos*, referring to the papyrus reeds used to make the paper upon which the original words of Scriptures were written by the biblical authors. From the time of Christ until the fifth century of our era, the Scriptures were usually known by the name *biblia*, meaning "the books" of the Bible. However, from the fifth century on, the complete collection of sixty-six books composing the Old and New Testaments became known as *biblos*, or the "Bible."

The overwhelming value of the Bible, in comparison with all other writings that fill the libraries of nations, was illustrated quite well by an experiment conducted by a London newspaper several years ago. The editor of this well-known London newspaper sent a letter to one hundred of the most important leaders in a variety of fields throughout the United Kingdom. These leaders included powerful members of the House of Lords, members of parliament, respected university professors, well-known authors, and wealthy businessmen — a list that included a representative sample of those who lead British society. The question asked by the editor in his letter was this: "Suppose you were sent to prison for three years and you could only take three books with you. Which three would you choose? Please state them in order of their importance." The replies were fascinating. Ninety-eight of these leaders choose the same book as the first choice on their list — the Bible. More surprising than their choice of reading was the fact that very few of these men were religious. Most of them did not even attend church regularly, and others were open agnostics or atheists. However, these men knew in their heart, that there was no other book in existence that could give them hope, joy, and peace in the midst of the fear and loneliness they would feel, surrounded by those hypothetical prison walls.

The German writer Heinrich Heine wrote about the marvellous and universal nature of the Bible: "What a book great and wide as the world, rooted in the abysmal depths of creation and rising aloft into the blue mysteries of heaven. . . . Sunrise and sunset, promise and fulfillment, birth and death, the whole human drama, everything is in this book. . . . It is the book of books, the Bible" (*Ludwig Boerne*, 1840).

There are a number of unique features of the Bible that provide overwhelming evidence that the Scriptures are truly inspired by God. The Word of God is unique among all other religious writings of man, as indicated by the features discussed below.

The Authority of the Bible

Moses and the prophets of the Old Testament repeatedly affirmed that they wrote the Bible under the direction of the Holy Spirit of God. More than 2500 times throughout the Old Testament the writers used expressions such as "This is what the Lord says," or "The word of the Lord came to . . ." to affirm the divine authority for their inspired statements. In addition, the New Testament continually declares that both it and the Old Testament were inspired by God. The apostle Paul wrote, "All scripture is given by inspiration of God, and is profitable for doctrine, for reproof, for correction, for instruction in righteousness" (2 Timothy 3:16). It is significant that the last book of the New Testament, the book of Revelation, confirms the inspiration of the Bible in its condemnation of anyone who would eliminate or change the words of Scripture. The apostle John warned, "And if any man shall take away from the words of the book of this prophecy, God shall take away his part out of the book of life, and out of the holy city, and from the things which are written in this book" (Revelation 22:19).

The Remarkable Unity of the Bible

The process by which the Bible was actually created is one of the greatest mysteries of the ages. The Bible contains sixty-six books written by forty-four men using three languages —- Hebrew, Aramaic, and Greek — over a period of sixteen centuries. No other book in history was written over such an extended period of time. Thirty-five centuries ago, Moses wrote the first five books of the Law, beginning with Genesis, which describes the creation of the whole universe, including mankind. Over the next millennium thirty-four other books were written by a diverse group of men as they were inspired by God to record a series of histories, laws, poetry, and prophecy. Finally a great man of God, Ezra, rose to unite the Jews into a renewed nation, following their return from seventy years of captivity in Babylon. In addition, Ezra was inspired by God to collect together all of the thirty-nine inspired books and to publish this as one collection called the Scriptures. Finally, at the end of the first century of the Christian era, the apostle John completed his astonishing prophecy, called the Revelation, which completed the canon of the New Testament. The Bible was written by men from widely different backgrounds including kings, generals, shepherds, prophets, tax collectors, and fishermen. Some of these writers were highly educated, such as Luke the physician and the brilliant Jewish teacher Paul. Other books of the Bible were written by uneducated men, including the shepherd Amos and Peter, a fisherman. Despite the radically different backgrounds of the writers who composed the message of the Bible over a period of sixteen hundred years, the Scriptures speak with one voice in its presentation of God's progressive revelation of His plan to redeem us from the consequences of our sinful rebellion.

There is no question that the Bible is the oldest book in the world with the most ancient portions written by Moses and Job approximately thirty-five hundred years ago. It is truly marvellous that this ancient writing is read by hundreds of millions of people every day in their search for the truths of God in the pages of the Scriptures. Another mystery is that although the Bible is the oldest book in the world and far and away the most published book in history with billions of copies in print, the sales of Bibles throughout the world in vast numbers of translations and versions is unprecedented. Despite the billions of copies of the Scripture in print, hundreds of millions of new Bibles are purchased throughout the world every year. Scholars estimate that over a billion people representing every nation and class of people on the planet call themselves Christians. Despite the diversity of writers and themes, the most brilliant men throughout history have reverently acknowledged that this book is the greatest literary masterpiece ever penned by man. Lastly, the very survival of the Bible in the face of the greatest persecution and censorship over thousands of years is inexplicable unless God preserved this book as His inspired gospel of salvation through the blood of Jesus Christ. The powerful, life-changing spiritual impact of the Bible on the lives of billions of readers is unprecedented in history.

1

Can We Trust the Bible As the Inspired Word of God?

During numerous conversations over the last few years, I have often been asked why I believe that the Bible can be trusted as the authoritative Word of God. These questions are legitimate and deserve to be answered. Fortunately, answers to these questions are available. *The Handwriting of God* will attempt to provide intelligent answers to the many questions raised by individuals who are honestly seeking the truth about God and those who want to know whether or not they can trust the Bible. Some of the questions addressed include the following:

Why should we believe that the Bible is the only genuine revelation of God when the world is full of hundreds of religious books that claim to reveal the wisdom of God to mankind?

Does the Bible bear any peculiar characteristics that uniquely identify the Scriptures as the only genuine revelation of God?

In what way is the Bible unique from all other religious books that claim our attention?

The Bible's claim to be the true Word of God has been widely rejected by philosophers, theologians, academic scholars, and millions of laymen in our generation. Why then should we pay attention to the message of this ancient book?

The Denial of the Verbal Inspiration of Scripture

The Bible claims that the very words of Scripture were inspired by God as His authoritative revelation to humanity. "The grass withereth, the flower fadeth: but the word of our God shall stand for ever" (Isaiah 40:8). However, it is very common today to find liberal theologians, mainline pastors, and the secular media expressing a complete denial of the verbal inspiration of the Scriptures. Tragically, there are some who belong to conservative denominations, which have historically upheld the doctrine of verbal and plenary inspiration of the Scriptures, who are beginning to experience doubts about the fundamental doctrines of the Christian faith and the inspiration of the Scriptures. Those who have retreated from the ancient doctrine and inspiration of Scripture suggest that there may be some inaccuracy in the words that have been transmitted down through the centuries. Logically, however, any inaccuracy in the text of the Bible would naturally involve inaccuracy in the statements of the Bible. These doubters even suggest the possibility of errors in the doctrines of the Bible's written revelation. This suggestion of inaccuracy is simply wrong.

The denial of verbal and plenary inspiration is also a denial of the supernatural power of God to both inspire the original writers and to preserve His message through the ages to communicate His doctrines to mankind. Logically, if the Bible contains inaccurate language, then it naturally follows that the text contains inaccurate statements, and therefore, we cannot have confidence in the authority of any scriptural doctrine. Such reasoning would replace the Bible's authoritative declarations such as "Thus saith the Lord," that have guided Christians for two thousand years with vague and tentative notions, such as "this biblical statement may (or may not) contain the words of God." This liberal approach of denying the accuracy of the Scriptures strips the Bible of its authority and weakens its usefulness as a rule of life for those who seek to follow God's will for their lives.

Sometimes people's motive for the denial of verbal inspiration is the desire to evade the clear teaching of the Scriptures in some area that restricts their immorality or freedom of action. This approach to the Bible is ultimately founded on an assumption of inaccuracy in both the words and the specific teachings of the Scriptures. In the end, this position will inevitably lead to a denial of the Bible itself, and finally, a denial of the supernatural claims of Jesus Christ as God, who is the One who reveals His will to us through the pages of Scripture.

Consider the implications of the position held by those who deny the verbal inspiration of the Bible. If God is truly a supernatural being who has caused these forty-four men to write His message, then what are we to make of the proposition that He was either unwilling or unable to cause these men to accurately record His revelation to humanity? If God is truly God then it is obvious that He could both accurately inspire the human authors to precisely record His message to humanity, as well as supernaturally preserve these precious words of spiritual wisdom through the centuries by ensuring the careful copying of the Scriptures by both the Jewish scribes and later the Christian scholars.

I cannot image a God who desired to convey His instructions for life, salvation, and eternity to a lost humanity who would be unwilling or unable to preserve His written revelation so that each generation would receive the genuine Word of God. The question of the trustworthiness of the Bible is one that is fundamental to all those who take the Scriptures seriously. The issue of our personal salvation is at stake. If the Bible is truly the inspired Word of God then we can have confidence as Christians in our eternal salvation. If the Bible is partially the Word of God and partially filled with human speculation, contradictions, scientific and historical errors, then it is a totally different Bible than the book that has been read reverently by Christians for the last two thousand years. If we cannot trust the Bible to tell us the truth on every page than we are left without any reason for confidence in our salvation. Therefore, the question of whether or not we can trust the Bible as the inspired and authoritative Word of God is one that everyone of us needs to determine for ourselves.

One of the glories of true science is that discoveries are as true today as they were when the first researcher made the original discovery. Statements that are true do not change as a result of the passage of time. When we proclaim the biblically demonstrated truth about God and salvation as found in the pages of the Bible, we are dealing with true statements inspired by God thousands of years ago. His words are as true today as they were when the Holy Spirit of God first inspired His prophets to record His unchanging revelation to those who seek the truth of God. While we constantly seek to expand our knowledge of science, history, et cetera, we do not progress by abandoning those things from our past that have been proven to be true. Rather, we build on the truth of past understanding and seek further understanding of God's revelation by continued study of His inspired Word.

Consider the attitude displayed by those who deny the inspiration of the Word of God. If these scholars truly loved the doctrines of God, but were forced by their textual and scientific discoveries to reluctantly abandon the doctrine of inspiration of Scripture, you would expect that they would announce with sorrow in their hearts that Christians could no longer be confident that the Bible was absolutely accurate and divinely inspired. However, after three decades of reading numerous articles and books written by those who deny the inspiration of the Bible, I believe the evidence is overwhelming that those who attack the verbal inspiration of the Scriptures do so with great fervor and enthusiasm. Rather than sadly express a reluctant conclusion that they no longer believe that the Bible contains the true words of God, these liberal religious writers almost invariably denigrate the so-called "ignorant" and "unlearned" views of those Christians who defend the orthodox belief that the Bible contains the true Word of God.

Truth is unchangeable. Truth and scientific knowledge advance as new discoveries are added to our store of knowledge. While researchers constantly add to their knowledge, those scientific discoveries that were true a century ago remain true today. When we expand our understanding of an area of study, we add additional facts without abandoning true statements discovered in the past. The only way modern theology can legitimately abandon past biblical doctrines is on the basis that they are now found to be false, not simply that they are old. The attempt to repudiate orthodox Christian beliefs based on the Bible on the basis that they are "obsolete" is simply a manifestation of cultural bias or the modern infatuation for that which is new or novel, at the expense of timeless and fundamental truth. When modern theologians claim that fundamental Christian doctrines are "not suited to our generation," they are actually condemning the attitudes of this generation. However, the unshakable truths of the Word of God remain true long after these theologians are forgotten. Just as genuine science can only progress on the basis of

its continuing adherence to the fundamental principles discovered in the past, it is equally true that genuine progress in our
understanding of theology will come from our continuing
adherence to the fundamental principles of biblical doctrine discovered through the ages by men of God who faithfully searched
the Scriptures to discover the doctrines of God.

Many people in our modern society cannot accept the reality
of the miracles and the supernatural events described in the pages
of the Bible. However, if there is a God, by definition, He is
supernatural and is therefore capable of both creating this
universe and producing the miracles described in the Scriptures.
A mother recently sent her son to a local Sunday School in the
hope that he would learn some values from the teaching of the
Bible. When he returned home she asked her son what his Sunday
School teacher had taught that morning. He replied, "Well, they
told us that the general Moses led his people to freedom from
slavery in Egypt. She told us how Moses used his radio to call in
an air-to-ground attack with advanced fighter planes and
powerful tanks to defeat the armies of the Egyptian pharaoh at the
Red Sea." His shocked mother questioned him further. "That isn't
how I remember my teachers telling me the story" she said.
"Well," said her son, "if I told you what the teacher actually said
you wouldn't believe me!"

This humorous account illustrates part of the problem modern
readers of the Bible have with the miracles and supernatural
elements of scriptural history. Yet, we cannot remove one part of
the supernatural element of the Bible without destroying its
integrity as the authoritative and inspired Word of God. The Bible
does not give its readers the option to pick and choose what parts
of the Bible appeal to us and to reject whatever we dislike. If the
Bible is what it claims to be, the inspired Word of God, then we are
faced with a fundamental choice: accept its authority or reject its
authority. However, many in our western society claim they are
Christians who love the Bible but yet reject large portions of its
testimony on the basis that they think that the Bible is out of date,
insensitive to modern social issues, and judgmental on certain
sexual behavior. They have set themselves up as judges of what
portions of the Bible pass their personal test of acceptability. How
can the Bible speak to them with authority regarding the eternal
issues of salvation, heaven, and hell when they are unsure

whether any particular passage of the Bible is actually inspired by God? Abandonment of any one issue in the Bible is an abandonment of the Bible in its entirety.

Those who denigrate the inspiration of Scripture often strongly assert that they have abandoned an outdated and ignorant view of the Bible. They claim they have replaced the outdated historic faith of the last two thousand years with a new sophisticated understanding that ignores the clear statements of Scripture and attempts to find the so-called "deeper meaning" of a "New Christianity" that has superseded the Gospel's literal statements about the historic Jesus of Nazareth. In the end liberal theologians abandon the very biblical principles that made Christianity powerful and capable of transforming the lives of men and women. These skeptics have replaced the living Christ with a New Age "Christianity." However, thousands of years ago, Jesus Christ Himself warned His disciples: "Ye are the salt of the earth: but if the salt have lost his savour, wherewith shall it be salted? It is thence forth good for nothing, but to be cast out, and to be trodden under foot of men" (Matthew 5:13). It is difficult for these people to worship fully the Jesus Christ that is revealed in the pages of the Scriptures when, in their minds, they have reduced the Scriptures to a collection of fallible opinions of human writers, who they believe were often mistaken in their statements.

However, a careful examination of the evidence will establish to the satisfaction of all unbiased readers that the Bible is truly the authoritative and inspired Word of God. In this controversy we should remember the inspired words of the apostle Peter: "For all flesh is as grass, and all the glory of man as the flower of grass. The grass withereth, and the flower thereof falleth away: But the word of the Lord endureth for ever. And this is the word which by the gospel is preached unto you" (1 Peter 1:24–25). The Jewish historian Flavius Josephus, who lived as a contemporary of the apostle Paul, wrote the following statement in his defense of the authority of the Word of God in his debate with Apion. In his description of the sacred books of the Old Testament, the historian Josephus declared that they wrote "according to the *pneustia* (inspiration) that comes from God." In another passage Josephus wrote, "After the lapse of so many centuries, no one among the Jews has dared to add or to take away, or to transpose any thing in the sacred Scriptures." Significantly, the Jewish scholar Philo, who lived from approximately 20 B.C. to A.D. 50, wrote about the authority of the Bible in his personal representation to the Roman Emperor Caligula. Philo stated that the oracles of the Old Testament Scriptures were *"theochrest oracles,"* which means that he declared that these Scriptures were produced under the authority and power of God Himself.

Does the Bible actually claim that it is truly inspired by God? Consider the scriptural evidence found in the words of the apostle Paul, who wrote the following declaration in his epistle to the Church in Rome: "What advantage then hath the Jew? Or what profit is there of circumcision? Much every way: chiefly, because that unto them were committed the oracles of God" (Romans 3:1–2). This statement by Paul affirms that the words of the Bible were not simply the words of men but that they were truly the inspired "oracles of God."

A Remarkable Description of How God Inspired the Scriptures

Throughout recorded history the proclamation of the message of the Bible has resulted in a response whose pattern appears predictable. First, the vast majority of the people reject the call of God to obedience and holiness in the Scriptures. Secondly, the elite religious, political, and business leaders almost invariably join this widespread rejection to the revelation of God's Word. Finally, a small minority of the people become believers in the Word of God and respond to the written revelation of God in personal repentance, obedience, and a genuine desire to see the will of God manifested in their lives and in the lives of their families. An example of the biblical record of this response is found in the words of Jeremiah the prophet, who was commanded to write his prophecies and deliver them to King Jehoiakim, the evil king of Judah. The nation of Judah was experiencing a period of total apostasy, under the leadership of King Jehoiakim, an evil king who hated God and His prophets. During these years of apostasy the Lord inspired His prophet Jeremiah to record His prophetic instructions to His Chosen People. While the leaders and the general population rejected God's written revelation, a small group of righteous individuals responded to the inspired Word of God with reverence and devotion.

This remarkable passage in the book of Jeremiah provides a unique insight into the process of how God actually inspired one of His prophets to record the direct words of God. It is fascinating to note that, even though the initial inspired words of God were physically destroyed by the actions of the evil king, God inspired His prophet Jeremiah to re-record these exact inspired words to preserve forever the declaration of God in the pages of the Bible. The prophet Jeremiah describes this event as follows:

> And it came to pass, that when Jehudi had read three or four leaves, he cut it with the penknife, and cast it into the fire that was on the hearth, until all the roll was consumed in the fire that was on the hearth. Yet they were not afraid, nor rent their garments, neither the king, nor any of his servants that heard all these words. Nevertheless Elnathan and Delaiah and Gemariah had made inter-cession to the king that he would not burn the roll: but he would not hear them. But the king commanded Jerahmeel the son of Hammelech, and Seraiah the son of Azriel, and Shelemiah the son of Abdeel, to take Baruch the scribe and Jeremiah the prophet: but the Lord hid them. Then the word of the Lord came to Jeremiah, after that the king had burned the roll, and the words which Baruch wrote at the mouth of Jeremiah, saying, *Take thee again another roll, and write in it all the former words that were in the first roll, which Jehoiakim the king of Judah hath burned.*
>
> (Jeremiah 36:23–28)

In this fascinating passage, the evil king of Judah actually burned in the fire the inspired written words of God recorded by Baruch, the scribe of Jeremiah the prophet, that warned of the coming judgment of God upon the wicked nation of Judah. Rather then repent of his sins, the wicked king Jehoiakim responded to the delivery of the written prophecy of Jeremiah by destroying the scroll. This destruction of the physical Bible has been attempted countless times throughout history, but the enemies of God have always failed to destroy His written message in the Scriptures. Just as King Jehoiakim tried to destroy the Scriptures, the evil Syrian king Antiochus Epiphanes attempted to eliminate the Bible when he ordered the burning of all of the religious scrolls in the Temple in 168 B.C. However, God overthrew the wicked king in

165 B.C. when the victorious family known as the Maccabees led the Jewish rebel soldiers to a miraculous victory over their pagan enemies. The Jews restored the system of sacrifice in the Temple, and the surviving Old Testament Scripture provided the inspired instruction that allowed the Jews to follow the Word of God.

Four and a half centuries later, the evil Roman emperor Diocletian ordered the destruction of the Scriptures throughout the Roman Empire in 303 A.D. However, to the amazement of the Christians, within a few years the miraculous conversion to faith in Christ by the Emperor Constantine ended three centuries of persecution against the Christians and their Holy Scriptures. In A.D. 325 Constantine, the emperor of Rome, sat down with the bishops of the Christian Church to affirm the essential beliefs of the faith based on the eternal Word of God. This remarkable history reveals that, despite great opposition to the Bible, the message of Jesus Christ continues to prosper. The history of this world shows that the Bible has triumphed over the violent opposition and indifference of evil men.

However, another key element in the revelation recorded in Jeremiah 36:23–28 is the precise record of how God inspired Jeremiah to create this inspired portion of the Word of God. Even though the king had physically burnt the original scroll in a fire, God commanded Jeremiah and his scribe to carefully re-create the scroll — word for word — exactly as the Lord dictated: "Take thee again another roll, and write in it all the former words that were in the first roll, which Jehoiakim the king of Judah hath burned" (Jeremiah 36:28).

The Original Manuscripts of the Scriptures

The above account is perhaps the most direct written record found in the Bible of how God actually inspired the human writer to record His precise revelation. This unusual biblical account described the destruction and replacement of the actual original manuscript on which the inspired prophet Jeremiah wrote the words of God. This account raises an interesting question regarding the original manuscripts of the Old and New Testament. When orthodox Christians affirm that the Bible is inspired and without error, they are referring to the original autographs or manuscripts, as written by biblical writers such as King David and the apostle Paul. Each translation in a modern language should attempt to reverently reproduce the inspired words of God in its own language. It is obvious that none of these original manuscripts are in our possession. Over the last several thousand years, these original manuscripts have been lost. As a result of the absence of these original manuscripts, some scholars have suggested that the claims that the original manuscripts are inspired and without error is meaningless. They are wrong. The claim that the original manuscripts are inspired and without error is fundamental and is supported by numerous statements from the Bible itself. Furthermore, the claim for inspiration of the original manuscripts protects us from the totally subjective interpretations of those who would deny the accuracy of the Word of God.

The tremendous scholarly work accomplished by the textual critics in the last century is supported by the exegesis or study of the historical background and grammar. The result of this scholarly work is that we have a high degree of confidence that the surviving manuscript copies of the Hebrew Old Testament and the Greek New Testament manuscripts are correct and accurate copies of the original manuscripts written by the biblical authors. The important point to note is that, as long as the words of the original manuscript were correctly and perfectly copied over the centuries, we still possess the precise inspired words of God.

As we will see in a later chapter that explores the astonishing phenomenon of the Bible Codes, recent discoveries by computer analysis of the Hebrew text of the Old Testament provide remarkable evidence that God has preserved the integrity of His Holy Scriptures from the time of their writing until today. Sometimes people have come to an incorrect assumption that there is major confusion as to the correct text of the Hebrew and Greek manuscripts that are translated into our present Old and New Testaments. However, the reality is that there is a tremendous degree of agreement between both liberal and conservative scholars as to the best text of the Bible in the original languages. Therefore, we have tremendous confidence that the Bible in our hands is an accurate transmission in our modern language of the inspired words of God, as delivered to the biblical authors thousands of years ago.

Does the Bible Claim That It Is Inspired and Infallible?

The Bible repeatedly declares that it is inspired directly by God Himself and that it is free from error. Several examples will prove this point. The Torah reveals that God actually wrote a portion of the Scriptures — the Ten Commandments — on tablets of stone with His finger. Moses recorded this event as follows: "And he gave unto Moses, when he had made an end of communing with him upon mount Sinai, two tables of testimony, tables of stone, written with the finger of God" (Exodus 31:18). King David confirmed the absolute accuracy and authority of the testimony of God recorded in the Bible in the following passage: "The law of the Lord is perfect, converting the soul: the testimony of the Lord is sure, making wise the simple" (Psalms 19:7). "For ever, O Lord, thy word is settled in heaven" (Psalms 119:89). Centuries later, the Gospel writer Matthew, who ministered for several years with Jesus of Nazareth, wrote, "For verily I say unto you, Till heaven and earth pass, one jot or one tittle shall in no wise pass from the law, till all be fulfilled" (Matthew 5:18). This statement declares that the very words and the spelling of words in the original Hebrew and Greek languages were inspired by God. The discovery of the phenomenal Bible Codes in the last ten years strongly suggests that Jesus was telling the precise truth when He declared that the exact spelling of the words found in the Bible was inspired by God thousands of years ago.

Years later, the Gospel writer John, the beloved disciple of our Lord, wrote, "For had ye believed Moses, ye would have believed me: for he wrote of me. But if ye believe not his writings, how shall ye believe my words?" (John 5:46–47). It is fascinating to note that Jesus compares the ancient words of Moses with His own words and declares that both statements are equally inspired and authoritative. Finally, the apostle Peter declared the authority and inspiration of the written Scriptures: "Knowing this first, that no prophecy of the scripture is of any private interpretation. For the prophecy came not in old time by the will of man: but holy men of God spake as they were moved by the Holy Ghost" (2 Peter 1:20–21). In this passage, the apostle Peter confirms that the authors of the Bible were directed by the power of God's Holy Spirit. This epistle of Peter describes the inspiration of Scripture in his statement that "holy men of God spoke as they were borne along by the Holy Spirit."

Some critics of the Bible's inspiration have tried to differentiate between the inspiration that is affirmed for the writings in the Old Testament from the writings found in the New Testament. These critics have wondered if the Bible's own declarations regarding its authenticity in the Old Testament is equivalent to the twenty-seven books found in the New Testament. However, a careful evaluation of the doctrines taught throughout the entire Word of God reveals that the whole Bible continuously declares that every passage from Genesis to Revelation is truly inspired of God; it is therefore without error. As evidence for this conclusion, we note that the apostle Peter wrote that the epistles of the apostle Paul were being twisted by the unlearned and the unstable "as they do the other Scriptures" (2 Peter 1:21; 3:16). In this letter, the apostle Peter clearly affirmed that all of Paul's writings were truly Scripture in the same manner that the whole of the Old Testament was Scripture. The twenty-one epistles of the apostle Paul comprise a majority of the twenty-seven books found in the New Testament. In another New Testament passage, Paul wrote, "The scripture saith, Thou shalt not muzzle the ox that treadeth out the corn. And, The laborer is worthy of his reward: (I Timothy 5:18). We should note that Paul's first quotation occurs in the Old Testament, in Deuteronomy 25:4. His second quotation can be found in Luke 10:7. It is fascinating to note that the apostle Paul connects these two quotations together and affirms that both statements are Scripture without qualification. This statement of Paul provides powerful evidence for the inspiration of the whole of the Bible, both the Old and New Testaments.

Even modern liberal New Testament scholars, including F. C. Grant and John Knox, admit that Jesus accepted the absolute infallibility of the Scriptures, as did the Jewish rabbis and Temple priests during Jesus' lifetime. Since Jesus and His disciples accepted the truthfulness of the Scriptures, those who follow Christ can be confident that the Bible is truly the Word of God.

2

The Bible's Astonishing Influence on the West

Western civilization is founded upon the Bible; our ideas, our wisdom, our philosophy, our literature, our art, our ideals come more from the Bible than from all other books put together. It is a revelation of divinity and of humanity.

William Lyon Phelps (*Human Nature in the Bible* [1922])

The British and Foreign Bible Society was created in the last century for the express purpose of providing the Holy Scriptures in every language to every individual and every nation throughout the world. This project's purpose was to achieve the universal distribution of the Scriptures throughout the globe. It received the support of virtually all levels of British society, from the aristocracy and royalty to the poorest subjects in the land. In addition, other Bible distribution societies were created throughout the British Empire to facilitate this goal. The virtually universal approval by British society of the Word of God was such that a well-known pastor, Reverend Benson, could write the following words in the introduction to *Benson's Bible Commentary*: "In such an age and nation, to say any thing in commendation of the Scriptures seems perfectly unnecessary; their truth, excellence, and utility being acknowledged by high and low, rich and poor, from one end of the land to the other. Who, indeed, that believes and considers the testimony which the Holy Ghost, speaking by the inspired writers, has given to the excellence of the Scriptures, can call their excellence in question?"

Another indication of the estimation of the importance of the Bible is found in the words of the brilliant writer Charles Dickens. He wrote, "The New Testament is the very best book that ever was or ever will be known in the world." When we compare the attitude of that society of two centuries ago to the contemporary attitudes of indifference or opposition to the Bible, we can recognize the vast changes that have occurred as a result of the continuing attack on the authority of the Word of God in this century.

Changing Attitudes about the Authority of the Bible

Charles Dickens' ringing endorsement of the obvious value of the Bible from 1815 illustrates the tragic transformation that has occurred in western society in the last 175 years. Today, the Bible, the greatest book ever written, has been almost exiled from our Congress and Parliaments, the courts of the land, and our schools. The result of this exile of the Scriptures is apparent to all who have eyes to see. The moral breakdown in modern society has produced an appalling situation in which America has a higher percentage of its population in prison than any other nation on earth. The level of crime and violence is frightening. The problem is that unless people are ruled by their own personal moral code, self-governed by absolutes of right and wrong, there will never be enough policemen or prisons to make our streets safe.

The beloved apostle Paul wrote about the great privilege that God had granted his Chosen People, the Jews. The chief advantage and responsibility they acquired from God was that "unto them were committed the oracles of God" (Romans 3:2). The apostle John revealed the overwhelming value of the written revelation of God to the Church in these inspired words: "Howbeit when he, the Spirit of truth, is come, he will guide you into all truth: for he shall not speak of himself; but whatsoever he shall hear, that shall he speak: and he will show you things to come (John 16:13)." The psalmist David declared that the wisdom and power of God was demonstrated by the fact that "He showeth his word unto Jacob, his statutes and his judgments unto Israel"

(Psalms 147:19). David concluded his praise to God for providing Israel with this written revelation in these words: "He hath not dealt so with any nation: and as for his judgments, they have not known them. Praise ye the Lord" (Psalm 147:20). It was Jesus Christ Himself who commanded His disciples as to "Search the Scriptures; for in them ye think [or rather, are assured] ye have eternal life: and they are they which testify of me" (John 5:39).

It is fascinating to note that after our Lord Jesus Christ rose from the dead and began to display His divine power in both heaven and earth, He appeared to his beloved disciples and enlightened their knowledge and understanding of the sacred Scriptures. Luke records these words of Jesus to His disciples about the revelation of God in the Scriptures: "And he said unto them, These are the words which I spake unto you, while I was yet with you, that all things must be fulfilled, which were written in the law of Moses, and in the prophets, and in the psalms, concerning me. Then opened he their understanding, that they might understand the Scriptures, And said unto them, Thus it is written, and thus it behoved Christ to suffer, and to rise from the dead the third day: And that repentance and remission of sins should be preached in his name among all nations, beginning at Jerusalem. And ye are witnesses of these things" (Luke 24:44—48).

These affirmations by Jesus Christ of the value of the Old Testament Scriptures, as well as the New Testament Scriptures, are as true for Christians today as they were during the life of Jesus. Unfortunately, a number of Christians today believe that the Old Testament is primarily, or only, a message to the Jewish people and that it has limited spiritual value for modern followers of Christ. Nothing could be further from the truth. The entire Word of God from the first word of the book of Genesis to the last word of the book of Revelation is equally valuable and precious for all those who claim to follow Jesus Christ as their Savior.

Unfortunately many believers neglect reading the Old Testament in the mistaken notion that God intended these Scriptures solely for the Jews. They have wrongly assumed that the Old Testament is of little use to Christians in our modern world. However, many of the greatest truths of God are revealed in the pages of the Old Testament. A careful evaluation of the New Testament reveals that both Jesus and the apostles continuously appealed to the authority of the Old Testament to support their doctrines and teachings.

For example, the apostle Paul wrote, " For whatsoever things were written aforetime were written for our learning, that we through patience and comfort of the Scriptures might have hope" (Romans 15:4). Later Paul declared, "Now all these things happened unto them for ensamples: and they are written for our admonition, upon whom the ends of the world are come" (1 Corinthians 10:11). Again and again Paul reminds his readers that the Old Testament is the bedrock of the revelation of God's great truths that form the foundation of the doctrines of the true Christian Church. He wrote to his beloved disciple Timothy to remind him of the foundation of his faith: "And that from a child thou hast known the holy Scriptures, which are able to make thee wise unto salvation through faith which is in Christ Jesus" (2 Timothy 3:15). The apostle Paul's most ringing endorsement of the inspiration and authority of the Scriptures is found in these words: "All scripture is given by inspiration of God, and is profitable for doctrine, for reproof, for correction, for instruction in righteousness. That the man of God may be perfect, thoroughly furnished unto all good works." (2 Timothy 3:16–17). In these words, from what many scholars believe is the last of the apostle's epistles, Paul confirms a fundamental truth: our Christian walk before God depends ultimately upon our conforming our life to the sacred words of the divinely inspired Scriptures.

The apostle Peter also declared the essential role of the inspired Word of God in the life of the individual believer in these words: "We have also a more sure word of prophecy; whereunto ye do well that ye take heed, as unto a light that shineth in a dark place, until the day dawn, and the day star arise in your hearts: Knowing this first, that no prophecy of the scripture is of any private interpretation. For the prophecy came not in old time by the will of man: but holy men of God spake as they were moved by the Holy Ghost" (2 Peter 1:19–21).

The reality is clear from direct biblical statements by both Jesus and the apostles that the New Testament doctrines are built upon the firm foundation of biblical revelation, as given in the Old Testament. This affirmation is proven by the frequent quotations by Christ and his apostles from the Old Testament — from the historical portions of Genesis to 2 Chronicles, the Psalms, and the great prophetic passages found in the later portions of the Old Testament.

It is fascinating to note the inspired words of Jesus Christ, following His resurrection from the grave, when He met two of His disciples on the road to Emmaus. After first reproaching them for not understanding the clear prophetic teachings found in the writings of the Old Testament, Christ teaches them: "And beginning at Moses and all the prophets, he expounded unto them in all the Scriptures the things concerning himself" (Luke 24:27). Later when Christ appeared to His disciples in the same Upper Room where they had celebrated the Last Supper, He announced, "These are the words which I spake unto you, while I was yet with you, that all things must be fulfilled, which were written in the law of Moses, and in the prophets, and in the psalms, concerning me. Then opened he their understanding, that they might understand the Scriptures" (Luke 24:44–45). Our understanding of the doctrines of Christianity depends to a great degree upon our understanding of the foundational truths found in the Old Testament.

When we fully understand the Old Testament revelation, we will begin to understand that Jesus Christ truly came to fulfill the law of God and to reconcile a lost humanity to God through His perfect sacrifice on the Cross for our sins. Then we can appreciate that all of the details of the Israelite worship in the Tabernacle and, later, in the Temple were a shadow of the ultimate fulfillment of God's plan to reconcile sinners to Himself through the shed blood of Jesus Christ at Calvary. Jesus of Nazareth, the Lamb of God, was prefigured in the ancient Temple sacrificial system.

Many of the New Testament books are unfathomable to Christians unless they understand the teaching of the Old Testament. In addition, the tremendous prophecies of the Old Testament enable us to grasp the marvellous sovereignty of God, as we witness the unfolding of these prophecies in the life, death, and resurrection of Jesus Christ. As we examine the forty-eight specific prophecies about the life of Jesus found in the passages of the Old Testament, written more than five hundred years before He was born, we marvel at the power of God to both foresee and to bring to pass His divine will in history. The pages of the Bible reveal astonishing details about the rise and fall of Assyria, Egypt, and Babylon. Although these powerful empires ruled the known world in their days of glory, the ancient Scriptures foretold that each in their turn would be destroyed and fall into ruin. Yet the Jewish people, one of the most insignificant of all of the many races inhabiting the ancient Middle East, were prophesied by God to continue to flourish to the end of time because they were God's Chosen People. Today, we look in vain for the Nabateans, the Moabites, the Edomites, or the Chaldeans — all powerful nations that fought against Israel long ago. The Jewish people still exert an incredibly positive influence throughout our world. Their influence is evident in medicine, science, literature, and many other fields. In a later chapter we will explore the mystery of the Jews' survival and their vital role in God's plan to redeem and reconcile humanity to Himself.

In the New Testament we find the revelation of the true character of God, as Jesus reveals Himself as the God of mercy and love, our gracious Redeemer, and the Savior of a sinful, lost humanity. The New Testament reveals the incredible sacrifice of Jesus Christ to reconcile mankind to God forever through His shed blood on Calvary.

The writings in the New Testament reveal the glorious nature and offices of Jesus of Nazareth, the Son of God who came to earth to suffer and die for our sins as God's perfect substitutionary sacrifice. The Gospels and Epistles reveal the true nature of the spiritual warfare that surrounds us in our Christian walk, as well as God's supernatural provision for our protection through our putting on "the whole armour of God." Paul commanded believers to "put on the whole armour of God, that ye may be able to stand against the wiles of the devil" (Ephesians 6:11).

The New Testament reveals our glorious privileges as Christians — most importantly, that the curse of death will be removed as the power of the grave is broken forever by Christ's resurrection power. The Gospels declare the resurrection glory that will be revealed in all who will freely accept the salvation offered through Christ's blood. The biblical writers tell us that our life here on earth is no more than a journey toward the Promised Land of heaven itself, where all who name the name of Christ will enjoy an eternal life of blessed immortality forever. An examination of the empty lives and dim spiritual expectations of those races that have never heard the Gospel of Christ reveals that the people in all ages and nations where the light of Jesus has not shined have lived in abject spiritual darkness without hope for eternal peace after death.

The Gospel of Luke recounts the wonderful promise that was announced by the priest Zacharias when he was filled with the Holy Ghost and prophesied in the Temple of the coming glory to be revealed in the birth of Jesus of Nazareth: "And thou, child, shalt be called the prophet of the Highest: for thou shalt go before the face of the Lord to prepare his ways; To give knowledge of salvation unto his people by the remission of their sins, Through the tender mercy of our God; whereby the day spring from on high hath visited us, To give light to them that sit in darkness and in the shadow of death, to guide our feet into the way of peace" (Luke 1:76–79). The history of the vast expansion of Christian missions throughout the nations of the world during the last two hundred years has fulfilled this Gospel promise, as the glorious spiritual light of Christ has been shed upon the lives of untold millions in virtually every nation on earth.

The Power of the Bible to Transform Lives

The transforming power of the Gospel of Jesus Christ is illustrated by an examination of the nations of central Africa that British and American missionaries explored during the last century in their desire to bring these tribes the saving message of the love of Christ. According to the writings of the explorers and missionaries Dr. David Livingstone and Henry M. Stanley, over half of all of the tribes they encountered during thousands of miles of exploration through eighteen-century Africa practiced cannibalism and other unspeakable pagan practices prior to the introduction of the saving Gospel of Christ. Truly, these peoples had sat "in darkness and in the shadow of death" until the glorious light of Jesus entered their lives. From 1800 on, thousands of faithful European and North American Christians gave up their family ties, their promising careers, and worldly success to travel halfway around the world as missionaries to share the wonderful truth that Jesus Christ died for our sins to set every one of us free if we would follow Him. As a result of their faithful efforts to share their faith, hundreds of thousands of African pastors and workers are now completing the Great Commission of Jesus Christ throughout the vast continent of Africa, where more than five hundred million people now live. Mission organizations estimate that over one thousand new churches are built every week in Africa today. Some studies indicate that up to half of Africa's population will be followers of Jesus Christ by the year 2000.

As an example of the marvellous power of the Word of God to spiritually transform both individuals and whole societies, we should consider the well-documented story of the events on Pitcairn Island. The true story of *Mutiny on the Bounty* has been retold numerous times in print, as well as in several famous movies. The fugitives from the mutiny on the British ship known as the *Bounty* took refuge on Pitcairn Island. They were hoping to escape the vengeance of the British navy. The following account was found in a quotation from the *Gospel Herald* (*7700 Illustrations*): "One part that deserves retelling was the transformation wrought by one book. Nine mutineers with six native men and twelve native (Tahitian) women put ashore on Pitcairn Island in 1790. One sailor soon began distilling alcohol. And the little colony was plunged into debauchery and vice. Ten years later, only one white man survived, surrounded by native women and half-breed children. In an old chest from the Bounty, this sailor one day found a Bible. He began to read it and then to teach it to the others. The result was that his own life and ultimately the lives of all those in the colony were changed. Discovered in 1808 by the USS *Topas*, Pitcairn had become a prosperous community with no jail, no whisky, no crime, and no laziness."[1]

Years ago an anonymous writer wrote a profound comment on the unique quality of the Bible: "Other books were given for our information, the Bible was given for our transformation." Throughout the centuries, those who have lived under the darkness of paganism and those who dwell today in spiritual darkness remain in the hopelessness of a closed grave, without purpose or meaning in life. To these people without hope, the universe is simply the accidental result of random chance. They dwell in a spiritual darkness of their own making, and, as a consequence, they live without hope or purpose in their lives. This bleak existential philosophy, which is widely taught throughout our world today, reduces life to meaninglessness. Relationships become mere accidental encounters. One cynical and ironic existentialist characterized his grim and pessimistic view of life as follows: "We are born naked, wet and hungry. From then on things get worse!" If we truly lived in a world without purpose or meaning then the ancient philosophy of the Epicureans — "Eat, drink, for tomorrow we die"— is a rational response.

Fortunately, there is an alternative view of life. Its meaningful purpose is revealed by the inspired Word of God and reverberates with hope, joy, and purpose. If we are living in a world of purpose and meaning, created by a supernatural God who is vitally interested in our lives, then we need to know the truth about our situation. Some who do not know the truth about the complete message of the Bible imagine that God wishes to curtail their joy and withhold from them the good things of life. Nothing could be further from the truth. Jesus Christ declared His purpose for humanity: "The thief cometh not, but for to steal, and to kill, and to destroy: I am come that they might have life, and that they might have it more abundantly" (John 10:10). The promise of faith in Christ gives us purpose, meaning, and an eternity with God.

In this day of government-mandated warning labels that must be affixed to packages of ant poisons and cigarettes, someone has ironically suggested that we might place a warning label on the covers of our Bibles — Warning: This Book is habit-forming. Regular use causes loss of anxiety, decreased appetite for lying, cheating, stealing, hating. Symptoms: increased sensations of love, peace, joy, compassion.

Testimonies about the Influence of the Bible

Some of the critics of Christianity denigrate the reverence that orthodox believers give to the precious Word of God. These modern critics suggest that the Bible is out of date and irrelevant to our sophisticated and highly technological world. Yet the enduring value of the Bible to provide an unchanging but totally relevant guide to the problems and challenges of human life has been affirmed by countless Christians throughout the last two thousand years.

In my earlier book, *The Signature of God*, I mentioned the remarkable study of American life conducted in 1830 on behalf of the French government by the brilliant writer and judge Alexis de Tocqueville. Alexis de Tocqueville was sent to America to study American society, its beliefs, and its prisons to discover the reason there was so little crime and so few prisoners in jail. America seemed a veritable paradise in comparison to the corruption and criminality that swept France during the period following the

French Revolution, a period in history in which the church and religion in general were totally repudiated by the French. After travelling across the nation for several years, Alexis de Tocqueville completed his study and wrote a fascinating book in 1840 entitled *Democracy in America*. He wrote about the true source of America's greatness as a nation and the real reason for her extremely low crime rate at that time.

> I sought for the greatness of the United States in her commodious harbors, her ample rivers, her fertile fields, and boundless forests-and it was not there. I sought for it in her rich mines, her vast world commerce, her public schools system and in her institutions of higher learning-and it was not there. I looked for it in her democratic Congress and her matchless Constitution-and it was not there. Not until I went into the churches of America and heard her pulpits flame with righteousness did I understand the secret of her genius and power. America is great because America is good, and if America ever ceases to be good, America will cease to be great![2]

Tragically, his analysis and prediction has proven to be correct. As America has progressively abandoned her rich spiritual heritage, based on the public and private reverence and teaching of the Bible, we have witnessed growing violence and crime from the lowest levels of society to the highest. Scandal and corruption in the highest political offices are now so commonplace that they seldom merit mention on the front pages of our newspapers. Our society has become so disillusioned by immorality and greed among business, military, religious, and political leaders that we are almost shell-shocked. Stories of sexual abuse of children and acceptance of bribes are so common that we rarely stop to register how far we have fallen from the high standards of public and private morality that existed in North America until the 1950s.

Can you imagine the shock of someone living in America in 1957 who had fallen into a coma that lasted for forty years, only to awake in 1997 to observe what has happened to our nation over the last four decades. He would be astonished. If he should ask the reason for this sorry state of affairs, the only rational answer would be to point to our society's public and private abandonment of the Bible during this same period. During the last forty years, the Bible has been relegated to the dusty bookshelves of our homes and libraries. The Bible is no longer considered relevant or authoritative by many in our modern educational establishments, government, courts, and even some churches. We have sown a wind of secularism, modernism, and flexible moral values. As a direct result, we are now reaping a whirlwind of immorality, sexually transmitted disease, corruption, and violent crime. The only hope for our national, spiritual, and institutional recovery is to return to the spiritual values based upon the unchanging Word of God that originally formed the foundation of our national life.

In light of the growing battle by secularist groups, such as the American Civil Liberties Union and People For the American Way, to banish the Bible from the courts, the schools, and any public places in our society, it might be enlightening to examine the attitude displayed towards the Word of God by the great leaders of the past who served as presidents of the United States. A small sampling of their publicly expressed views on the supreme value of the Bible is quite instructive.

The first president of the United States of America, George Washington, wrote, "It is impossible to rightly govern the world without God and the Bible." John Quincy Adams, the sixth president of the United States wrote, "So great is my veneration of the Bible, that the earlier my children begin to read it the more confident will be my hope that they will prove useful citizens of their country and respectable members of society." Adams also declared, "I have for many years made it a practice to read through the Bible once a year. My custom is to read four or five chapters every morning immediately after rising from my bed. It employs about an hour of my time, and seems to me the most suitable manner of beginning the day. In what light soever we regard the Bible, whether with reference to revelation, to history, or to morality, it is an invaluable and inexhaustible mine of knowledge and virtue." President Andrew Jackson referred to the Bible as the foundation of the nation: "That book, sir, is the rock on which our republic rests."

In a letter to his friend Mr. Speed, written during the tragic years of the Civil War, President Abraham Lincoln wrote, "I believe the Bible is the best gift God has ever given to man. All the good from the Saviour of the world is communicated to us through this book." Lincoln also gave this suggestion to those who wondered how they should approach the Word of God: "Take all this book upon reason that you can, and the balance on faith, and you will live and die a happier and better man."

In this century, President Woodrow Wilson declared in a speech he gave on May 7, 1911, "A man has found himself when he has found his relation to the rest of the universe, and here is the Book in which those relations are set forth." President Wilson was so committed to the importance of the Bible to the life of this republic that he called for daily Bible reading by all citizens to strengthen the moral fiber and destiny of the American nation: "I ask every man and woman in this audience that from this day on they will realize that part of the destiny of America lies in their daily perusal of this great Book." President Herbert Hoover suggested that the key to the unique strengths of American democracy and her stable institutions is to be found in the pages of the Holy Scriptures. Hoover wrote, "The whole of the inspiration of our civilization springs from the teachings of Christ and the lessons of the Prophets. To read the Bible for these fundamentals is a necessity of American life." Another president, the beloved Dwight D. Eisenhower, indicated his own profound love for reading the pages of the Scriptures: "To read the Bible is to take a trip to a fair land where the spirit is strengthened and faith renewed." Many more examples could be given but these quotations reveal the profound understanding of these great military and political leaders of the United States. This nation was founded upon the principles of the Word of God.

Those who love Jesus Christ as their Lord and Savior need to reawaken their passion for daily reading of the Bible. It is truly the source of our spiritual food and sustenance. I read a fascinating account of the profound love for the Scriptures that was experienced by a village in eastern Poland in the years before World War II, when the Bible was virtually unavailable to the average citizen. A few years before the war, a colporteur named Michael Billester visited this small village near the Russian border. A colporteur was a travelling missionary whose mission was to place Bibles in the hands of those who had never possessed the Word of God. When Bellester passed through this Polish hamlet, he gave a humble villager a Bible. The man read the Scriptures avidly and was converted. He then shared this precious Bible with others.

Ultimately, through that one Bible, more than two hundred villagers and farmers in the area became followers of Christ.

When Michael Billester revisited the village a few years later in the summer of 1940, hundreds of these new converts gathered to worship God and hear Billester preach the Gospel. Usually he would ask new Christians to share their testimony, but this time Billester suggested that each believer recite their favorite verse of Scripture. At this suggestion, one of the new Christians stood up and asked, "Perhaps we have misunderstood. Did you mean verses or chapters?" In astonishment Mr. Billester asked, "Do you mean to say there are people here who can recite chapters of the Bible?" It turned out that these new Christians so loved their precious Bible that each of them had memorized, not only chapters, but whole books of the Bible. Thirteen of them could recite the Gospel of Matthew and Luke and half of Genesis. One man had committed all the Psalms to memory. All together, the two hundred converts had memorized almost the entire Bible. The Bible had been passed around from family to family and read in their meetings every Sunday. The old Book had become so worn with use that its pages were hardly legible (taken from an article in the *Sunday School Times* quoted from *7700 Illustrations*)[3]. If every Christian today had an equally strong passion to read and memorize the precious Word of God, we would witness a spiritual revival and transformation of our families and nation.

The apostle Paul raised a profound question about our responsibilities as Christians to our neighbors and to those in other lands who have never heard the Gospel. Paul asks, "How then shall they call on him in whom they have not believed? And how shall they believe in him of whom they have not heard? And how shall they hear without a preacher?" (Romans 10:14).

The real question is, how can we who are Christians, in possession of the Good News revealed through the inspired Old and New Testament, fail to take every opportunity to share this incredible revelation of divine truth with those in our western society, as well as those in the rest of the world who have not yet encountered the reality of Jesus Christ? How can we who have received the unsearchable riches of God's grace and the glorious hope of redemption for mankind, as declared to us through the Scriptures, stand aside with indifference in light of the coming judgment on mankind if they choose to reject the only way of salvation promised by God.

The Bible's Influence on the West

When we examine the social situation in England in the years before the Evangelical Revival of the Wesleys, we find a moral abyss without hope. The Bible was not preached in the churches, and it was virtually unread by millions of citizens in their homes. Before the Evangelical Revival, led by John and Charles Wesley, public morality and spiritual values had collapsed in England "to a degree that has never been known in any Christian country."[4] A number of contemporary writers such as Pope and Samuel Johnson provided striking evidence that the nation was at the point of moral collapse in the early 1700s. However, into this great spiritual darkness, God mercifully sent the light of His written revelation of truth, the Bible.

Two centuries ago the Lord sent the written Word of God as the only hope for revival. Two great evangelists, John and Charles Wesley, preached their biblically based message of salvation throughout the nation. In 1769, John Wesley created the incredibly successful Sunday school movement, with the goal of teaching the Bible to millions of young children. Sunday schools prospered throughout the British Empire and produced a marvellous increase in understanding of the Bible in the hearts of millions. The Bible-based preaching of the Wesley brothers was used by God to give birth to a spiritual revolution in England that created a reformed nation based on the principles of the Word of God.

It is important to note that John Wesley declared that the Gospel was meant to transform both the individual as well as society: "We know no Gospel without salvation from sin. . . . Christianity is essentially a social religion; to turn it into a solitary religion is indeed to destroy it." Our Christian faith, if it is real, must reveal itself in our treatment of those around us. As a result of this revival, Christianity transformed every aspect of the society. John Wesley declared that "a doctrine to save sinning men, with no aim to transform them into crusaders against social sin, was equally unthinkable."[5] The Christian revival that began in England ultimately spread throughout the world, bringing millions to a personal faith in Jesus Christ.

Many people in our society imagine that many of the positive distinguishing characteristics of Western culture are the results of political democracy. However, I would challenge my readers to consider the features and institutions of our modern society: universal, free education for every child, regardless of wealth; virtually universal health care; massive charities; anti-slavery and child labor laws; women's rights; and basic human-rights laws. What is the true origin of these beneficial institutions that we all take for granted as the fruits of our democratic government? The answer will surprise many people, including Christians. These institutions and laws are the result of a "back to the Bible" movement led by the powerful Evangelical Revival in England and North America that began with the Weslyian spiritual revival movement in the 1800s. It is the application of the principles of the Word of God that produced the wonderful institutions of Western society that are the glory of our modern world. The Bible is the source of the greatest benefit that God has provided to mankind.

The return to biblical values by the evangelical Christian movement in the 1700s created the first real hope for the people of England to improve their lives since the first introduction of Christianity to the British Isles more than a thousand years earlier. The widespread reading of the Bible in the common language of the people produced the greatest religious revival in history. England was raised from moral destitution to greatness, as the biblical principles were practically applied to the challenges and issues of society. Free universal education, charity hospitals, anti-slavery and child labor laws, together with hostels for the poor, were created by Christians who were motivated by their love of Jesus to help their weaker brothers and sisters. It is no exaggeration to declare that the return to the Bible transformed the character of England. In truth, it was the distribution of the Bible throughout the Western world that transformed England from a moral wasteland into a country that was proud to send the Bible to every nation on earth. Our only hope for our nation's spiritual health today is a similar revival based on a return to the unchanging Word of God.

Notes

1. *Gospel Herald (7700 Illustrations)*.

2. Alexis de Tocqueville, *The Democracy in America* (1840).

3. *Sunday School Times (7700 Illustrations)*.

4. Bishop George Berkeley, *Discourse Addressed to Magistrates and Men in Authority* (1738).

5. Henry Carter, *The Methodist*. 174.

3

The Impact of Jesus on the World

The evidence is overwhelming that Jesus of Nazareth made a greater impact on the culture, history, religion, attitudes, and laws of the Western world than any other person or group of men. Unlocking the mystery of the awesome influence of the life of Jesus of Nazareth will enable us to understand who Jesus really is. The evidence that will be examined throughout this book reveals overwhelming proof that both the Old and New Testaments declare that Jesus is God. The acceptance of the deity of Jesus of Nazareth brings us to that point where we must choose to accept or reject Jesus Christ's claims on our life and soul.

An examination of the writings of many modern liberal theologians reveals that they have concluded that Jesus of Nazareth was simply a prophet, a man of God who was a great teacher and moral leader. However, they reject out of hand the orthodox biblical teaching of the Scriptures that Jesus is God. Consequently, liberal theologians and preachers usually reject the supernatural elements in the Bible that surround the life of Jesus, including His virgin birth, His miracles, and His physical resurrection from the dead. There are a number of logical contradictions in this widely held theory. This view of Christ completely ignores the tremendous historical evidence from the Gospels, as well as independent historical records that confirm the historical reality of the life, death, and resurrection of Jesus Christ. This historical evidence is explored in detail in my earlier book, *The Signature of God.*

As one confirmation of the historical truth of the crucifixion of Jesus, consider that the supernatural darkness that covered the earth while Jesus hung on the Cross was recorded by several pagan historians. Matthew recorded this event: "Now from the sixth hour there was darkness over all the land unto the ninth hour" (Matthew 27:45). However, a contemporary pagan historian named Thallus also wrote about this astonishing event in A.D. 52, only twenty years after the resurrection of Christ. Thallus wrote that the darkness totally covered the face of the earth at the time of the Passover in A.D. 32. The writer Julius Africanus, writing in approximately A.D. 220, records, "This darkness, Thallus, in the third book of his *History*, calls, as appears to me without reason, an eclipse of the sun."[1] Julius explained that Thallus' theory was unreasonable because an eclipse of the sun cannot occur at the same time there is a full moon. The moon is almost diametrically opposite the sun during full moon making a solar eclipse impossible. The priests of Israel carefully calculated the time of the full moon to set the date of the Passover Feast. The Gospels record that it was at the season of the Passover full moon that Christ died.

There are two important points here. First, a pagan historian who was alive at the time Jesus' death occurred has confirmed that darkness covered the earth at the very time recorded in the Gospels. Secondly, the fact that there was a full moon present makes it certain that this darkness was not an eclipse but that it was a supernatural event. Another remarkable historical reference to this darkness is found in the writings of Phlegon. He noted the seemingly impossible fact that this "eclipse" occurred at the time of the full moon during the reign of Tiberius Caesar as emperor of Rome. Further, Phlegon wrote that the darkness covered the earth for precisely three hours, from the sixth to the ninth hour, precisely the time period that is recorded in the Gospels.

One of the problems with this liberal view of Jesus as a mere man is the logical necessity that either Jesus or the Gospel writers must have totally fabricated the supernatural events of His life and resurrection. How can Jesus or His followers be credited with launching the greatest moral revival in the history of mankind if they lied about the events, miracles, and resurrection of Jesus?

How could Jesus be called a wise and moral teacher of ethics if He or His disciples engaged in the greatest deception in history — claiming that He was God and that He could forgive sins — if He was only a man according to their view.

In addition to these problems, there is an incredible and arrogant assumption in this viewpoint that suggests that the people living in Judea and throughout the Roman Empire in the first century were ignorant fools who believed stories about supernatural miracles without any logical evaluation or historical evidence. However, this view of the population of the first century as simple-minded is totally contradicted by the letters, speeches, and historical documents from that era which have survived the centuries. Both the Jewish people and the Romans were as intelligent as our population today.

One factor in considering just how improbable the liberal theory of Jesus as a mere man truly is the history of the growth of Christianity in the first century. If the liberal theologians are correct, then Jesus performed no miracles, died on the cross as a criminal, and was never seen again. However, the history of the period reveals that His disciples quickly recovered from their shock at His death and that, within fifty days, they met to launch the most powerful spiritual movement in history, which has impacted literally billions of lives. Furthermore, during the seventy years following Christ's death, hundreds of thousands of Christians endured the most horrible persecution, torture, and martyrdom rather than deny their faith in the risen Lord. Remember that these Christians refused to save their lives by denying Jesus' resurrection at a time when thousands of believers who were eyewitnesses to the events of Christ's life were still alive.

Another factor to consider is the transformation in the behavior of the disciples. What could possibly account for the sudden transformation from an attitude of helplessness, fear, and despair among the eleven disciples at the Cross to an attitude of joy and bold confidence in declaring the Good News of the risen Savior that these men demonstrated to the whole of the known world? The only rational answer is that they personally witnessed the resurrected Jesus of Nazareth with their own eyes and personally experienced His supernatural empowerment through the Holy Spirit. It is noteworthy that the writers of the New Testament repeatedly affirm that they were eyewitnesses of these events. For example, Luke the physician tells us that his written account is based on eyewitness reports. "Even as they delivered them unto us, which from the beginning were eyewitnesses, and ministers of the word" (Luke 1:2). The apostle Peter confirmed that he personally witnessed the glory and majesty of Jesus in His resurrection body. "For we have not followed cunningly devised fables, when we made known unto you the power and coming of our Lord Jesus Christ, but were eyewitnesses of his majesty" (2 Peter 1:16).

The history of this persecution, which began during the reign of Emperor Nero within thirty years of the Cross, reveals that these followers of Jesus were noteworthy for going to their painful deaths with hymns and prayers. Is it probable — is it even possible to imagine that hundreds of thousands of intelligent people would endure torture and martyrdom rather than deny their faith in the risen Jesus if they had the slightest doubt that He was truly God and that His resurrection, attested to by eyewitnesses, was the guarantee that they too would arise one day through His victory over death and sin? The only logical explanation is that these people were absolutely convinced that Jesus was the Son of God because they personally were eyewitnesses or they had heard from other eyewitnesses trustworthy accounts of the death and resurrection of Jesus. The staggering growth of the Christian faith, despite the most horrendous persecution, provides powerful evidence that these people were supernaturally motivated to reach the world with the good news of Jesus Christ. It is estimated that up to one-half of the population of the Roman Empire were followers of Jesus within one hundred years of His resurrection.

Does It Really Matter If Jesus Actually Rose from the Grave?

Some religious writers have questioned if it really matters whether or not the resurrection of Jesus actually occurred as an historical event. The answer: Absolutely! The historical truth of the Gospel account of the life, teachings, death, and resurrection of Jesus of Nazareth is of supreme importance to Christians today, as well as to all believers throughout the last two thousand years. If Jesus of Nazareth never died and rose from the dead on that first Easter Sunday, Christians are fools to follow Him. However, the overwhelming historical evidence proves that we are not fools. Those who follow Jesus Christ as their Lord and Savior are basing their life and their hope for eternity on the historical reality of the greatest fact and miracle in human history — the physical resurrection of Jesus of Nazareth. The apostle Paul declared openly that the historical truthfulness of the physical resurrection of Jesus was the foundation and most essential truth of Christianity: "And if Christ be not risen, then is our preaching vain, and your faith is also vain" (1 Corinthians 15:14). Paul correctly announced that our faith in Christ would be in vain and a useless lie if Jesus' body was still in the ground. Furthermore, he logically pointed out that the forgiveness of our sins and, consequently, our reconciliation with God in heaven are totally dependent upon the fact that Jesus, as the Son of God, paid the price of our sins on the Cross and rose victorious over death and sin. Paul wrote, "And if Christ be not raised, your faith is vain; ye are yet in your sins" (1 Corinthians 15:17).

It is interesting to note that the doctrine of physical resurrection from the dead was held by many Jews during the time of Christ, as well as in later centuries. Paul appealed to this faith in the resurrection, held by the Pharisees, during his trial. The Jewish Talmud that records in great detail the theology and doctrines of the ancient Jewish faith makes this statement about the resurrection: "He who maintains that the resurrection is not a biblical doctrine has no share in the world to come" (*Mishneh Sanhedrin* 10.1. c. 200). From Genesis to Revelation, the Bible teaches us that the purpose of the life, death, and resurrection of Jesus is to reconcile a lost and sinful humanity to our holy God through His perfect sacrifice of His innocent blood in full payment of the price of our sins. The Word of God teaches us that Jesus, the Son of God, demonstrated His power to defeat sin and death forever through His resurrection

Some liberal and agnostic scholars argue that the examination of the validity of the historical evidence about Jesus of Nazareth is a waste of time. While many scholars concede that the archeological and manuscript evidence confirms the historical reality of the life and death of Jesus Christ as Christians affirm, they claim that this has little, if any, religious importance today. Some liberal theologians argue, "What difference does it ultimately make whether or not Jesus was actually born in Bethlehem as the son of Mary and lived with his family in Nazareth?" These liberals ask, "What is the relevance of the fact that Jesus taught for three and one-half years and was crucified by Rome on a charge of sedition, as long as we can spiritually experience the inner Christ and live our lives in the light of His inspired teachings?" They believe they can escape from guilt for sin and find meaning for their lives through the mere idea of Christ's atonement of our sins as portrayed by the symbolic "myth" of the death of Jesus on the Cross. Modern liberal theologians argue that, if Jesus the Christ, "God incarnated in man," lives within our spirits, it matters very little whether or not the historic Jesus, the physical son of Mary, actually lived and died in Israel two thousand years ago. However, they are absolutely wrong!

It matters very much whether or not Jesus of Nazareth actually lived, died, and rose from the dead two thousand years ago. If the critics are correct and the Gospels are merely myths, then we are still trapped in our guilt and sins. The forgiveness of our sins and our hope for redemption and an eternity in heaven with God depend on the historical reality of the actual sacrifice of the blood of the Lamb of God to atone for our sins on the Cross. If Jesus never lived, died, and rose from the dead as the Gospels record, the symbol of "Christ" would lose all of its relevance and meaning. The word "Christ" would simply become an imaginary religious concept that would be divested of all objective reality. Divorced from the historical Jesus of Nazareth, as taught in the inspired Scriptures, this subjective "Christ" can mean anything one chooses it to mean.

However, there is another matter to consider. If the liberal theologians are correct in their belief that Jesus was basically a myth, it is virtually impossible to understand how the dynamic Christian faith could have come into existence among a group of intensely persecuted people who chose to die in martyrdom for their faith in the reality of the resurrected Jesus and His divinity. How could the concept of "Christ" have incarnated itself in the hearts of hundreds of millions of people throughout the Roman Empire if there was no actual historical Jesus of Nazareth who rose from the grave to inspire this extraordinary religion? The only reasonable answer is that this extraordinary religion of Christianity could not have occurred unless Jesus of Nazareth actually lived, died, and rose from the dead, as the Gospels affirm.

The Bible's Progressive Revelation of God

In Genesis, we witness the God of power in His marvellous powers of creation. In the Torah, we find the record of the history of the Patriarchs, their Exodus from Egypt, and the giving of the Law. We witness the God of justice and mercy revealed in the pages of the Scriptures. In the balance of the Old Testament, especially the Psalms, Proverbs, and Ecclesiastes, we see the God of wisdom. However, in the Gospels, we finally receive the revelation of the God of love and mercy revealed in Jesus Christ.

The Gospel of John records that three women each named Mary, were present at the crucifixion of Jesus. "Now there stood by the cross of Jesus His mother, and His mother's sister, Mary the wife of Cleophas, and Mary Magdalene. When Jesus therefore saw His mother, and the disciple [John] standing by, whom He loved, He saith unto His mother, Woman, behold thy son! Then saith He to the disciple [John], Behold thy mother! And from that hour that disciple took her unto his own home" (John 19:25–27). This moving passage reveals the profound love of Jesus for His mother, Mary, and His loyal friend John. In the primitive attitudes of the ancient Middle East, it was common for a rabbi to comment "Thank God that I was not born a woman" as part of his customary morning prayers. Some of the peoples in the ancient Middle East denied that women even possessed souls. The status of women in the time preceding the life of Jesus was very restricted in comparison to that of men. In contrast to this ancient attitude that tended to minimize the role of women, Jesus surrounded Himself with women disciples who were often the first to recognize Him as their Messiah and respond to His message about the need for personal repentance. In this way, Jesus elevated forever the role of women by treating them as equal in spiritual and social value to men. Edith Hamilton wrote that "the Bible is the only literature in the world up to our century which looks at women as human beings, no better and no worse than men."[2]

Despite the constant attacks in our generation on the biblical doctrine that Jesus is the Son of God, the world's fascination with the character and teachings of Jesus continue to grow with each generation. Sometimes it seems as though the critics are winning, but the truth is that the Christian faith has triumphed throughout the globe to the point that more than a billion people today acknowledge Jesus of Nazareth as the Son of God. The spiritual history of the last two thousand years reveals an astonishing increase in the numbers who follow Christ over the centuries. The profound and lasting spiritual influence of the teachings of Jesus and the significance of His death and resurrection are beyond calculation. Jesus personally transformed the formal, ceremonial, and external religion of Temple worship into a powerful and spiritually dynamic experience with God for each individual believer. He introduced humanity to a universal faith that united all men and women as the children of God under the providence of our heavenly Father. Thus, Jesus Christ made possible a previously unknown brotherhood of man that transcended race and ethnic backgrounds. Jesus changed our age-old fear of death into a glorious anticipation of being reunited with Him in a heaven of indescribable splendor. Further, He guaranteed our own immortality through His glorious victory over death and the grave.

Jesus introduced humanity to a new revelation of the fundamental law and command of God — that we should love God with our whole mind, body, and soul. In addition, Jesus taught us to love our neighbour as ourselves. He went further and taught us the revolutionary concept that we should love our enemies and care for those who hurt us. By working as a carpenter in Joseph's business for many years, Jesus honored physical labor and acknowledged the value of those who toil. This was a radical change in attitude because the aristocracy and priesthood of the ancient world usually looked with contempt upon those who toiled for a living. The Lord also changed forever the way adults would look at children by surrounding Himself with young people and declaring "of such is the kingdom of God." This was a revolutionary change in attitude from the prevailing ancient cultural attitude that held children to be of little value. Jesus elevated forever the precious value of every single person regardless of their position, capabilities, age, sex, or race because each of us is made in the image of God. These principles taught by Jesus motivated the reformers during the past several centuries to finally put an end to slavery. The prominent position of women as followers of Jesus and His dignified treatment of women ultimately led to a transformation of the rights and roles for women in Western society. If we will examine the lives and attitudes of the great reformers of the past and present, we will often find that the wellspring of their motivation to improve their society is their love of Jesus Christ and the inspiration they derive from the contemplation of His life and teachings, as found in the Word of God.

The writer Madonna Kolbenschlag wrote a fascinating book in 1988, called *Lost In the Land of Oz*, in which she describe the central role of Jesus Christ to the essence of Christianity: "For the Christian, Jesus is the Way. All things are measured by his Way: by his healing grace, his call to forgiveness and purity of heart, nonviolence and a concern for justice; by his relinquishment of earthly power and dominance; affection of agape (sacrificial Love) as a new basis for kinship, of change of heart as the requirement for righteousness, and of the transcendent power of suffering."[3]

One Solitary Life

Years ago an anonymous writer summed up the extraordinary influence and impact of human life of the one solitary life of Jesus of Nazareth. While many of us have read this beloved passage it is worthy of repetition because these words reveal the awesome influence of the life of Jesus as the Son of God.

He was born in an obscure village, the child of a peasant woman. Until He was thirty, He worked in a carpenter shop and then for three years He was an itinerant preacher. He wrote no books. He held no office. He never owned a home. He was never in a big city. He never travelled two hundred miles from the place He was born. He never did any of the things that usually accompany greatness. The authorities condemned His teachings. His friends deserted Him. One betrayed Him to His enemies for a paltry sum. One denied Him. He went through the mockery of a trial. He was nailed upon a cross between two thieves. While He was dying, His executioners gambled for the only piece of property He owned on earth: His coat. When He was dead He was taken down and laid in a borrowed grave.

Nineteen centuries have come and gone, yet today He is the crowning glory of the human race, the adored leader of hundreds of millions of the earth's inhabitants. All the armies that ever marched and all the navies that were ever built and all the parliaments that ever sat and all the rulers that ever reigned — put together — have not affected the life of man upon this earth so profoundly as that One Solitary Life.[4]

Notes

1. Julius Africanus. *Ante Nicene Fathers.* 200.

2. Spokesmen For God: The Great Teachers of the Old Testament. 1948.

3. Madonna Kolbenschlag. *Lost in the Land of Oz.* 1988.

4. Anonymous writer.

4

The Incredible History of The Bible

The remarkable history of the writing, the preservation, and the profound influence of the Bible on the Western world is an extraordinary story that will help us to understand our Western culture and history.

How Did We Get Our Present Bible?

King David was a man greatly beloved by God. David was a very passionate man who loved God and His Scriptures with all of his heart, mind, and soul. In addition to his diligent study of the Bible, God inspired David to record His inspired words for the instruction of future generations. The psalmist wrote these words, "Thy word is a lamp unto my feet, and a light unto my path" (Psalms 119:105). However, David knew that a mere reading of the Word of God would not transform our lives. Rather, he taught us that those who desire to know God must study the Scriptures with the assistance of the Holy Spirit to gain a deeper understanding of the great truths that will change our lives. David wrote, "I am thy servant; give me understanding, that I may know thy testimonies" (Psalms 119:125). It is vital that Christians understand the history of both the creation of the Bible and how the Word of God was supernaturally preserved and translated through the ages. Unfortunately, few people today know the remarkable history of how the Bible was created and preserved. This study will produce a greater confidence in God's miraculous preservation of His inspired Scriptures from the ancient times, when the biblical writer recorded the inspired words of God, down through the centuries until these words were printed recently in your personal Bible.

The Canon of the Old Testament

Both Jewish and Christian scholars generally agree that Ezra, the great leader of the Jewish captives who returned to Israel from Babylon in 536 B.C., collected all of the sacred scrolls of the Hebrews and published them as the Scriptures (our Old Testament). During the earlier reign of King Josiah, a priest by the name of Hilkiah found a scroll in the Temple that contained the written law of God. The righteous king commanded that the people join him in the Temple to hear his reading of the Scriptures (2 Kings 22). King Josiah led his people in a genuine revival of worship, based on the laws of God as revealed in the Torah. However, this history of King Josiah's revival explains that the Scriptures were suppressed for many years by the previous wicked kings of Judah and Israel, including the evil King Manasseh. This spiritual revival under the leadership of King Josiah led to a renewal of the reading of the scrolls of the Scriptures, which the Jews ultimately carried to Babylon during their seventy years of captivity.

When the Jewish exiles returned to the Promised Land God raised up Ezra as their spiritual and political leader to restore both the nation and their religious worship. Ezra gathered together all of the available scrolls, including the five books of the Law, the historical records, the prophetic writings, the Psalms, and all the other scrolls. Under the supernatural inspiration of God, Ezra prepared a complete edition of these sacred writings and thus established the canon of the Old Testament Scriptures. The word *Canon* is derived from a Hebrew and Greek source meaning a type of cane or measuring rod. The word canon was first used as a reference to the approved, authoritative, and inspired books of the Bible by bishops of the Christian Church during the fourth century after Christ.

Ezra divided these sacred scrolls into three sections: (1) The Torah (the Law or Pentateuch); (2) Nevi'im (the Prophets); (3) The

Ketuvim, or Hagiographa (the Holy Writings). The Jewish historian Josephus, who lived at the time of the apostle Paul, mentions
this threefold division of the Hebrew Scriptures in his history of
the Jewish people: "We have only twenty-two books which we
believe to be of divine authority, of which five are the books of
Moses. From the death of Moses to the reign of Artaxerxes, the son
of Xerxes king of Persia, the prophets who succeeded Moses have
written in thirteen books. The remaining four books contain
hymns to God, and moral precepts for the conduct of life." It is
likely that the books of Chronicles, Ezra, Nehemiah, Esther, and
Malachi were placed in the canon of Holy Scripture during the
lifetime of Simon the Just, the last of the great religious leaders of
the Great Synagogue.

The Jews refer to the Hebrew Bible (the Old Testament) as the
"Tanakh." This word is derived phonetically as an acronym from
the Hebrew words for the three divisions: Torah — Nevi'im —
Ketuvim = TaNaKh. Naturally many Jews resent the Christian
identification of their sacred books of Tanakh as the Old Testament because they reject the concept that God has added twenty-
seven additional, inspired books of Scripture to the Bible in the
form of the New Testament. However, God Himself chose to refer
to this new revelation of His covenant as His "new covenant" in
the words of the prophet Jeremiah: "Behold, the days come, saith
the Lord, that I will make a new covenant with the house of Israel,
and with the house of Judah" (Jeremiah 31:31). The word
"testament" that is universally used by Christians to refer to both
sections of the Bible is derived from the words of Jesus Christ in
the Gospel account of the Last Supper with His disciples: "For this
is my blood of the new testament, which is shed for many for the
remission of sins" (Matthew 26:28). The word "testament" is
related to a will or a covenant that disposes of one's estate after
their death. The expressions "Old Covenant" and "New Covenant" would be equally accurate names for the Old and New
Testaments.

The first section of the Hebrew Bible, the Torah or Law, con-
tains five books: Genesis, Exodus, Leviticus, Numbers, and
Deuteronomy. The second section, The Prophets, contains Joshua,
Judges-Ruth, Samuel, Kings, Isaiah, Jeremiah-Lamentations,
Ezekiel, Daniel, a scroll with the twelve Minor Prophets, Job, Ezra,
Nehemiah, and the book of Esther. The third section, the

Hagiographa (the Writings) include the Psalms, Proverbs, Ecclesiastes, and Song of Solomon.

It is interesting to note that the number of books or scrolls in the Old Testament has changed from ancient times, but the total inspired text of the Scriptures was preserved faultlessly by God's providence. While the arrangement of the Scriptures changed, the inspired text of the Bible was not altered in the slightest. The Jews joined together several related books such as 1 and 2 Samuel into one book called Samuel. The following sets of books were joined together: Judges and Ruth, 1 and 2 Samuel, 1 and 2 Kings, 1 and 2 Chronicles, Ezra and Nehemiah, Jeremiah and Lamentations, and the twelve Miinor Prophets. Apparently, the Jews combined these thematically linked books to reduce the number of the sacred scrolls in the Hebrew Scriptures to twenty-two, the precise number of letters in the Hebrew alphabet. Numerous early writers, including Josephus and Jerome refer to the ancient Jewish canon containing just twenty-two books, allowing one volume for Ezra-Nehemiah. In the Latin Vulgate (common language) translation of the Bible, the book Ezra-Nehemiah was divided into 1 Ezra and 2 Ezra (Nehemiah) around A.D. 400. However, it is worthwhile to note that these changes and combinations of books into larger scrolls did not add or subtract a single letter or word from the Hebrew Bible.

The Jews divided the text of the first five books of the Bible, the Torah, into fifty-four sections. This division may date back to the days of Moses, but it is more likely that these sections were established during the lifetime of Ezra, when the canon of Old Testament was established. In addition, these sections of the Torah were divided into verses for the first time at this point. Every Sabbath day throughout the year, each one of these fifty-four sections would be read in turn in the synagogue. The ancient Hebrew calendar had an extra intercalary (leap) month that they added to the end of the year approximately every third year to adjust their 360-day calendar to the solar calendar of 365.25 days. In these intercalated (leap) years, there were thirteen months that produced, as a consequence, fifty-four weekly Sabbaths. Thus the Jews would read each of the fifty-four sections in the course of that year. In the other years without the leap month, which had only fifty-two Sabbaths, the leaders of the synagogue would combine together two short sections on two particular Sabbaths to enable them to cover the whole of the Torah in a yearly reading.

However, during the terrible persecution by the evil Syrian king Antiochus Epiphanes who conquered Israel for three years between 168 B.C. and 165 B.C., the reading of the Torah was forbidden under severe punishment. Instead, the Jewish priests substituted the reading of Torah portion with the reading of one of fifty-four sections from the writings of the prophets every Sabbath day. When the Jewish people succeeded in defeating the Syrian army in 165 B.C. the reading of the sections from the Torah was restored. However, the Jewish priests chose to continue to read the sections of the Prophets as a second lesson every Sabbath day after reading the Torah section.

The Targums, or Paraphrases of the Hebrew Bible

When the Jewish exiles returned from the seventy years of captivity in Babylon, most of the people had lost their under-standing and use of the Hebrew language. Naturally, during the seventy years of captivity, they had learned to speak the Chaldean (Babylonian) language as their common tongue. Consequently, after the return from Babylon, the priest would first read the Torah portion in the original Hebrew and then he would interpret the Hebrew portion to the people using the Chaldee language that they understood. The division of the fifty-four sections of the Torah into verses made it more convenient to read both the Hebrew Scriptures and the *Targums* which were written para-phrases or commentaries on the relevant Scripture written in the Chaldee language.

This practice apparently began in the days of Ezra, as his book describes his reading the Torah to the people in the rebuilt Temple. The leaders then explained the text in the common Chaldee language to allow the people to understand the Scrip-tures. The book of Nehemiah records this practice as follows: "The Levites, caused the people to understand the law: and the people stood in their place. So they read in the book in the law of God distinctly, and gave the sense, and caused them to understand the reading" (Nehemiah 8:7–8). The two major *Targums* (paraphrases) were the *Targum of Jonathan* and the *Targum of Onkelos*. Although spoken commentary on the Scriptures in the Chaldee language was common for centuries, the Jews did not possess written paraphrases before the time of Onkelos and Jonathan, both of whom lived just before the birth of Jesus. These written commentaries or paraphrases of the Bible in the Chaldean language became known as *Targums*, which contained paraphrases combined with commentary on the Scriptures by the Targum interpreters. The *Targum of Jonathan* was written by Jonathan ben Uziel, a famous scholar who was himself taught by the brilliant sage Hillel the Great during the reign of King Herod the Great. The date of the writing of the *Targum of Onkelos*, who commented only on the five books of Moses, is not certain, but likely it preceded the time of Jesus as well. Onkelos the Proselyte likely was descended from Gentile converts to Judaism. His Targum was considered so valuable that it was almost treated as inspired literature in the synagogue.

The *Targums* are valuable in helping us to understand both the Old Testament as well as the New. They provide tremendous evidence that the present Hebrew text is genuine because the detailed commentaries confirm that the original Hebrew text is identical to our present Hebrew text. In the Targums we find the explanation of many difficult words, phrases, and customs found in the Hebrew Bible. In addition, some of the idioms, phrases, and unusual forms of speech found in the New Testament can be better understood through studying these Targums. Lastly, these Jewish commentaries reveal clearly that the ancient Jewish sages interpreted the Old Testament prophecies about the Messiah precisely as we Christians understand them today. This will be dealt with in a future chapter on the prophecy of Isaiah 53 about the suffering Messiah.

The Division of the Bible into Chapters and Verses

The Scriptures were not divided into the chapters we find in our modern Bible until approximately 1240. Hugo de Sancto Caro, more commonly known as Hugo Cardinalis, after he became a cardinal in the church, created the division of the Bible into its present form of chapters to facilitate the reader's ability to find any particular portion of Scripture. Hugo wrote a Bible commentary entitled *Comment on the Scriptures* and created a valuable concordance based on the Vulgate Latin Bible, which enabled a reader to find any passage in which a particular word or phrase occurs from Genesis to Revelation. Hugo realized that it would improve immensely the usefulness of his concordance if he divided the Bible's text into sections (chapters), which were then numbered. Until Hugo's time, the books of the Bible had no divisions at all which made it very difficult to find a particular passage. Imagine the difficulty you would have in finding a favorite passage, such as "For God so loved the world," if the whole book of John had written out as one paragraph with no divisions, chapters, or verses. Hugo's division of the Bible into sections has now become the chapter divisions universally used in the billions of Bibles printed in the last seven centuries. However, Hugo did not subdivide the chapters into the numbered verses found in our present-day Bibles. Interestingly, Hugo placed the letters of the alphabet, A, B, C, D, et cetera in the margins of the Bible at an equal distance from each other. This helped identify the approximate position in the chapter where a particular passage was located.

Over two centuries later, in A.D. 1445, a famous Jewish rabbi, Mordecai Nathan, subdivided the chapters created by Cardinal Hugo into the individually numbered verses we find in our modern Bibles. Rabbi Nathan created a *Concordance to the Hebrew Bible* to assist Jews in their study of the Word of God. While he used the same chapter divisions created by Hugo several centuries earlier, Rabbi Nathan further subdivided the chapters into individually numbered verses. Once Rabbi Nathan's Bible was published, this division of the Scriptures into chapters and verses became so popular and useful that every Bible printed since that day has followed this same method. It is ironic and quite fitting that the Jews borrowed the Christian Hugo's division of the Bible into chapters, while the Christians borrowed the division of the sacred Scriptures into verses created by the Jewish Rabbi Nathan. For the last five centuries, all students of the Scriptures, both Christians and Jews, have benefited immensely from these inventions.

A number of scholars, including Dr. H. Prideaux, have suggested that Ezra was inspired by God to make several editorial additions to some of the books of the Bible in order to connect several sections of the Bible together or to complete the final pages of a particular book. If this suggestion is correct, then we would have a logical explanation for a number of problems and puzzles in the Bible that have been used by atheists to attack the inspiration and authority of the Scriptures. A multitude of biblical statements affirm the total inspiration of the Bible, including Paul's declaration that "all Scripture is given by inspiration" (2 Timothy 3:16). These scriptural declarations provide a strong witness to the fact that any such editing by Ezra would have been as equally inspired by God as the writing of the original author.

There are a number of puzzling verses in the Bible which can be explained on the basis of this principle. For example, the final chapter of Deuteronomy records the details of the death and burial of Moses, as well as the commencement of the leadership of Joshua. Since the five books of the Law, including Deuteronomy, are ascribed in the Bible to Moses, a number of critics have pointed to these verses as an obvious error because Moses could not have recorded his own death and burial. However, it would be very natural and necessary for the inspired writer Ezra, who was inspired by God to write his own book as well as to gather together the books of the Old Testament, to add the final details of the death and burial of Moses to the final chapters of Deuteronomy under the same inspiration of God as moved Moses to record the pages of the Torah.

My friend Yacov Rambsel is the author of two best-selling books on the phenomenal Bible Codes that reveal that the name *Yeshua* (Jesus) is encoded at equally spaced intervals in every major messianic prophecy. His books are entitled *Yeshua: The Name of Jesus Revealed in the Old Testament* and his latest release *His Name Is Jesus*. Recently I asked Yacov to research the Hebrew text of the last chapter of Deuteronomy to discover if anything significant was encoded in this passage at equal letter sequences. The fascinating story of the phenomenal Bible Codes is revealed in a later chapter of this book. To my amazement, Yacov found that the name "Ezra" was actually encoded in this passage regarding the death and burial of Moses, a passage that many scholars believe was actually written by Ezra the scribe. The first verse of the last chapter of Deuteronomy reads, "And Moses went up from the plains of Moab unto the mountain of Nebo, to the top of Pisgah, that is over against Jericho. And the Lord showed him all the land of Gilead, unto Dan" (Deuteronomy 34:1). Beginning at the very first verse of Deuteronomy 34, describing the death and burial of Moses, we find the name of the scribe Ezra is encoded at an interval of every forty-seventh letter left to right, beginning with the third letter in the first word of the verse. In addition, the name "Ezra" also occurs in the encoded phrase "I pray Ezra" in Deuteronomy 34:4, beginning with the third letter of the thirteenth word of this verse at an interval of every second letter spelled left to right.

There are many other difficult passages in the Bible that are used to support objections to the doctrine of the inspiration and authenticity of the Scriptures. Another example is Genesis 22:14 where the verse reads "As it is said to this day, In the mount of the Lord it shall be seen." The problem is that Mount Moriah, where Abraham offered Isaac, was not called "the mount of the Lord" until King Solomon built the Temple almost a thousand years after the life of Abraham. Therefore, it is likely that another person (probably Ezra) added this statement to the original words of Moses to explain the passage.

In Genesis 36:3, we find this passage: "And these are the kings that reigned in the land of Edom, before there reigned any king over the children of Israel." This statement would not make sense until centuries later, when Israel began to be ruled by kings, beginning with Saul and David. While it is certainly possible that God inspired Moses to record the details of his death and burial and the future monarchy of Israel, these particular passages do not appear to be written in the normal language of direct prophecies as we find throughout the Scriptures. It is probable that Ezra added these finishing comments under the inspiration of God to complete the Divine revelation.

Another example is found in Exodus 16:35: "And the children of Israel did eat manna forty years, until they came to a land inhabited; they did eat manna, until they came unto the borders of the land of Canaan." However, the death of Moses (Deuteronomy 34) had occurred before the Jews crossed the Jordan River at the time of Passover and began to eat the new corn of the Promised Land after the manna had ceased to fall from heaven. Therefore, it is more probable that Ezra added this inspired explanatory verse rather than Moses.

Apparently, Ezra also changed the names of several cities that were no longer known in his time by their ancient names. For example, the book of Genesis records the fact that Abraham's small armed force fought against the five Canaanite kings "unto Dan." The passage reads, "And when Abram heard that his brother was taken captive, he armed his trained servants, born in his own house, three hundred and eighteen, and pursued them unto Dan" (Genesis 14:14). Since the name of Dan as a city or territory was unknown at the time when Abraham lived, it is possible that Ezra was inspired by God to change the name of the city, which was known as Laish in the days of Moses, to the name Dan, the new name given to the city by the Danites who conquered it centuries after the days of Moses.

Pharoah Ptolemy Philadelphus was the king of Egypt in 285 B.C. Philadelphus was known as a great scholar and lover of knowledge. He created the largest library in the ancient world at Alexandria, Egypt. His wealth and power enabled him to acquire volumes from many nations throughout the known world. The Jewish tradition is that the king of Egypt sent representatives to Israel to gather the greatest Jewish sages for the purpose of translating the ancient Hebrew Scriptures into the Greek language. Greek was the common language of the known world following the conquest of the Middle East by Alexander the Great in 330 B.C. These Jewish scholars reportedly produced a Greek version of the five books of the Torah in the Old Testament, called the Septuagint, or "version of the Seventy." The word Septuagint was based on an ancient tradition that the king of Egypt employed seventy or seventy-two interpreters to produce this invaluable translation. It is probable that a small group of scholars produced the Greek translation which was later approved as a correct and authoritative version of the Jewish Bible by the seventy members of the Sanhedrin of Alexandria, the highest Jewish court of law in Egypt. The remaining books of the Old Testament were translated into the Greek language by scholars in later years and added to the Septuagint version over a period of years until it ultimately contained all of the books of the Old Testament. The Hellenist or Greek speaking Jews used the Septuagint version for several centuries before the birth of Jesus to approximately A.D. 128.

The Jewish people gradually abandoned the Greek Septuagint version and created another Greek language version because the Christians constantly quoted from the Septuagint version, especially the messianic prophecies, to prove that Jesus of Nazareth had fulfilled these predictions. A Jewish convert by the name Aguila, from the city of Sinope in the province of Pontus joined Rabbi Akiba, the most famous Jewish teacher of his day, and was given the responsibility of creating a new Greek translation of the Old

Testament in A.D. 128. It is interesting to note that Jesus and His disciples, as well as the early Church writers, almost invariably quoted from the Septuagint Greek version rather than from the Hebrew original, indicating the great respect Christians held for this version.

Curiosities About the Bible

Over the last thirty-five years of Bible study I discovered numerous curious details regarding the publication of the Bible that I found fascinating. When I first began to consider publishing my first book *Armageddon — Appointment With Destiny* I decided to create a publishing company to publish my books in order to maintain control over the process and enable us to offer the books to various ministries and mission groups throughout the world. Today these books are published in numerous foreign languages including French, Spanish, Portuguese, Korean, Japanese, Mandarin, Cantonese, Russian, Polish, Ukrainian and Romanian. My interest in publishing naturally led me to examine the history of the printing of the Bible over the centuries. Centuries ago the printing of a Bible was a time consuming and very exacting process. Naturally, any publisher is mortified when he finds that a book contains typographical errors and he does his best to immediately correct such errors in his next printing. However, in past centuries it was much more difficult to produce a perfect printed text because each letter of type was set by hand. In my research I found that several of the most notorious cases of typographical errors resulted in the particular editions of these Bibles being rejected by the printer and destroyed.

Printing Errors in Past Bibles

The So-called "Wicked" Bible

In 1631 a wealthy religious businessman commissioned a printer in England to publish ten thousand copies of the Bible, an enormous sized printing for that time period. However, one of the printer's apprentices made a tragic error during the process of manually typesetting the passage containing the Ten Commandments. While typesetting the verse Exodus 20:14, the apprentice inadvertently dropped the word "not" from the commandment, "Thou shalt not commit adultery." The buyer indignantly demanded that the entire ten thousand misprinted "Wicked"

Bibles must be destroyed and replaced with a corrected edition. In addition, the court fined the printer three hundred pounds, a considerable sum in those days. That unfortunate result must have made subsequent printers of Bibles much more careful in their typesetting.

The "Printers" Bible

However, in 1702 another printer's apprentice was typesetting the Book of Psalms. When he came to Psalm 119:161 which reads, "Princes have persecuted me without a cause," for some unknown reason, he carelessly typeset the verse as follows: "Printers have persecuted me without cause." Perhaps this was an unconscious complaint about his employer.

The "Bugs" Bible

In 1551 a translator inadvertently mistranslated Psalm 91:5. In the original Scriptures it reads, "Thou shalt not be afraid of the terror by night." However, when he completed his translation, the printer rendered the verse as follows: "Thou shalt not be afraid of the bugs by night." Unknowingly, the printer printed the translated Bible with the error. Thereafter this edition became known as "the Bugs Bible."

Lest you think that such notorious errors in typesetting a Bible cannot happen anymore as a result of modern spell checkers and word processors, think again. A very large Bible publisher in the United States, which shall remain nameless, produced a new Bible several years ago in the familiar Red Letter Edition which prints the actual words of Jesus in red ink to differentiate them from the rest of the biblical text. Since the color of text is different for that particular verse the printers use a separate film that solely contains the particular red letter verse containing Christ's words. The rest of the black text that appears on that page is produced from a separate film plate. The printers had carefully used both the red letter and black letter film together to produce the four Gospels. However, when they began to print the New Testament book — Timothy — the printer was not used to using the red letter film and when he printed that particular page he used only the black letter film leaving a blank space on the page where the particular verse with Jesus' words should have appeared in red ink. When they discovered the error it was too late because thousands of these Bibles had been printed and bound in leather. The publisher knew that people would not accept a Bible with a missing verse, especially the words of Jesus. The only thing they could do was to destroy the misprinted Bibles at great cost.

The Lost Books Mentioned in the Bible

While God has preserved the totality of His inspired Scriptures in the present Old and New Testaments, the Bible refers to at least fourteen ancient books that are no longer in existence. These curious texts are referred to in a number of biblical passages as the official royal historical records of the kings of Israel and Judah plus numerous other texts containing the prophecies of various seers such as the prophet Nathan. While these particular books are lost to history there is no reason to believe that they were inspired by God. It is obvious that a person may be used of God in one instance to write a divinely inspired book of Scripture while other examples of their writing would not be inspired but the result of his normal intellect. God is capable of sovereignly preserving His holy Scriptures as demonstrated by our present complete Bible.

In the Old Testament, the book of Numbers 21:14 refers to *The Book of the Wars of the Lord*, while Joshua 10:13 describes *The Book of Jasher*. In 2 Kings 11:41 we find a reference to *The Book of the Words of the Days of Solomon*, and *The Book of the Chronicles of the Kings of Judah* is referred to six times in 1 and 2 Kings, including 1 Kings 14:29: "Now the rest of the acts of Rehoboam, and all that he did, are they not written in the book of the chronicles of the kings of Judah?"

There are nineteen references throughout the historical books of the Old Testament to the lost *Book of the Chronicles of the Kings of Israel*, which was certainly the royal historical chronicle of the nation that would be updated to record the history of each succeeding king. Three additional missing books with the titles *The Book of Samuel the Seer, the Book of Nathan the Prophet*, and *The Book of Gad the Seer* are referred to in 1 Chronicles: "Now the acts of David the king, first and last, behold, they are written in the book of Samuel the seer, and in the book of Nathan the prophet, and in the book of Gad the seer, with all his reign and his might, and the times that went over him, and over Israel, and over all the kingdoms of the countries" (1 Chronicles 29:29–30).

Two other lost books, *The Prophecy of Ahijah the Shilonite*, and *The Visions of Iddo the Seer*, along with *The Book of Nathan the Prophet*, are referred to in 2 Chronicles 9:29: "Now the rest of the acts of Solomon, first and last, are they not written in the book of Nathan the prophet, and in the prophecy of Ahijah the Shilonite, and in the visions of Iddo the seer against Jeroboam the son of Nebat?" There is a reference to *The Book of Shemaiah the Prophet* and *The Book of Iddo the Seer* in 2 Chronicles 12:15: "Now the acts of Rehoboam, first and last, are they not written in the book of Shemaiah the prophet, and of Iddo the seer concerning genealogies?" The missing *Book of Jehu* is referred to in 2 Chronicles 20:34. In 2 Chronicles 33:19 we find a reference to *The Sayings of the Seers*, which may be a separate book or may be a reference to one of above books.

A tantalizing reference to a book written by the prophet Isaiah is found in 2 Chronicles 26:22: "Now the rest of the acts of Uzziah, first and last, did Isaiah the prophet, the son of Amoz, write." There is a reference to three thousand parables of King Solomon together with his songs, that may refer to a missing book of Solomon that appears in 1 Kings 4:32: "And he spake three thousand proverbs: and his songs were a thousand and five."

5

The Reason Many Reject The Bible

Why have so many individuals in our generation rejected the teachings of the Bible and the claims of Jesus Christ to be the Son of God? Throughout the greater part of the last two thousand years, the vast majority of all classes within the nations of Western Europe and North America have willingly accepted that the Bible is the true Word of God and that Jesus Christ was sent by God to bring salvation to mankind. However, approximately a century ago, a strong attack on Christianity and the Holy Scriptures began in European universities among the academic community. During the following decades, a large majority of the scholars in the universities, the mainline Protestant churches, and the secular media began to openly reject the claims of Christianity and deny the accuracy of the historical statements found in the Bible regarding Jesus' miracles, His virgin birth, and His resurrection.

As a result of a century of growing attacks on the Bible most North Americans and Europeans believe today that the Scriptures contain scientific, historical, and archeological errors that prove that the Bible is simply a work produced by less advanced and, perhaps, ignorant authors thousands of years ago, who wrote from a perspective of limited human knowledge. The negative spiritual consequences of this widespread belief that the Bible is not the accurate and inspired Word of God is incalculable.

Attacks on the Accuracy of the Bible

As a result of the relentless attack on the truthfulness of the Scriptures by the academic community, the educational establishment, the secular media, and liberal clergy, the majority of people in our culture are convinced that the Bible is simply compiled of stories by ancient men writing to the best of their natural ability thousands of years ago. This widespread rejection of the supernatural origin of the Scriptures has caused many liberal theologians, pastors, and rabbis to abandon their confidence in the Scriptures as the inspired Word of God. A theological statement made at the Central Conference of American Rabbis (1985) is just one example that demonstrates this loss of faith in the clear assertions of the Bible: "We reject as ideas not rooted in Judaism, the beliefs both in bodily resurrection and in Gehenna and Eden."

The consequence of this widespread rejection in our culture of the supernatural claims of the Bible has been profound. The Ten Commandments, which were accepted for thousands of years as the bedrock of divine law, have now been rejected by our courts of law, the Congress, and our schools. The repudiation of these divinely inspired Ten Commandments has set our legal-justice system adrift on an ocean without a moral anchor or a compass to direct our justice system. If there is no reliable revelation from God of absolute right and wrong, then mankind is free to choose its own standards of right and wrong without any reference.

If there is no absolute right and wrong — good and evil — as revealed for all time by an Almighty and holy God, then man is free to set his own standards, based on constantly changing cultural opinions expressed by votes, polls, referendums, and laws. This shift in the basis of moral values is reflected in our current laws on abortion. According to modern values, if the mother would rather not have the responsibility of bearing a particular child at a particular time, she can terminate her inconvenient pregnancy. Currently, a mother can choose to abort her unborn child in the last day of the ninth month of her pregnancy. According to this "new morality," a doctor can now legally plunge a pair of scissors into the skull of a child just a few minutes before this child would naturally enter the world as a healthy baby. He can legally use a suction device to suck the brains out, facilitating the crushing of the skull of the baby. Then he is able to withdraw the now lifeless body, and refer to the child as an aborted "piece of flesh." The incredible justification for this morally repugnant procedure is that the mother's health must be protected. However, the law does not define the "health of the mother" in any meaningful way. If the mother decides that she does not want to give birth to a live child for any reason whatsoever, the doctor can lawfully destroy the child's life by this horrendous torture called "partial birth abortion."

Many of those working in the abortion industry admit that the "health justification" for most abortions is motivated by a simple desire to escape the economic inconvenience or emotional embarrassment of a child's birth. Furthermore, an overwhelming majority of obstetricians agree that even when the physical health of a woman is serously compromised by her pregnancy, there is no circumstance in which this barbaric technique is medically necessary. It's sole purpose is to provide a means for abortion at the end of a pregnancy that will ensure that the mother and doctor will escape charges of murder. After the U.S. government hearings on the "partial birth abortion" were over, a pro-abortion witness admitted that this disgusting procedure was not nearly as rare as the testimony had suggested.

We have arrived at a time when, every year, over one and one-half million North American women decide to kill their unborn children to avoid the social or economic inconvenience of an unwanted child. Remember that at the same time as these abortions occur, millions of North American couples are desperately seeking to adopt newborns. Despite this overwhelming demand for new babies for adoption, the "family planning" network almost always suggests to the pregnant woman that she abort rather than give birth and place her child in a loving home with parents willing to raise it properly.

Modern philosophers and liberal theologians have contemptuously rejected the literal truth of the Bible. In its place, they have attempted to create a new "Christian" religion that would be unrecognizable to the early Church or to the hundreds of millions who have experienced faith in Jesus Christ, as revealed in Scripture over the last two thousand years. These modernists and rationalists have rejected altogether the supernatural element in the Bible, along with the accounts of miracles, prophecies, the virgin birth, and the resurrection of Jesus from the tomb. However, true Christianity cannot be divorced from the physical resurrection of Jesus of Nazareth without losing its very reason for being. If Jesus' body still lies moldering in some unknown grave in Israel, then the billions of Christians over the last two thousand years are fools. As Clement C. J. Webb wrote in his 1935 book *The Historical Element in Religion*, "A Christianity without the belief in the resurrection of Christ as an historical event would be another Christianity than that which the world has hitherto known."[1]

Modern liberals have rejected the supernatural elements in the Bible, yet they attempt to call themselves "Christians" while repudiating the defining elements of the orthodox Christian faith. For example, the liberal theologian Emil Brunner wrote that the orthodox belief of Christians since the time of Christ has "killed" what he terms the true conception of revelation as "personal encounter" with Christ. Incredibly, Brunner claims that orthodox belief in the literal truth of the Bible's accounts has created virtually irreparable damage to the concept of "faith" as he holds it. In his book *Revelation and Reason* (p. 168), Emil Brunner condemned the orthodox Christian belief in the literal truth of Scripture:

> All Christian faith is based, according to this theory, upon faith in the trust-worthiness of the Biblical writers. The whole edifice of faith is built upon them, upon their absolute and complete inspiration. What a fearful caricature of what the Bible itself means by faith. And on what a quaking ground has the Church of the Reformation, in its (orthodox) perversion, placed both itself and its message! We owe a profound debt of gratitude to the historical criticism that has made it quite impossible to maintain this position. This mistaken faith in the Bible has turned everything topsy-turvy. It bases our faith-relation to Jesus Christ upon our faith in the Apostles. It is impossible to describe the amount of harm and confusion that has been caused by this fatal perversion of the foundations of faith; both in the Church as a whole and in the hearts of individuals.[2]

Emil Brunner also wrote that "revelational events must be

separated from anything like propositional revelation." By this statement, Brunner declares that his subjective experience of the revelation of Christ is not related to or dependent upon the written statements about the life, teaching, death, or resurrection of Jesus found in the Bible. Obviously, such a personal "revelational event" is totally subjective and therefore cannot be tested or measured against anything as objective as the doctrines or testimony of Scripture. This kind of subjective faith or "Christianity" is grounded solely within the internal beliefs or assumptions of the individual and is, therefore, unrelated to historic Christian faith. In this subjective approach, people are free to create their own "Christ" in their imagination without reference to any historical record of Jesus, His teachings, or His actions. The problem is that such a "Christianity" has nothing to do with Jesus Christ.

However, orthodox Christians throughout the ages simply believed that the supernatural God who created this universe also possesses the ability to inspire the human writers to accurately record His revelation to humanity, as affirmed by the clear statements of the Bible. Logically, if a supernatural God exists who truly cares for His creatures, there is no difficulty in concluding that He could have supernaturally inspired these writers to record His precise words. Furthermore, such a supernatural God could have preserved His divine written revelation down through the centuries in order to continue to communicate His genuine revelation to all generations of mankind. The underlying assumption of the majority of those who contemptuously reject the inspiration of the Scriptures is that a supernatural God with miraculous powers does not exist.

The theologian Emil Brunner expressed his totally subjective experience of "Christ" in contrast to the literal, orthodox Christian faith based on the teachings of the Bible. Brunner wrote the following statements expressing his views of the essentials of Christianity:

> Substituting the idea of revelation as personal encounter for the orthodox one of system I may as a believer become as contemporary with Christ as was Peter . . . No longer must I first of all ask the Apostle whether Jesus is really Lord. I know it as well as the Apostle himself, and indeed I know it exactly as the Apostle knew it; namely, from the

Lord Himself, who reveals it to me . . . Being thus
contemporaneous with Christ the believer now shares in
the grace and glory of God. Being face to face with Christ
as his contemporary also means having the true content of
revelation . . . We must say quite clearly Christ is the Truth.
He is the content; He is the "point" of all preaching of the
Church; but He is also really its content.[3]

A careful examination of these statements reveals that these
modern liberal theologians have created a new religion that bears
no resemblance to the orthodox Christian faith. Rather, these
modern theologians have created a new "Christianity" that can be
infinitly adjusted to suit their own desires because they deny the
fundamental doctrines of historic orthodox Christianity and they
reject the truthfulness of the Gospel account about Jesus. The
criteria for accepting or rejecting a particular statement of the
Scriptures seems to be whether or not it agrees with their personal
religious preferences.

If these critics were honest, they would admit they are no
longer Christians because they vehemently and contemptuously
reject every major doctrine of the apostolic Christian faith.
Meanwhile, they reject the literal truth of biblical statements while
suggesting that they have discovered some deeper, subjective
truth behind these scriptural statements. They often claim to have
a profound experience of "Christ" while they denigrate the
historical reality of the biblical accounts of the life, death, and
resurrection of Jesus Christ.

The "Christ" and the "Christianity" of the modernist liberal
theologians has become an extremely flexible philosophical creation of their own making, absent of any of the supernatural
elements or the objective historical facts recorded in the Bible that
they find so objectionable. They reject as embarrassing the Bible's
teaching of the historical reality of the virgin birth of Jesus, His
identity as the Son of God, the accuracy of His words as recorded
in the Gospels, His supernatural miracles, His resurrection, and
His ascension. Having stripped away any historical or supernatural reality from Jesus of Nazareth, they are then free to create a
new "Christ" limited only by their own imagination. The word
"Christ" has become an empty vessel for the liberal theologians
into which they can pour whatever New Age philosophical or

religious concepts they imagine. If these liberal theologians were to physically take a pair of scissors and cut out from the sacred pages of the Scriptures every verse referring to the supernatural, the prophecies, the miracles, and the statements of Jesus that they reject, the Bible that remained in their hands would be a mere fraction of the one that Christians have treasured for thousands of years. If they doubt this truth, I would challenge them to take a highlighter and highlight the few verses in the Bible that they still accept unreservedly to be literally true. This experiment would reveal to many liberals, who reject the literal statements of the Scripture, that their "acceptable" Bible has been reduced to a shadow of the inspired volume that has profoundly affected billions of lives over the last two thousand years.

Bishop John Spong's Attack on Fundamental Biblical Beliefs

The controversial Episcopalian Bishop John Spong is known for his prominent attacks on Christians who believe the fundamental doctrines of the Word of God. Bishop Spong claims that there are three main paths for Christians to take in addressing the words of the Bible. These alternatives are described in his words as "ignorant fundamentalism," "vapid liberalism," and his own unique path. However, Spong's path is merely another example of a modernist liberalism that results in a wholesale rejection of the orthodox doctrines of Christianity. The bishop claims he wants to free Christians and Jesus from "2000 years of misunderstanding." Spong declares that the Gospel writers and Paul never intended their "stories" to be taken literally. As a result of his denial of the reality of the New Testament accounts Bishop Spong openly admits his rejection of the foundational doctrines of the orthodox Christian faith. He denies the reality of the virgin birth, the reality of the miracles and prophecies, details of the crucifixion, and the resurrection of Jesus. As a result of his rejection of the literal meaning of Scripture, Spong logically feels no need to submit morally to the Bible's condemnation of homosexuality. Therefore, the bishop proudly proclaims his endorsement of homosexuality and the fact that he oversees twenty-three openly homosexual priests in his Newark, New Jersey Episcopalian diocese.

While Spong despises fundamentalist, orthodox Christians (like myself) as "uniformed, unquestioning, and ignorant," he is forced to admit that the fundamentalist churches are rapidly growing because biblical literalism appeals to people's need for certainty. Spong rejects the Genesis account of the beginning of man's sinful disobedience and states that "the fall of man . . . no longer makes sense." He then dismisses as "no longer believable" the Bible's revelation, in which "Christ has been portrayed as the divine rescuer — sent to save the fallen human creature from sin and to restore that creature to the goodness of his or her pre-fall creation."[4] Together with many liberal theologians and modern religious writers, Bishop Spong condemns as "ignorant" those who uphold the orthodox Christian, biblically based beliefs that have sustained billions of believers for two thousand years.

However, anyone who observes the religious attitudes exhibited today in America and Europe recognizes the utter failure of this liberal, anti-literal, anti-Bible, and anti-Christian religious viewpoint to motivate people to join the shrinking congregations of liberal mainline denominations. Spong admits that the fundamentalist, Bible-believing churches are growing at an unprecedented rate, while the liberal mainline churches that reject the Bible's teaching "shrink every day in membership." He complains, "The only churches that grow today are those that do not, in fact, understand the issues and can therefore traffic in certainty. They represent both the fundamentalistic Protestant groups and the rigidly controlled conservative Catholic traditions." In other words, Spong believes the successful and growing Bible-believing churches "do not, in fact, understand the issues," primarily because they still espouse traditional, orthodox Christian beliefs.

Bishop Spong admits, "The churches that do attempt to interact with the emerging world (rejecting historic orthodox Christian beliefs) are for the most part the liberal Protestant mainline churches that shrink every day in membership and the silent liberal Catholic minority that attracts very few adherents. Both are, almost by definition, fuzzy, imprecise, and relatively unappealing. They might claim to be honest, but for the most part they have no real message." Incredibly, although Spong himself admits the liberal mainline Protestant position is "fuzzy, imprecise, and relatively unappealing," he presents his own slight variation of that same "fuzzy" liberal position that also rejects the orthodox, literal view of the Bible. Spong wants to create a new "Christianity" that is stripped of the following doctrines that have been fundamental to the orthodox faith for centuries: the reality of the historical Jesus Christ as described in the Gospels, His status as the Son of God, His role as the Savior for our sins, and the truth of His physical resurrection from the dead.

However, once someone divorces their "Christianity" from the statements about the Jesus of the Bible, they have, in reality, created a new religion or myth that has nothing to do with Jesus of Nazareth or with God's biblical revelation of salvation, heaven, or hell. In other words, Bishop Spong's new "Christianity" is a new religion that, apart from the name "Christian," would be unrecognizable to the disciples of Christ or to the vast majority of followers of Jesus of Nazareth over the last two thousand years. When Christianity is divorced from the historic written documents of revelation that guided it for centuries, theologians and religious leaders are free to create whatever doctrines or myths they desire because there is no longer any agreed standard against which their statements can be measured. However, their new "faith" is no longer Christian in any meaningful sense of the word. If the words of the Bible are no longer meaningful according to their normal grammatical-historical usage, then liberal religious leaders are free to re-create their "mythical" Jesus, and Christianity itself, into any shape or teaching that appears popular at the moment. However, this divorce from historic and biblical Christian faith should be obvious to anyone who compares these beliefs against the unchangeable Word of God.

Sincere, long-suffering Christians who have sat in the pews of these "fuzzy, imprecise and relatively unappealing" liberal churches are finally leaving in sadness and frustration because the preaching from the pulpit no longer provides spiritual sustenance or meaningful guidance for their lives. Sitting in church Sunday after Sunday, they have heard a vague message that denies that the Bible truly means what it says when it promises forgiveness for sins and guilt or when it offers a real heavenly home. Their liberal "ship of faith" has lost its anchor and is now drifting hopelessly on the ocean of ever-changing theological opinion. It is no wonder that millions in recent years have abandoned liberal churches in their earnest search for an orthodox, biblically-based Christian church that confidently bases its faith and teaching on the unchanging, inspired Word of God.

A fascinating Gallop Poll completed several years ago

examined the attitudes of many people by asking this question: "What is your number one personal goal for the next year?" It was fascinating and encouraging for Christians to note that 57 percent of the respondents declared that their number one personal goal was to find a strong personal relationship with God. This outcome suggests that millions of our fellow citizens are longing for a more meaningful relationship with God. The conservative, orthodox, Bible-believing churches are growing at an unprecedented rate worldwide because hundreds of millions are seeking a spiritual meaning and certainty in their life that can only be found in a reliance in the unshakable truths expressed in the Word of God. Many people are seeking a biblically based faith that produces the spiritual confidence to affirm the historic Christian statement: "I know in whom I have believed, and am persuaded that he is able to keep that which I have committed unto him against that day" (2 Timothy 1:12).

Notes

1. Clement C. J. Webb, *The Historical Element in Religion* (1935).

2. Emil Brunner, *Revelation and Reason* (Philadelphia: 1946) 168.

3. Emil Brunner, *Revelation and Reason* (Philadelphia: 1946) 98–171.

4. John Shelby Spong, *Rescuing the Bible from Fundamentalism* (San Francisco: Harper Collins, 1991) 35.

6

The Sacred Mystery of the Trinity

"Hear, O Israel: The Lord our God is one Lord."

Deuteronomy 6:4

Many Christians and virtually all non-Christians acknowledge that the mystery of the Trinity is the most profound and difficult of all biblical doctrines to understand. During my years at Bible college in Philadelphia, I can remember many late-night conversations with my fellow students as we vainly attempted to come to terms with this difficult concept. As a result of numerous conversations over thirty-five years with both pastors and laymen, I have come to believe that many Christians do not have a clear understanding of the great scriptural truths about the triune nature of God. Unfortunately, many pastors and Bible teachers in our generation have failed to teach this vital doctrine, perhaps because of its obvious difficulty. However, the sad result of this failure is that many Christians are unable to express clearly in either thought or word their understanding of the true nature of God as revealed in the Bible. Surely, we who love God with all our heart and have dedicated our lives to His service need to come to a full, mature understanding of the great biblical truths regarding the nature of God. It is obvious that the only source of true knowledge about God's nature must be found in the genuine written revelation of God, as found in the Holy Scriptures. However, in this study we will also examine the writings of the Early Church about the nature of God. Finally, I will share some fascinating research that will reveal an extraordinary discovery — the greatest of the Jewish rabbis in the years before Jesus was born taught, in the clearest language possible, about the sacred mystery of the Trinity.

When we examine the pages of the Bible, we find that there is a deep mystery concerning the nature of God, beginning with the opening verses of the Scriptures. From the initial verses in the book of Genesis through to the closing promises found in the book of Revelation, we discover numerous inspired statements that affirm that there is only one God. However, it is equally clear that the Word of God constantly affirms, often in the very same verses, that this same God, is revealed in three persons or three manifestations. This seeming contradiction has puzzled millions of thoughtful believers over the centuries. The infinite and omnipresent nature of God is far beyond the power of our finite minds to understand perfectly. However, while we still struggle to appreciate the inner mystery of His triune nature, the truth of the Trinity has been taught throughout the Scriptures from Genesis to Revelation.

One of my favorite biblical commentators is the brilliant Russian writer Ivan Panin, who completed an exhaustive study of the Word of God to discover its marvellous doctrines and the phenomenal textual features within the Scriptures. He once wrote, "I used to doubt God. Now I only doubt my knowledge of Him."[1] While the doctrine of the Trinity is beyond our ability to fully appreciate, it is not fundamentally contrary to reason. This is a study that needs to be approached with a holy reverence, an open heart, and an obedient spirit that will examine the inspired statements of the Scriptures to learn from its sacred pages what our Lord reveals regarding His divine nature.

What does the Bible actually teach about the Trinity, the triune nature of God? The scriptural revelation of the nature of God can be succinctly described in one sentence.

The Bible declares that there is one God who is revealed to us as Father, Son, and Holy Spirit, each of whom has distinct personal attributes; however, there is no division regarding nature, essence, or being.

This statement sums up every significant point that the Scriptures teach us about the doctrine of the Trinity, as held by orthodox Christian believers in all denominations during the last two thousand years. While the Bible clearly describes this triune or threefold nature in its constant use of the words *Father, Son,* and *Holy Spirit,* the Scriptures also declare authoritatively that there is only one God. As we consider these passages that describe God, we need to fix our mind on the truth that God is one God, not three. Because of the lack of biblical teaching about this important doctrine of the Trinity, some believers who are young in their faith have misunderstood the true nature of God. Some immature believers unfortunately imagine that they will see three individual Gods — the Father, Son, and Holy Spirit — sitting on three separate thrones when they arrive in heaven. This is a profound misunderstanding of the true doctrine of the Trinity.

Let us examine the teaching of the Bible itself to learn what these inspired passages can teach us about the nature of God. First, the Bible repeatedly and emphatically rejects the pagan idea of polytheism (the view that there are many gods). In ancient times polytheism was virtually universal, with the exception of the Jews and Christians. The Hindus of India believe that there are millions of gods. The various ethnic groups making up the vast Roman Empire acknowledged thousands of different gods. However, the teaching of the Bible, from the first pages of Genesis to the last verses of Revelation, has declared that there is only one God.

Jesus Taught the Trinity

Consider the profound words of Jesus Christ that reveal His authoritative teaching about the triune nature of God, or the Trinity: "Believe me that I am in the Father, and the Father in me: or else believe me for the very works' sake . . . And I will pray the Father, and he shall give you another Comforter, that he may abide with you for ever" (John 14:11,16). In this one verse Jesus affirmed that He and the Father were one. At the same time, He identified himself and the Father as two distinct persons under the titles of His own name and that of "the Father." Then Jesus promised His Church that the Father would answer the prayer of Jesus and send "another Comforter," referring to the Holy Spirit, as the third person in the Triune God. A careful examination of these words of Jesus reveal clearly that He taught the unity of God expressed in three distinct persons: the Father, the Son, and the Comforter (the Holy Spirit).

The word "Trinity" comes from the Latin word *trinitas*, or the word *trinitus*, which means "three in one" or "threefold." This word expresses the clear teaching of the Church on the profound biblical doctrine of the nature of God, as revealed in the Scriptures, as a Trinity in unity.

The Unity and Attributes of God

The Bible teaches repeatedly that there is only one God. Numerous examples from the Scriptures could be sighted, but these few verses will suffice to prove the truth of this important doctrine. Moses, the great lawgiver of the Jews, declared, "Thou shalt have no other gods before me" (Exodus 20:3). Moses also declared the unity of God in the famous words of the "Shema," the daily affirmation of righteous Jews throughout the world for thousands of years: "Hear, O Israel: The Lord our God is one Lord" (Deuteronomy 6:4). However, there is a mystery found in the Hebrew words of this declaration that we will study more deeply later in this chapter. The prophet Isaiah also declared the unity of God in his prophetic words, "I am the Lord: that is my name: and my glory will I not give to another, neither my praise to graven images" (Isaiah 42:8). Isaiah also wrote of God in the following words: "To whom will ye liken me, and make me equal, and compare me, that we may be like?" (Isaiah 46:5). The prophet Malachi wrote of one God when he said, "Have we not all one father? hath not one God created us?" (Malachi 2:10).

One of the most important attributes of God is that He is both eternal and uncreated. In other words, there was never a time when God did not exist. Therefore, God has no beginning and no ending. The Scriptures reveal the eternal nature of God in numerous passages, including the words of King David in the Psalms: "Before the mountains were brought forth, or ever thou hadst formed the earth and the world, even from everlasting to everlasting, thou art God" (Psalms 90:2). Jesus Christ confirmed His eternal nature in these words: "Verily, verily, I say unto you,

Before Abraham was, I am" (John 8:58). Furthermore, the Bible teaches us that God is omnipresent, which means that He is simultaneously everywhere throughout His creation, not only in awareness but in His actual divine presence. This omnipresence of God was alluded to by King Solomon, as recorded in the book of Kings at the building of the Temple: "But will God indeed dwell on the earth? Behold, the heaven and heaven of heavens cannot contain thee; how much less this house that I have builded?" (1 Kings 8:27). The Scriptures also declare that God is unchangeable, that His nature will remain the same forever. The prophet Malachi wrote, "For I am the Lord, I change not" (Malachi 3:6). This inspired declaration by Malachi confirms that God's nature, as expressed in the Trinity in unity, did not change when the Son incarnated in the body of the Christ child, Jesus of Nazareth, 2000 years ago. In other words, the Father, the Son, and the Holy Spirit have always existed as the Trinity.

The Father, the Son, and the Holy Spirit Are Called God

Now that we have examined the passages that affirm there is only one God, we need to explore the other passages of Scripture that also teach us clearly that God the Father, God the Son, Jesus, and God the Holy Spirit are all identified and named as God. Paul wrote the following letter referring to both the Father and Jesus as God: "To Timothy, my dearly beloved son: Grace, mercy, and peace, from God the Father and Christ Jesus our Lord" (2 Timothy 1:2). Paul again affirms that both are God in his letter to the Church at Philippi: "And that every tongue should confess that Jesus Christ is Lord, to the glory of God the Father" (Philippians 2:11). In the Gospel of John we find a clear declaration by the beloved disciple, John, that both Jesus and the Father are God. "No man hath seen God at any time; the only begotten Son, which is in the bosom of the Father, he hath declared him" (John 1:18).

Jesus, the Son of God, Created the Universe

However, while John reveals that Jesus and the Father are both God, he also reveals that it was Jesus, the Son of God, as the Word (Logos) of God, who created the entire universe and everything within it. I am constantly surprised to find that many Christians have assumed that God the Father created everything. However, a careful examination of the Scriptures reveals that the act of creation was committed to Jesus, the Son of God. "In the beginning was the Word, and the Word was with God, and the Word was God. The same was in the beginning with God. All things were made by him; and without him was not any thing made that was made" (John 1:1–3). This teaching is confirmed by the letter Paul wrote to the Ephesians Church: "And to make all men see what is the fellowship of the mystery, which from the beginning of the world hath been hid in God, who created all things by Jesus Christ" (Ephesians 3:9). The Psalmist David alludes to the fact that the Son is the One who created all things by identifying the Creator as "the Word of the Lord." Later in this chapter we will examine the scriptural evidence that "the Word of the Lord" is often used as an Old Testament title for the Son of God, the second person of the Trinity. David declares, "By the word of the Lord were the heavens made; and all the host of them by the breath of his mouth" (Psalms 33:6).

The Bible continually refers to the Holy Spirit as a distinct person of the Godhead who teaches, acts, witnesses about Christ, and dwells within the spirit of the believer as the Spirit of God. At the end of His earthly ministry, Jesus Christ promised His disciples that He would send them "a Comforter" to guide and direct them after He ascended to heaven. "And I will pray the Father, and he shall give you another Comforter, that he may abide with you for ever; Even the Spirit of truth; whom the world cannot receive, because it seeth him not, neither knoweth him: but ye know him; for he dwelleth with you, and shall be in you" (John 14:16–17). This passage reveals the three divine persons of the Trinity. However, this verse also clearly identifies the Holy Spirit as the person of God the Comforter, who will indwell the believers. King David also wrote about the divine Holy Spirit as a separate person of the Trinity when he appealed to God (the Father) in the following words: "Cast me not away from thy presence; and take not thy holy spirit from me" (Psalms 51:11). Additionally, in the New Testament, Jesus identified the Holy Spirit as both God and as a distinct person of the Trinity. Jesus taught about the Holy Spirit as God in His conclusion to the Lords Prayer, which was addressed to "Our Father." Jesus taught, "If ye then, being evil, know how to give good gifts unto your children: how much more shall your heavenly Father give the Holy Spirit to them that ask him?" (Luke 11:13). These Scriptures obviously teach the threefold nature of God as we describe it under the word "Trinity."

The Bible Teaches the Trinity

We have examined the scriptural teaching that there is only one God. In addition, we have examined the Scriptures that teach that the Father, the Son, and the Holy Spirit are three distinct persons of the Godhead. We now need to look at the Scriptures that reveal the three persons as one God. One of the most significant passages revealing this teaching about the Trinity is found at the beginning of the ministry of Jesus when John baptized our Lord. The Gospel of Matthew records, "And Jesus, when he was baptized, went up straightway out of the water: and, lo, the heavens were opened unto him, and he saw the Spirit of God descending like a dove, and lighting upon him: And lo a voice from heaven, saying, This is my beloved Son, in whom I am well pleased" (Matthew 3:16–17). In this well-loved passage we observe Jesus, the Son of God, being baptized by John and the Holy Spirit of God descending upon Him. Simultaneously, God the Father speaks from heaven saying, "This is my beloved Son."

This critical passage clearly reveals the three distinct persons of the Trinity acting as individual persons, yet in perfect harmony as the Trinity of God. It is significant that at the end of His ministry on earth, Jesus Christ instructed His disciples by giving them His Great Commission: "Go ye therefore, and teach all nations, baptizing them in the name of the Father, and of the Son, and of the Holy Ghost" (Matthew 28:19). Since baptism is the most profound profession of faith, devotion, and worship, which is due only to God, the words of Jesus confirm that "the Father, the Son, and the Holy Ghost" are equally God, as taught in the biblical doctrine of the Trinity. This teaching of the Trinity also appears in the final benediction, in which the apostle Paul concludes his second inspired letter to the church at Corinth. Paul gave them his blessings in the names of the three persons of God, as revealed in the Trinity, "The grace of the Lord Jesus Christ, and the love of God, and the communion of the Holy Ghost, be with you all. Amen" (2 Corinthians 13:14).

The Trinity As Taught in the Old Testament

The unusual language used by Moses in the first verses of the book of Genesis presents a great mystery regarding the nature of God and His creation of this universe and mankind. The first verse of the Bible records the creation of the heavens and the earth by God. However, the inspired writer used the word *Elohim* אלהים "Gods," which is the plural name for God, rather than the singular name *Jehovah* יהוה "God." It is fascinating to note that Moses uses this plural name for "God" *Elohim* אלהים more than five hundred times in the first five books of the Bible. The mystery is that the plural name of God *Elohim* appears with a singular verb each time. The normal laws of grammar demand that the plural form of the noun must agree with the plural form of the verb. However, throughout the Scriptures, we find that the plural noun for God *Elohim* appears invariably with the singular form of the verb, such as we find in the first verse of Genesis. Here the singular verb "created" ברא *bara* occurs with the plural noun *Elohim* אלהים in Genesis 1:1: "In the beginning God created the heaven and the earth." The Hebrew Scriptures record this passage as follows [reading from right to left in the Hebrew]:

"the heavens and the earth." "*Elohim* (Gods)" "created" "In the beginning"

בראשית　　　ברא　　　אלהים　　　את השמים ואת הארץ

[plural noun for Gods] [singular verb]

There is only one logical solution to this problem. If there is no grammatical agreement between the plural noun *Elohim* and the singular verb "created," then there must be an overriding logical agreement that demands the unusual grammatical construction found in these sentences. The logical agreement is that the word *Elohim* clearly reveals the sacred mystery of the nature of God as a Trinity. In other words, Genesis 1:1 reveals this declaration: "In the beginning the Trinity (the Father, Son, and Holy Spirit) created the heavens and the earth."

The Teaching of the Early Church on the Trinity

The early Church upheld the biblical doctrine of the Trinity universally from the Day of Pentecost in A.D. 32 throughout the last two thousand years. An examination of the early Church writings will verify their unwavering support for this teaching found in the writings of both the Old and New Testament. The real value of these ancient Christian writings is that they are the best interpreters of the doctrine of the Trinity as it was preached by Jesus and the apostles. As some of these early Christians were taught by those who personally knew the apostles, they would have been in an excellent position to understand the true meaning of the New Testament teachings. Some critics of the doctrine of the Trinity have complained that the word "Trinity" cannot be found in the actual Hebrew or Greek words of the Scriptures. However, the truth of this doctrine is taught clearly from Genesis to Revelation. Many scholars believe that the word "Trinity" was used for the first time in reference to this biblical doctrine during a church council held at Alexandria, Egypt in A.D. 317. However, the history of the early Church reveals that this doctrine of the Trinity was taught by Jesus Christ, His disciples, and the apostles. The Trinity of God was the universal belief of the church from the very beginning of the Christian era. For example, the secular Greek writer Lucian, in his book *Philopatris*, written in A.D. 160, confirmed the well-known belief of the Christians in the Trinity. Lucian described the first generations of Christians confessing their faith in God in the following words: "The exalted God . . . Son of the Father, Spirit proceeding from the Father, One of Three, and Three of One."[2]

Some critics and theologians have claimed that the doctrine of the Trinity was unknown until the Council of Nicca in A.D. 325, where they claim it was invented by the unanimous collusion of the Church fathers in that council. However, this claim is totally contradicted by the many writings of the early Church from Christ to A.D. 325. I will share some passages from several of these writers to establish this fact. In addition, the orthodox Christian faith has continued to teach the Trinity for two thousand years, from the resurrection of Jesus Christ until today.

One of the earliest of the manuscripts written by Church leaders is the *Shepherd of Hermas*. He was a brother of Pius, the bishop of Rome. Some scholars believe Hermas is the person mentioned in the apostle Paul's epistle to the Romans (16:14). Hermas wrote, "The Son of God is more ancient than any created thing, so that He was present in council with His Father at the creation."[3]

Justin Martyr was a great leader and writer in the early

Church in A.D. 150. His writing declares that the doctrine of the Trinity was proclaimed with great clarity from the earliest ages of the Church. Justin and many of the early Church fathers wrote that it was Jesus Christ who appeared as God to Moses in the burning bush. He criticized the Jews for confusing the roles of God the Father with that of His Son in the passages of the Old Testament. Justin Martyr wrote,

> The Jews, who think that it was always God the Father who spoke to Moses, (whereas He who spoke to him was the Son of God, who is also called an Angel, and an Apostle) are justly convicted both by the prophetical spirit, and by Christ himself, for knowing neither the Father nor the Son. For they, who say that the Son is the Father, are convicted of neither knowing the Father, nor of understanding that the God of the universe has a Son: who, being the first-born Word of God, is also God.[4]

Justin Martyr also wrote the following statement in his *Dialogue With Trypho*. He establishes a general rule that wherever God appears or converses with any man in the Old Testament, as in Genesis 17:22, we should understand that the passage is referring to Jesus as God the Son.

> Now that Christ is Lord, and substantially God the Son of God, and in times past appeared potentially as a man and an angel, and in fiery glory as He appeared in the bush. and at the judgment of Sodom, has been proved by many arguments."[5]

The Council of Sirmium was held in A.D. 351 to deal with a number of heresies that were beginning to plague the Church. This council established a creed as a clear statement of the teaching of the Church regarding the Trinity. In one of its comments on this subject we find the following words: "If any one say that the Father did not speak the words, 'Let us make man,' to His Son, but that he spoke them to Himself, let him be anathema."[6] The declaration "Let him be anathema" means "Let him be accursed or cut off from the Church." This statement shows how strongly the Trinity was held to be an essential doctrine of the faith by the early Church.

The Mystery of the Trinity Revealed in Ancient Jewish Writings

A few years ago I made a fascinating discovery in the ancient writings of the Jewish sages that were recorded thousands of years ago during the centuries surrounding the life of Jesus Christ and the destruction of the Second Temple in A.D. 70. This discovery suggests that the mystery of the Trinity was understood by some of the greatest of the ancient Jewish sages and writers. Furthermore, this doctrine of the Trinity was recorded in the writings of these great Jewish teachers and sages in their *Targums* (paraphrases of Scripture) and their commentaries (including the *Zohar*).

Both Christians from Gentile backgrounds and Jewish Messianic believers accepted the teaching of the Bible from Genesis to Revelation that shows that God has revealed Himself throughout the Scriptures in the form of the three persons of the Godhead, or as the Jewish sages wrote, "three manifestations" or "three emanations."

Many students of the Bible will be as astonished as I was when I first discovered these provocative ancient Jewish theological writings. They helped me understand why so many of the Jews in Israel and throughout the Roman Empire rapidly accepted the claims of Jesus of Nazareth to be both the Messiah and the true Son of God. Any student of the history of religion knows that the Jewish people, together with the Muslims, have historically rejected the truth of Christianity, primarily because they reject the claims that Jesus is the Son of God. The Jews and Muslims generally reject Christ because they believe that Christianity teaches polytheism, that we believe there are three Gods, not one. They generally fail to understand that Christians believe and uphold the biblical teaching that there is only one God. Both Jews and Muslims understand the truth that is clearly expressed numerous times in the Old Testament that there is only one God, but because they misunderstand the biblical teaching about the Trinity, they reject Christianity without examining the claims of Christ.

The question that occurred to me several years ago was this: Why did hundreds of thousands of Jews accept the claims of Jesus to be the Son of God? We know from early Church history that many of those who first accepted the Gospel throughout the Roman Empire were Jews. The apostle Paul and other Jewish Christian missionaries were accepted as teachers and worshippers in the Jewish synagogues throughout the empire for one hundred years, from the resurrection of Jesus in A.D. 32 until the rebellion against Rome in A.D. 135. During the three years of battle for Jewish independence led by the general Simeon Bar Kochba, many of his followers (including the famous Rabbi Akiba) declared that Bar Kochba was Israel's true messiah.

Naturally the Jewish Christian believers were forced to withdraw from the Jewish forces fighting against Rome because, as followers of Jesus Christ as the true Messiah, they could not acknowledge the false claims of Simeon Bar Kochba. Unfortunately, this rejection was treated as treason by the Jews who were involved in a life and death struggle with six legions of the cruel Emperor Hadrian. The war for Jewish independence ended in A.D. 135 with the massacre of one and a half million men, women, and children in the Jewish army and their civilian followers. From A.D. 135, the Jews that were believers in Jesus were no longer welcome in the Jewish synagogues. The great schism began between Jews and Christians that has tragically continued for the last two thousand years.

However, to return to my question: Why did many Jews in the first century of this era accept the claim that Jesus is God, while most Jews in later centuries have rejected this claim out of hand? I believe the answer can be found in these ancient Jewish *Targums* and the *Zohar*, which we will examine in this chapter. These writings clearly reveal that the Jews in the centuries surrounding the life of Jesus Christ understood that the sacred Scriptures taught that there was a profound mystery regarding the triune nature of God. That mystery is revealed in the *Targums* and the *Zohar*. There is One God, who is revealed in three persons — the Trinity. Since these *Targums* were read in the synagogue every Sabbath day, these concepts would have been widely known to religious Jews in that day. I believe that the evidence we will examine will prove that these writings prepared many Jews to accept the claim of Jesus to be the Son of God because their greatest religious teachers, including Rabbi Simon ben Jochai and Rabbi Eliezer, writers of the *Zohar*, and the writers of the *Targums*,

Jonathan ben Uziel and Onkelos the Proselyte, all taught the mystery of God expressed as "Three in One."

In the remaining pages of this chapter, I will share a number of fascinating ancient Hebrew writings from the distant past that reveal that these brilliant Jewish writers anticipated the New Testament's revelation that Jesus was truly the Son of God. It was natural that the Jews in the first century found it difficult to accept the claims of Jesus of Nazareth to be the Son of God and to be "equal with the Father." The obvious problem faced by Jewish religious scholars when they encountered the unusual name Elohim אלהים, the plural name for God, repeatedly in the Bible was the question, Why would God identify Himself in the plural form? One of the ways these Jewish scholars escaped the clear suggestion of the plurality of persons in the Godhead, as found in the word Elohim, was to claim that this expression was simply an example of the "royal plural form" used by kings and queens to express their royal nature. The famous Rabbi Aben Ezra, writing around A.D. 1100, suggested this as a solution. The "royal plural" is an unusual plural form of speech used by such royalty as Queen Victoria when she uttered her famous line, "We are not amused."

While this evasion regarding "Elohim" as a "royal plural" appears in numerous Jewish commentaries on the Scriptures, it does not solve the problem. There is no evidence that this royal plural form of speaking was ever used in ancient biblical days. The kings and leaders of Israel and the leaders of surrounding pagan nations, such as King Nebuchadnezzar or King Cyrus, never used this form of speech. In fact, it is a comparatively modern invention that was created by medieval monarchs to emphasize their elevated status to rule their kingdoms in accordance with the theory of the "divine right of kings." However, all of the leaders and kings in the Scriptures speak in the singular form, never in the plural form of address. The normal mode of royal speech in biblical times was always the same singular form used by King Nebuchadnezzar in the book of Daniel: "Therefore I make a decree . . ." (Daniel 3:29). Therefore, the plural name for God Elohim אלהים must refer to the mystery of the plurality and unity of God in the Trinity.

The *Zohar*

The *Zohar* is a fascinating book written by Rabbi Simon ben Jochai and his son Rabbi Eliezer in the years following the Roman army's tragic destruction of the Temple in Jerusalem in A.D. 70. For many years father and son were forced to hide from the troops of the Roman emperor who had passed the death sentence on them both. The *Zohar* is held in great reverence by Jewish scholars, and has also been of great interest to many Christian scholars in past centuries, beginning with Pico della Mirandola (a medieval scholar), who wrote Latin summaries of its teachings. Pico della Mirandola was the first Christian writer to conclude that significant parallels existed between some of the deeper doctrines of Christianity and Judaism, as found in the writings of the *Zohar*. He believed that the doctrines of the Trinity, the doctrine of original sin, and the mystery of the incarnation of Christ were referred to in the ancient *Zohar*.

The Christian writer Petrius Galatinus published his book, *De Arcanis Catholicae Veritatis*, which illustrated his research into the ancient Jewish teachings of the *Zohar* which paralleled several of the major doctrines of the Church. Other Christian researchers on the *Zohar*'s teaching include the writer Gasparellus, Kircher, and Knorr von Rosenroth. The fascinating book *Kabbalah Denudata* by Knorr von Rosenroth was published in 1677 and later translated into English almost two centuries later. His book is valuable for Christian scholars unfamiliar with the Hebrew and Aramaic languages who wish to examine the teachings of the *Zohar*.

Many of the most difficult areas of the Scriptures are discussed and debated in the pages of the *Zohar*. The primary value for Christians is the deeper understanding we can gain as to what the Jewish religious leaders truly thought about the teachings of the Old Testament, including the mystery of the Trinity. I was amazed when I first read the English translations of this book because I discovered that these brilliant Jewish sages had come to a clear understanding of the mystery of the Trinity two thousand years ago. This important discovery of the teaching of the Trinity by the ancient Jewish sages helps us to understand why many Jews accepted the teaching of John the Baptist and Jesus of Nazareth during the first century of this era. Although many Jews naturally rejected Jesus' claims to be the Messiah and the Son of

God, many Jews accepted that Jesus was the fulfillment of the ancient prophecies of the Old Testament. In addition, the fact that the ancient Jewish sages spoke of the mystery of the plural nature of God prepared many in the Jewish nation to accept Jesus' claims that "I and my Father are one" (John 10:30).

The Trinity As Taught by the Ancient Jewish Sages

Do the ancient Jewish books such as the *Zohar* and the *Targums* actually refer to the Trinity and clearly describe the plural nature of God? Let me present the evidence, and you will be able to judge for yourself. Consider the following statements:

"How can they (the three) be One? Are they verily One, because we call them One ?

How Three can be One, can only be known through the revelation of the Holy Spirit."[7]

According to the *Zohar*, one day Rabbi Simeon ben Jochai was teaching his son Rabbi Eliezer about the mystery of the triune nature of God. He instructed his pupil by saying, "Come and see the mystery of the word יהוה, Jehova: there are three steps, each existing by itself; nevertheless they are One, and so united that one cannot be separated from the other."[8]

Rabbi Simeon ben Jochai indicates in another passage of the *Zohar* that these three steps as revealed in *Elohim* אלהים (God) are three substantive beings or three divine persons united in one.

The Ancient Holy One is revealed with three Heads, which are united in One, and that Head is thrice exalted. The Ancient Holy one is described as being Three; it is because the other Lights emanating from Him are included in the Three. Yet the Ancient One is described as being two. The Ancient One includes these two. He is the Crown of all that is exalted; the Chief of the chief, so exalted, that He cannot be known to perfection. Thus the other lights are two complete ones, yet is the Ancient Holy One described complete as one, and He is one, positively one; thus are the other lights united and glorified in because they are one.[9]

Rabbi Simeon ben Jochai wrote a fascinating passage recorded in the *Zohar* that is as clear a discussion of the mystery of the

Trinity as you could find in any Christian theology text. Rabbi Simeon comments on the text found in Deuteronomy 32:39: "See now that I, I am he, and Elohim is not with me."[10]

> He said: "Friends, here are some profound mysteries which I desire to reveal to you now that permission has been given to utter them. Who is it that says, 'See now that I, I am He?' This is the Cause which is above all those on high, that which is called *the Cause of causes*. It is above those other causes, since none of those causes does anything till it obtains permission from that which is above it, as we pointed out above in respect to the expression, 'Let us make man.' 'Us' certainly refers to two, of which one said to the other above it, 'Let us make,' nor did it do anything save with the permission and direction of the one above it, while the one above did nothing without consulting its colleague. But that which is called 'the Cause above all causes,' which has no superior or even equal, as it is written, 'To whom shall ye liken me, that I should be equal?' (referring to Isaiah 40:25), said, 'See now that I, I am he, and Elohim is not with me,' from whom he should take counsel, like that of which it is written, 'and God said, Let us make man.'"

Another book written by Rabbi Simeon ben Jochai, known as *The Propositions of the Zohar*, records the mystery of the Shechinah glory of God in these words.

> . . . the exalted Shechinah comprehends the Three highest Sephiroth; of Him (God) it is said, (Ps. lxii. 12), "God hath spoken once; twice have I heard this." Once and twice means the Three exalted Sephiroth, of whom it is said: Once, once, and once; that is, Three united in One. This is the mystery.[11]

Another famous Jewish scholar, Rabbi Eliezer Hakkalir, who lived at the time of Rabbi Simeon ben Jochai, also taught the scriptural doctrine that there were three distinct Beings revealed in the one unified Godhead. In his commentary on Genesis 1:1, Rabbi Hakkalir wrote the following:

> When God created the world, He created it through the

Three Sephiroth, namely, through Sepher, Sapher and Vesaphur, by which the Three הויות (Beings) are meant . . . The Rabbi, my Lord Teacher of blessed memory, explained Sepher, Sapher, and Sippur, to be synonymous to Ja, Jehovah, and Elohim meaning to say, that the world was created by these three names.[12]

Rabbi Bechai, in his commentary on Genesis 1:1 (p. 1, col. 2) explained that the word Elohim אלהים is compounded of two words, הם and אל, that is, "These are God." The plural is expressed by the letter jod (י).

Another extraordinary reference to the Trinity is found in the *Zohar* :

> Here is the secret of two names combined which are completed by a third and become one again. "And God said Let us make Man." It is written, "The secret of the Lord is to them that fear him" (Psalm 25:34). That most reverend Elder opened an exposition of this verse by saying "Simeon Simeon, who is it that said: 'Let us make man?' Who is this Elohim?" With these words the most reverend Elder vanished before anyone saw him . . . Truly now is the time to expound this mystery, because certainly there is here a mystery which hitherto it was not permitted to divulge, but now we perceive that permission is given." He then proceeded: "We must picture a king who wanted several buildings to be erected, and who had an architect in his service who did nothing save with his consent. The king is the supernal wisdom above, the Central Column being the king below: Elohim is the architect above . . . and Elohim is also the architect below, being as such the Divine Presence (Shekinah) of the lower world.[13]

The Shema: "Hear O Israel, the Lord Our God Is One Lord."

Every religiously observant Jew makes a daily affirmation of his faith in speaking the Shema, the inspired words of Scripture, as recorded in Deuteronomy 6:4: "Hear O Israel, the Lord our God is one Lord." In these sacred words, the speaker first uses the singular name of God, יהוה "Jehovah," then the plural name, אלהים "our God" (strictly, "Gods"), and then again the singular name, יהוה "Jehovah," and concluded with אחד "One." Most people hearing this affirmation would assume that the simple meaning is a direct declaration that "there is only one God." This biblical statement does declare that there is only one God — a statement accepted whole heartedly by both Jews and Christians. However, as pointed out earlier in this chapter, the mysterious use of the plural name for God, *Elohim* אלהים, suggests that this passage also contains God's revelation of His mysterious nature as Three in One and One in Three. When I searched the ancient Jewish books that were written during the period from the return from the captivity in Babylon in 536 B.C. to the destruction of the Second Temple in A.D. 70 I was amazed to find that many prominent Jewish sages taught the mystery of the Trinity based on this very passage in Deuteronomy 6:4.

We need to carefully read the words of this ancient teaching found in the *Zohar* regarding the deeper meaning and mystery of God found in Deuteronomy 6:4: "Hear, O Israel: The Lord our God is one Lord." Although the language is awkward, it clearly teaches the Trinity.

> We have said in many places, that this daily form of prayer is one of those passages concerning the Unity, which is taught in the Scriptures. In Deut. vi. 4, we read first יהוה "Jehovah", then, אלהים "our God," and again, יהוה "Jehovah," which together make one Unity. But how can three Names [three beings] be one? Are they verily one, because we call them one? How three can be one can only be known through the revelation of the Holy Spirit, and, in fact, with closed eyes. This is also the mystery of the voice. The voice is heard only as one sound, yet it consists of three substances, fire, wind, and water, but all three are one, as indicated through the mystery of the voice. Thus are (Deut. 6:4) "The Lord, our God, the Lord," but One Unity, three Substantive Beings which are One; and this is indicated by the voice which are One; and this is indicated by the voice which a person uses in reading the words, "Hear, O Israel," thereby comprehending with the understanding the most perfect Unity of Him who is infinite; because all three (Jehovah, Elohim, Jehovah) are read with one voice, which indicates a Trinity.[14]

This statement from the *Zohar* is an incredible acknowledgment of the nature of God, as revealed in the Scriptures, as a Trinity. Rabbi Menachem of Recanati, writing in his *Commentary on the Pentateuch* about the Deuteronomy 6:4 passage, also clearly describes the mystery of the Trinity, the threefold Unity of the Godhead. Rabbi Menachem wrote about these mysteries and concluded, "These are secrets which are revealed only to those who are reaping upon the holy field, as it is written 'The secret of the Lord is with them that fear Him'" (Psalms 25:14). Rabbi Menachem wrote the following on the Trinity:

> "Hear, O Israel, the Lord our god is one Lord." This verse is the root of our faith, therefore Moses records it after the ten commandments. The reason (that there is said יהוה, Lord, אלהים, our God, and יהוה, Lord) is, because the word שמע does not here signify "Hear;" but "to gather together, to unite," as in 1 Samuel 15:4, "Saul gathered together the people." The meaning implied is The Inherent-Ones are so united together, one in the other without end, they being the exalted God. He mentions the three names mystically to indicate the three exalted original Ones.[15]

Let Us Make Man in Our Image

Moses recorded God's creation of man in the first chapter of Genesis. The inspired account read, "And God said, 'Let us make man in our image.'" The question that has been asked by many Christian and Jewish commentators is this: Who did God refer to as "us" when he stated "Let *us* make man in our image?" The answer is this: God referred to the other members of the Trinity when He said "Let us. . . ." This statement clearly refers to the Trinity.

In Genesis 1:26 God says, "Let us make man in our image." In this passage we find God definitely speaking of the Godhead in the plural form using the word "us." Then, we find a sentence in which the word "God" is written in the singular tense (Genesis 1:27). Therefore, this passage suggests that God as revealed in plurality is yet One God. In Genesis 11:5, Moses speaks of God using the singular noun, "And the Lord came down to see the city." However, in the seventh verse of this passage God Himself speaks in the plural form "us": "Go to, let us go down, and we will confound their language." This transformation from the singular form of God to the plural reveals the mystery of the Trinitarian nature of God as declared in the doctrine of the Trinity.

In the prologue to the *Zohar* we find the following statement that suggests the clear knowledge of the Jewish sages about the plurality of the One God.

> The fourth precept is to acknowledge that the Lord is God, as we read: 'Know this day, and lay it to thy heart that the Lord, he is God' (Deuteronomy 4:39); namely, to combine the name *Elohim* "God" with the name *Jehovah* "Lord" in the consciousness that they form an indivisible unity.[16]

The latest English translation of the *Zohar* also contains fascinating passages revealing the knowledge of the ancient Jews about the Trinity.

> All those supernal lights exist in their image below — some of them in their image below upon the earth; but in themselves they are all suspended in the "firmament of the heaven." Here is the secret of two names combined which are completed by a third and become one again. "And God said, Let us make Man. . . ."[17]

In the second Psalm, we read, "Thou art My Son; this day have I begotten Thee." It is interesting that Rabbi Simeon ben Jochai comments in *The Propositions of the Zohar* on this passage:

> There is a perfect Man, who is an Angel. This Angel is Metatron, the Keeper of Israel; He is a man in the image of the Holy One, blessed be He, who is an Emanation from Him; yea, He is Jehovah; of Him cannot be said, He is created, formed or made; but He is the Emanation from God. This agrees exactly with what is written, Jeremiah 23:5, of צמח דוד, David's Branch, that though He shall be a perfect man, yet He is "The Lord our Righteousness.[18]

In this incredible passage from *The Propositions of the Zohar* we can see the ancient Jewish sages understood the mystery of the Trinity and the realization that the "Son of God" is truly the Holy One of God.

The Trinity Was Also Taught in the Ancient Jewish Targums

As I mentioned in an earlier chapter, the *Targums* were a series of paraphrases and commentaries on the Jewish Bible written in the Chaldean language that were read in the synagogue every Sabbath day. The two major commentaries were written by Jonathan and Onkelos. *The Targum of Jonathan* was written by Jonathan ben Uziel, a famous scholar who was a student of the great Jewish scholar Hillel the Great during the decades before the birth of Christ. *The Targum of Onkelos*, which contained commentary on the five books of Torah, was written around the same time period. Jewish scholars believe that Onkelos the Proselyte was probably descended from Gentiles who had converted to Judaism. Both *Targums* were considered virtually as inspired as the Bible itself and were read in the synagogue after the reading of the Torah in Hebrew.

These *Targums* are valuable because they allow us to understand exactly how the ancient Jewish sages interpreted these important biblical passages that deal with the mystery of the nature of God. While only the words of Scripture itself are authoritative in teaching us the true doctrines of God, we can learn a great deal from examining the writings of the ancient Jewish scholars who understood the nuances of the Hebrew text. Furthermore, these *Targums* provide a precious insight into the true understanding of the Trinity by the Jewish sages who lived before the birth of Jesus. Let's examine these *Targums* to understand exactly what they taught about the nature of God.

In the so-called *Jerusalem Targum,*written by Jonathon ben Uziel, we find a commentary on the passage in Genesis that describes God's destruction of Sodom and Gomorrah: "Then the Lord rained upon Sodom and upon Gomorrah brimstone and fire from the Lord out of heaven" (Genesis 19:24). The Targum describes the Lord (יהוה) in this passage as "the Word of the Lord," which is a title for Jehovah suggesting the second person of the Trinity that appears often throughout these paraphrases: "And the Word of the Lord caused to descend upon the people of Sodom and Gomorrah, brimstone and fire from the Lord from heaven."[19]

The Targum on Exodus 3:14 reveals God's declaration of His eternal identity using the same title of "the Word of the Lord" to describe God. "And God said unto Moses, I AM THAT I AM: and he said, Thus shalt thou say unto the children of Israel, I AM hath sent me unto you" (Exodus 3:14). The *Jerusalem Targum* on Exodus 3:14 reads as follows: "And the Word of the Lord said unto Moses: I am He who said unto the world, Be! and it was: and who in the future shall say to it, Be! and it shall be. And He said Thus thou shalt say to the Children of Israel: I Am hath sent me unto you."[20]

The Angel of the Lord and the Angel of the Covenant

The ancient Jewish commentary by Rabbi Bechai (col. 1, p. 35) that describes Abraham's obedience to God's call for him to sacrifice Isaac provides an extraordinary insight into the writer's appreciation of the Trinity. Moses records in Genesis 22:11 that "the angel of the Lord" was the person of the Trinity that intervened to prevent the sacrifice of Isaac. "And the angel of the Lord called unto him out of heaven, and said, Abraham, Abraham: and he said, Here am I."[21] This portion of the deepest teaching of the great sages of Israel provides powerful evidence for the fact that some of the Jewish writers in ancient times understood the mystery of the Trinity:

> It is necessary that thou shouldest understand what in this section (Abraham's sacrifice) is related; namely, that He who is tempting is God, and He who is restraining is the *Angel* of the blessed God. . . . The eyes of Abraham's understanding were opened, that this *Angel* was not one of the intelligences, but one of the Inherent Ones, which cannot be separated, nor cut off one from the other. If this *Angel* had been one of the intelligences, Abraham would not have obeyed his voice, when restraining him to do what God had commanded him; yea, an *Angel* would have no authority to say, "Thou hast not with holden thy son from *Me*, but would have said, from Him." But this *Angel* was one of the Inherent Ones, the great *Angel* . . . and in fact it was that *Angel* of whom it is said, "for my name is in Him."

Another famous sage, Rabbi Moses ben Nachman, wrote about this mysterious Angel of the Lord, the great Lawgiver, that appeared to Moses in the flames of the burning bush. Rabbi Nachman points out that the Bible refers to this appearance of God to Moses as the Angel of the Lord in Exodus 3:2: "And the angel of the Lord appeared unto him in a flame of fire out of the midst of a bush." However, only two verses later Moses declared that it was the Lord God who was speaking to him from the burning bush: "And when the Lord saw that he turned aside to see, God called unto him out of the midst of the bush, and said, Moses, Moses. And he said, Here am I" (Exodus 3:4). These Jewish sages obviously understood that the Scriptures taught that the Angel of the Lord was truly God. Rabbi Nachman commented as follows:

> It is said: "An Angel of the Lord appeared unto him in a flame of fire," and (*Elohim*) אלהים, "God called unto him." This is all one, namely, whether he saith "The *Angel*, or (*Elohim*) אלהים, "God spake to him out of the midst of the bush". . . Therefore be not astonished that Moses hid his face before this *Angel*; because this *Angel* mentioned here is the *Angel, the Redeemer*, concerning whom it is written; "I am the God of Bethel;" and here, "I am the God of thy father, the God of Abraham, the God of Isaac, and the God of Jacob." It is the same of whom it is said, "My name is in Him."[22]

The significance of this study of the Trinity is that it will enable us to appreciate the biblical revelation of the mysterious nature of God who is revealed to us as the Father, the Son, and the Holy Spirit. As we grow and mature as Christians we need to come to a fuller understanding of the deeper truths taught to us by the beloved Scriptures. The apostle Paul shared this wonderful blessing with the Church at Ephesus that I would like to use to conclude this chapter. "Blessed be the God and Father of our Lord Jesus Christ, who hath blessed us with all spiritual blessings in heavenly places in Christ" (Ephesians 1:3).

Notes

1. Ivan Panin.

2. Lucian, *Philopatris* (A.D. 160).

3. *Shepherd of Hermas*, 1, III, Similitude 9, 12, 118.

4. Edward Burton, *Testimonies of the Ante-Nicene Fathers to the Divinity of Christ* (1829).

5. Edward Burton, *Testimonies of the Ante-Nicene Fathers to the Divinity of Christ* (1829).

6. The Council of Sirmium, *Ath. de Synodis*, vol. 1 (A.D. 351) 743.

7. *Zohar*, vol. ii. p. 43, versa., 22.

8. *Zohar*, vol. iii. Amsterdam edition. 65.

9. *Zohar*, vol. iii. Amsterdam edition. 288.

10. Rabbi Simeon ben Jochai, *Zohar*.

11. Rabbi Simeon ben Jochai, *The Propositions of the Zohar*, cap. 38, Amsterdam edition. 113.

12. Rabbi Eliezer Hakkalir, *The Book of Creation*. 28–29.

13. *Zohar*, vol. 1, Soncino Press edition. 90–91.

14. *Zohar*.

15. Rabbi Menachem, *Commentary on the Pentateuch*, Venice edition. 267.

16. *Zohar*, vol. 1, Soncino Press edition. 51.

17. *Zohar*, vol. 1, Soncino Press edition. 90–91.

18. Rabbi Simeon ben Jochai, *The Propositions of the Zohar*.

19. Jonathon ben Uziel, *Jerusalem Targum*.

20. Jonathon ben Uziel, *Jersualem Targum*.

21. Rabbi Bechai, col. 1, 35.

22. Rabbi Moses ben Nachman.

7

The Incredible Bible Codes

Several years ago computer scientists in Israel discovered a staggering phenomenon — encoded words hidden within the text of the Bible. Within the Hebrew text of the Old Testament they found hidden codes that revealed an astonishing knowledge of future events and personalities. The existence of these codes can only be explained if God inspired the writers to record His precise words.

An Astonishing Discovery

Rabbi Michael Dov Weissmandl, a brilliant Czechoslovakian Jewish scholar in astronomy, mathematics, and Judaic studies, found an obscure reference to these codes in a book written by a fourteenth-century rabbi, Rabbeynu Bachayah. This reference described a pattern of letters encoded within the Torah, the first five books of the Bible. This discovery during the years before World War I inspired Rabbi Weissmandl to search for other examples of codes hidden within the Torah. During the war years, he found that he could locate certain meaningful words, phrases, and word pairs, such as "hammer" and "anvil," if he found the first letter and then skipped forward a certain number of letters to find the second one, and the same number again to find the third one, and so on. As an example, he found the letter tav (ת), the first letter of the word *Torah* תורה, the Hebrew word for "law," within

the first word of Genesis 1:1, "Beginnings" *Bereishis* בְּרֵאשִׁית.
Then, by skipping forward fifty letters, he found the second letter
vav ו. He continued to skip forward fifty letters and found reysh ר
and finally the last letter hey ה, completing the spelling of the
word *Torah* תורה. The rabbi was astonished to find that many
significant words were hidden within the text of the Torah at
equally spaced intervals. These intervals varied from every two
letters up to hundreds of letters apart.

Although Rabbi Weissmandl found many encoded names by
manually counting the letters in the text, he did not record his
code discoveries in writing. Fortunately, some of his students did.
Over the following decades, students in Israel who had heard
about his research began searching the Torah for themselves to
ascertain whether or not such codes actually existed. Their discoveries ultimately resulted in research studies at Hebrew University
that have proven the validity of the codes, now known as Equidistant Letter Sequence (ESL) codes. In the last decade, the introduction of sophisticated high-speed computers has allowed
Jewish scholars at Hebrew University to explore the text of the
Torah in ways that were unavailable to previous generations.

In 1988 three mathematics and computer experts at Hebrew
University and the Jerusalem College of Technology (Doron Witz-
tum, Yoav Rosenberg, and Eliyahu Rips) completed an astonishing research project that followed up Rabbi Weismandl's original
research. As a result, they published a paper in August 1994 called
"Equidistant Letter Sequences in the Book of Genesis" in one of
the most prominent mathematical and scientific journals in the
world, the American mathematics journal *Statistical Science.*

In one experiment, the scientists arbitrarily chose three hundred Hebrew word-pairs that were logically related in meaning,
such as "hammer" and "anvil," or "tree" and "leaf," or "man" and
"woman." They asked the computer program to locate any such
word pairs anywhere in the Genesis text. Once the computer
found the first letter in the Hebrew word for "hammer," it would
look for the second letter at various intervals or spaces between
letters. If the program could not locate the second letter of the
target word "hammer" following the first letter at a two-letter
interval, it would search at a three-letter interval, then a four-letter
interval, and so forth. Once it located the second letter at, say, the
twelve-letter interval, it would then skip forward at the same

twelve-letter interval looking for the third letter, and so on through all 78,064 Hebrew letters in the book of Genesis. The computer also looked for coded words by checking in reverse order.

After the program had examined the text for each of the three hundred word pairs, the researchers were astonished to find that every single word-pair had been located in Genesis in close proximity to each other. As mathematicians and statisticians, they were naturally astounded because they knew it was impossible for humans to construct such an intricate and complicated pattern beneath a surface text, such as Genesis, which tells the history of the beginnings of the Jewish people. The odds against the three hundred word pairs occurring by random chance in the text of Genesis was staggering! The bottom line is that only a supernatural intelligence, far beyond our human ability, could have produced the intricate pattern of secretly coded words found in the Bible.

The Bible Codes Speak of Future Events

That was only the beginning of the story. In a 1994 follow-up paper, the team of researchers recorded the results of a new experiment involving their search for pairs of encoded words that related to events that occurred thousands of years after Moses wrote the Torah. They selected the names of thirty-four of the most prominent rabbis and Jewish sages who lived from the beginning of the ninth to the end of the eighteenth century. These Jewish sages had the longest biographies found in the *Encyclopedia of Great Men in Israel*[1], a well-respected Jewish reference book. They asked the computer program to search the text of the Torah for close word pairs coded at equally spaced intervals that contained the names of the famous rabbis, paired with their dates of birth or death (using the Hebrew month and day). The Jewish people celebrate the memory of their famous sages by commemorating the dates of their deaths. Incredibly, the computer program found every single one of the thirty-four names of these famous rabbis embedded in the text of Genesis. Each name of a rabbi was paired in significantly close proximity to the actual date of his birth or the date of his death. The odds against this occurring by chance were calculated by the Israeli mathematicians to be only one chance in 775,000,000!

The scientists and editors at the *Statistical Science* journal who reviewed the experimental data were naturally amazed. They demanded that the Israeli scientists run the computer test program again on a second sample group. This time they searched for the names of a second group of thirty-two prominent Jewish sages listed in the encyclopedia. To the astonishment of the skeptical reviewers, the results were equally successful with the second set of famous sages. The combined test revealed that the names and dates of the births or deaths of every one of the sixty-six most famous Jewish sages were encoded in close proximity within the text of Genesis.

Despite the fact that all of the science journal reviewers previously denied the inspiration of the Scriptures, the overwhelming evidence from the data was so strong that the journal editors reluctantly agreed to publish the article in its August 1994 issue under the title "Equidistant Letter Sequences in the Book of Genesis." Robert Kass, the editor of *Statistical Science*, wrote this comment about the study: "Our referees were baffled: their prior beliefs made them think the Book of Genesis could not possibly contain meaningful references to modern day individuals, yet when the authors carried out additional analyses and checks the effect persisted. The paper is thus offered to *Statistical Science* readers as a challenging puzzle." After three years of careful analysis by many scholars throughout the world, the experiment remains credible.

In October 1995, an article in *Bible Review* magazine by Dr. Jeffrey Satinover, reported that the mathematical probability that these sixty-six names of Jewish sages paired with their dates of birth or death occur by chance in an ancient text like Genesis is less than 1 chance in 2.5 billion! Interestingly, the researchers attempted to discover codes by running the computer program to test other religious Hebrew texts other than the Bible, such as the Samaritan Pentateuch. The Samaritans developed their own variant text of the five books of Moses, called the Samaritan Pentateuch, which differs in numerous small textual details from the standard Masoretic text of the Hebrew Bible. Despite the surface similarity of the two texts, the researchers could not detect significant numbers of word pairs in the Samaritan Pentateuch or any other Hebrew text. Similar tests were run on other Hebrew literature including the Jewish *Talmud* and a Hebrew translation of Tolstoy's novel *War and Peace*. The researchers also analyzed the Jewish Apocryphal books including *Tobit* and *Maccabees*. No significant codes were found in any of these non-biblical texts. Similar experiments were used to analyze sample texts written in other languages, such as English and German, but the tests failed to discover significant ELS codes in any other text.

The *Bible Review* article provoked an onslaught of letters (mostly critical) to the editor. Dr. Satinover responded to his critics as follows: "The robustness of the Torah codes findings derives from the rigor of the research. To be published in a journal such as *Statistical Science*, it had to run, without stumbling, an unusually long gauntlet manned by some of the world's most eminent statisticians. The results were thus triply unusual: in the extraordinariness of what was found; in the strict scrutiny the findings had to hold up under; and in the unusually small odds (less than 1 in 62,500) that they were due to chance. Other amazing claims about the Bible, Shakespeare, and so forth, have never even remotely approached this kind of rigor, and have therefore never come at all close to publication in a peer-reviewed, hardscience venue. The editor of *Statistical Science*, himself a skeptic, has challenged readers to find a flaw; though many have tried, none has succeeded. All the [basic] questions asked by *Bible Review* readers — and many more sophisticated ones — have therefore already been asked by professional critics and exhaustively answered by the research. Complete and convincing responses to even these initial criticisms can get fairly technical" (*Bible Review*, November 1995).

The Incredible Hitler and Holocaust Codes

The Israeli Jewish code researchers naturally wondered if these incredible Bible Codes might reveal anything about the Holocaust, the greatest tragedy in the history of the Jewish people. When they asked the computer program to search for the target words *Hitler*, *Nazis*, and *Holocaust*, the computer found that each of these target names were encoded in a cluster of codes within a passage in Deuteronomy 10:17–22. The word *Hitler* in Hebrew, היטלר, is spelled out at a 22-letter interval. Several of the names of concentration death camps were found embedded within this text, beginning with the second to last appearance of the Hebrew letter bet ב in this passage. The researchers counted every 13th letter from left to right and discovered that the coded letters spelled out the phrase *b'yam marah Auschwitz*, which means "in the bitter sea of Auschwitz." As they carried the counting forward another thirteen letters, they came to the letter resh ר. From the resh, they counted every 22nd letter from left to right and connected to the word היטלר *Hitler*, the greatest enemy of the Jews. The actual names of two of the Nazi concentration camps, *Auschwitz* and *Belsen*, were also encoded close to *Hitler* and *Berlin* in a cluster of encoded words hidden within the text of Deuteronomy. In addition, the researchers found the words *Germany*, *Poland*, *genocide*, *plagues*, *cremetoria*, *Fuhrer*, and *Mein Kampf*.

The researchers found that Deuteronomy 33:16 also contained a hidden message about the Nazi Holocaust. Beginning with the first Hebrew letter mem מ, they counted every 246th letter from left to right and found the encoded word *Melek Natzim*, which means as the "King of the Nazis." This passage revealed another fascinating code found in Deuteronomy 32:52. Beginning with the letter aleph א and counting from left to right every 670 letters spells the name *Aik'man*, a Hebrew variant of the name "Eichmann." Adolph Eichmann was the wicked Nazi official who designed the Final Solution, the evil system of concentration death camps used in the Holocaust. The series of hidden codes dealing with the Holocaust concluded in Deuteronomy 33:21. Many Jews have asked why the prophecies of the Bible say nothing about the Holocaust, the worst tragedy in the history of God's Chosen People. The discovery of the Bible Codes in the closing years of this century reveal that God encoded prophetic words about the Holocaust within the text of the Bible.

Note: The word "interval" indicates the number of Hebrew letters that are skipped in the orginal biblical passage to spell out the encoded word in equally spaced intervals (ELS). If the interval number in brackets is positive (22) then the encoded word begins at the indicated passage and reads right to left, skipping the indicated number of Hebrew letters. However, if the interval number in brackets is preceded by a minus sign (–13), the encoded word begins at the indicated passage and reads left to right, skipping the indicated number of Hebrew letters.

The Holocaust Codes

Encoded Name	Hebrew	Interval	Begins at:
Hitler	היטלר	(22)	Deut. 10:17
Auschwitz	אושויץ	(–13)	Deut. 10:21
Holocaust	שואה	(13)	Deut. 10:20
Germany	גרמניה	(–933)	Deut. 33:28
Crematorium for my sons	כבשן לבני	(134)	Deut. 31:28
The Holocaust	השואה	(50)	Deut. 31:16
Plagues	מגפות	(–134)	Deut. 32:32
Eichmann	אייכמן	(9670)	Deut. 32:52
Hitler	היטלר	(–3)	Num. 19:13
Mein Kampf	מין קאמפ	(9832)	Num. 22:1
Auschwitz	אושויץ	(–536)	Deut. 33:24
In Poland	בפולין	(–107)	Deut. 32:22
King of the Nazis	מלך נאצים	(–246)	Deut. 33:16
Genocide	רצח עם	(–22)	Deut. 33:21
The Fuhrer	הפירר	(5)	Deut. 32:50

The discovery of complex Hebrew codes that reveal supernatural and prophetic knowledge about the future has caused tremendous consternation in the academic community. The Bible Code phenomena challenges the long-held beliefs of liberal scholars, who generally reject the supernatural origin, as well as the verbal inspiration, of the Bible. In 1996, I published my book *The Signature of God*, which analyzed the archeological and scientific evidence that supported the inspiration and authority of the Scriptures. In this book, I presented numerous Bible Code discoveries, as well as those discovered by my friend Yacov Rambsel that reveal the name of Jesus encoded in the messianic passages of the Old Testament. Many Christians throughout the world viewed these code discoveries as powerful new evidence of the inspiration of the Word of God. Yacov and I have independently researched the phenomenon of the Bible Codes for the last six years. In the past twelve months, we have worked together to carefully examine a number of significant codes that will be fascinating to all those who love Jesus Christ as their Savior and Lord. These code discoveries will be revealed in the next two chapters.

A Word of Caution about the Bible Codes

Bible Codes are found only in the orthodox Hebrew text of the Old Testament

No one has been able to locate detailed, meaningful Bible codes in any other Hebrew literature outside the Bible. Experimenters have carefully examined other Hebrew writings for the existence of codes including the Jewish *Talmud*, the *Mishneh*, the Apocryphal writings of *Tobit* and *Maccabees*. They even examined modern Hebrew literature such as translations of *War and Peace*. However, the scientists found no significant pattern of codes in any other Hebrew literature outside the Old Testament. Several researchers have told me they found indications of codes in the Greek of the New Testament but no detailed research has been published to date.

Bible Codes cannot be used to accurately foretell future events.

One cannot discover meaningful encoded information about a future event until the event occurs. Otherwise, it is impossible to know what target word to ask the program to search for. However, once an event occurs, such as the War in the Gulf, we can ask the computer to look in the Bible text for such target words as "Saddam Hussein" or "General Schwarzkopf." The encoded information about a future event cannot be discovered in the biblical text in advance of the event because you wouldn't know what to ask the computer to look for. In other words, the Bible Codes can confirm that the Scriptures contain encoded data about historical events that occurred centuries after the Scriptures were written. However, the codes cannot be used to foretell future events. Even if you correctly guessed at the right target words for a future event, such as the assassination of a prominent politician, and you found the name of the person and the word "killed," you would still not know anything certain about the future. Until the event occurs, any suggestion that the occurrence of these two code words means that the politician would be killed would be merely a guess.

The Bible prohibits us from engaging in foretelling the future. A recent book called *The Bible Code*, by agnostic writer Michael Drosnin, claims that he, himself, discovered codes that allowed him to predict future events. However, a careful examination of his claims reveals that the encoded information he discovered is insufficient to allow anyone to confidently predict any future event. Michael Drosnin may have made a guess about a particular, tragic future event based on his discovery of the encoded name "Yitzchak Rabin." However, it was simply a guess. There was not enough information in the code he discovered to allow him to confidently affirm that a particular future event, namely the assassination of Yitzchak Rabin, would actually occur. Michael Drosnin claims that he warned the Prime Minister of Israel about the danger of assassination based on the fact that he found that one of the eight letters of the encoded words "Yitzchak Rabin" happened to appear in the surface text of Deuteronomy 4:42, which reads in Hebrew "assassin that will assassinate."

However, it was impossible to know in advance of the event what this particular combination actually meant. It could easily have meant that Prime Minister Rabin might order the assassination of some terrorist in the future, or it could easily have meant nothing at all. The point is that the limited information from the encoded words can only be accurately interpreted after the fulfillment of an historical event, such as the Holocaust, the Gulf War, or the crucifixion of Jesus Christ. The Lord did not place these codes within the Bible to enable men to play at becoming prophets of future events. The Bible repeatedly forbids fortune telling.

Both the major Israeli code researchers, including Professor Eli Rips, and all of the Christian researchers, including Yacov Rambsel and myself, deny that the Bible Codes can be used to accurately predict future events. The information encoded in the Bible can only be accurately interpreted after a historical event has actually occurred. Then, we can compare the details of the historical event with the encoded information in the Bible to determine whether or not God had encoded these prophetic details centuries before the events occurred. In this manner, the Bible Codes give God the glory, not the human researcher. The prophet Isaiah declared these words of God, "I will not give my glory unto another" (Isaiah 48:11).

Bible Codes do not reveal any hidden theological sentences, teachings, or doctrines.

There are no secret sentences, detailed messages, or theological statements in the encoded words. God's message of salvation and His commandments for holy living are only found in the normal, surface text of the Scriptures. The Bible Codes can only reveal key words, such as people's names, places, and occasionally, dates (using the Hebrew calendar), which provide confirmation of the supernatural inspiration and origin of the Scriptures.

The Bible Codes have nothing to do with numerology.

The phenomenon of the Bible Codes has nothing to do with numerology. Numerology is defined by the authoritative Webster's *Dictionary* as "the study of the occult significance of numbers." Numerology is connected with divination or foretelling the future and is clearly forbidden by the Bible. There is nothing occult or secret about the codes. This phenomenon was openly published in scientific and mathematical journals, taught, and broadcast since it was first discovered twelve years ago.

The particular interval between the Hebrew letters, the actual number of letters to be skipped, has no importance or significance. The codes have nothing to do with "the occult significance of numbers." Obviously, the coded words are found at various intervals (i.e., by skipping 2, 7, 61, or more letters). However, the significance or meaning of the encoded word does not relate to the particular interval (the number of letters skipped). Either a particular word is spelled out in Hebrew letters at equal intervals or it is not. Anyone can examine a particular encoded word and verify for themselves that these words are truly spelled out at ELS intervals. Computer programs such as Torah Codes and Bible Scholar are publically available to allow anyone to verify these codes for themselves. These programs can be ordered from our company if you wish to personally research the Bible Codes.

Why Did God Place These Hidden Bible Codes in the Bible?

For almost seventeen centuries, from the time of Emperor Constantine's conversion in A.D. 300 until the beginning of our century, the Bible was generally accepted by the majority of Western culture as the inspired and authoritative Word of God. However, we have witnessed an unrelenting assault on the authority of the Bible by the intellectual elite, the academic community, liberal theologians, and the media during the last hundred years. Most people in our culture have been exposed to countless attacks on the authority and accuracy of the Scriptures throughout high school, university, and from the mass media. I believe that God has provided this extraordinary new evidence in the form of the Bible Codes to prove to this generation of skeptics that the Bible is truly the Word of God. The complex nature of these codes means that the phenomenal discovery of these encoded words could not have occurred until the development of high-speed computers during the last fifteen years. In a sense, God secretly hid these incredible codes within the text of the Bible thousands of years ago with a time lock that could not be opened until the arrival of our generation and the development of sophisticated computers. In His prophetic foreknowledge, God knew that our generation would be characterized by an unrelenting attack on the authority of the Scriptures. No previous generation needed the additional scientific evidence provided by the discovery of these codes as much as our present skeptical generation.

The discovery of these incredible Bible Codes provides powerful evidence to our skeptical generation that God truly inspired the writers of the Bible to record His message to mankind. These encoded words describing the names of people, places, and dates provide powerful evidence to any unbiased inquirer that they can trust the supernatural message of the Bible.

Hundreds of years ago a famous rabbi, known as the Vilna Gaon, lived and taught in the city of Vilna, Latvia, near the Baltic Sea in northern Europe. This brilliant and mystical Jewish sage taught his students that God had hidden a vast amount of information secretly encoded within the Hebrew letters of the Torah. Consider the fascinating and suggestive statement about the hidden codes by this famous Jewish sage.

> The rule is that all that was, is, and will be unto the end of time is included in Torah from first word to the last word. And not merely in a general sense, but including the details of every species and of each person individually, and the most minute details of everything that happened to him from the day of his birth until his death; likewise of every kind of animal and beast and living thing that exists, and of herbage, and of all that grows or is inert. (Vilna Gaon, Introduction to *Sifra Ditzniut*)

There is a tradition that a number of codes were discovered in past centuries by various Jewish sages, including Rabbeinu Bachya, Moses Maimonides, and the Vilna Gaon. Since World War II Rabbi Michael Weissmandl and others have taught about these codes. There is an interesting statement suggesting knowledge of the codes in the Jewish mystical writing known as the *Zohar*. "The entire Torah is replete with Divine Names. Divine Names run through every single word in the Torah" (*Zohar* II, 87a). In approximately A.D. 1200, the brilliant Jewish sage Moses Maimonides, known as Ramban, made a curious comment about this statement in the *Zohar* that indicated he understood that there were complex codes hidden in the Torah. He said that the hidden codes provided another reason why a Torah scroll should be considered as unfit for use if even one single letter was missing from the text. The removal or addition of a single letter from the Hebrew text would eliminate the codes found hidden within that section of text. Also, there is a suggestive statement in the *Talmud* that refers to the codes: "Everything is alluded to in the Torah" (*Talmud Tan'anis* 9a). Other references to the existence of the Bible Codes are found in the following passages: *Zohar* II, 161a; *B'reishis Rabah* 1:1; *Tanchuma* 1:1; *Raya M'hemna*; and *B'reishis* 23a.

ELS Bible Code Analysis Using Computer Programs

The primary method used by researchers to find the coded words is called *equidistant-letter sequence* (ELS). During the last six years I have analyzed the Hebrew Scriptures using this method with several computer programs I obtained in Jerusalem during the 1991 War in the Gulf. These computer programs enable a researcher to discover various Bible Codes for themselves through the examination of particular Hebrew letters that are distributed at equal intervals, (i.e., fifth, tenth, seventeenth letter, throughout the text). I use the Torah Codes computer program that allows a researcher to personally search for any encoded word within the first five books of the Old Testament. In addition, the Bible Scholar computer program will print out the text of any passage of the Old Testament in Hebrew or English from Genesis to Malachi. This will allow a researcher with a MacIntosh or IBM-compatible computer to verify a particular code discovery reported by any other researcher. These computer programs are allowing thousands of Bible students to begin searching the biblical text to both verify the code discoveries of others and to conduct independent research on their own. Anyone familiar with computers who is fascinated by this research project can personally participate by acquiring such a computer program. In addition, they will find that a Hebrew-English Interlinear Bible and a Hebrew-English dictionary are helpful in their research.

The Bible Codes: Equidistant-Letter Sequence

The Hebrew word for "equidistant sequence" is *shalav* שלב, which means either "equally spaced rungs on a ladder" or "several objects equally spaced from one another," such as letters in a text.

I invited my friend Yacov Rambsel to a scholarly Bible conference in January 1997 held at Tyndale Theological Seminary in Dallas, Texas. I presented the phenomenon of the Bible Codes to this group of academics and Hebrew scholars. I illustrated numerous encoded words, as shown in my book *The Signature of God*, including a number of Yacov's discoveries of the name of Jesus *Yeshua* encoded in the Old Testament. After discussing numerous codes found in the Hebrew text, I introduced Yacov to the group for an in depth discussion about the method of analysis used in our research. One of the scholars asked if we had discovered any direct reference to the Bible code phenomenon encoded in the Scriptures itself.

The Encoded Phrase "Equidistant-Letter Sequence"
Shalav A'ot

Immediately, Yacov and I entered the Hebrew word *shalav* שלב, which means "equidistant," into the Torah Codes computer program on my Powerbook 1400 laptop computer to search the Scriptures for this target word. In just a few minutes, we were able to report to this group that we had discovered the encoded words "equidistant" *shalav* שלב in every one of the five books of the Torah. The full phrase, "equidistant-letter sequence" *shalav a'ot*, was found in the Hebrew text at equal intervals in Genesis through Deuteronomy. One example of this insight is found in Genesis 20:2, at equal intervals of every 5th letter from right to left. This example from Genesis 20:2 that we presented to the scholars at the Dallas conference is illustrated below.

Genesis *Bereishis* בראשית 20:2 says, "And Abraham said of Sarah, his wife, She is my sister: and Abimelech king of Gerar sent, and took Sarah." The Hebrew text for this verse, according to the Masoretic text, is given below. I have removed the spaces between each word and enlarged every fifth letter to emphasize the Hebrew letters that spell out the words "the lattice work of the equidistant-letter sequence."

ויאמראברהמאלשרהאשתואחתיהוא
וישלחאבימלךמלדגלרויקחאתשרה

Starting with the enlarged heh (ה) on the second line to the far left and counting every fifth letter from left to right, we find the encoded words *hacharak oht shalav* שלב אות החרד, which means, "the latticework of the equidistant-letter sequence." It was fascinating to discover that God had encoded in every one of the five books of the Torah the Hebrew letters of the words "equidistant-letter sequence" *shalav a'ot* שלב אות, the actual words used by the modern Israeli researchers to describe the Bible Codes phenomenon. This phrase was encoded in the following passages: Genesis 20:2, every fifth letter from left to right; Exodus 35:21–24, every 38th letter from left to right; Leviticus 10:10, every 78th letter from left to right; Numbers 1:45, every 89th letter from left to right; Deuteronomy 13:19, every 61st letter from left to right.

Answers to Criticism and Questions about the Codes

Michael Drosnin's book, *The Bible Code*, published in the late spring of 1997, caused a great sensation in the secular community and the Christian community. Although this book appeared almost one year after my book, *The Signature of God*, and the books of several Israelis about the codes, *The Bible Code* was extensively promoted by its publisher in virtually every major media outlet from CNN, to *TIME* magazine, to "The Oprah Winfrey Show." The result is that the whole world is now talking about the phenomenal Bible Codes. On balance, I believe this publicity will prove positive in that it will create a curiosity about the phenomenon in the minds of tens of millions of readers who would otherwise never read about the codes in a Christian book like this. Perhaps God will use this secular approach to the Bible Codes to draw many people into a closer examination of the Bible with the result that many will be introduced to Jesus Christ. Naturally, I have received many letters and questions on radio talk shows about my response to Drosnin's book *The Bible Code.*

Firstly, I believe the book is fascinating in its reporting of many additional code discoveries by Israeli code researchers. Unfortunately, the author Michael Drosnin reveals that he is somewhere between an atheist and an agnostic in his rejection of the existence of God, despite the overwhelming evidence of the supernatural origin of the Bible that is obvious to any unbiased reader of the incredible code discoveries. While he admits that only a supernatural being could have produced the Bible Codes three and a half thousand years ago, Drosnin firmly rejects the conclusion that the author of the codes is God.

Can the Bible Codes Allow Us To Correctly Predict the Future?

Many readers have written to ask if we could use the Bible Codes to discover the name of the Antichrist or tell of any other future events. The answer is "no." A much greater objection to Drosnin's book is his false claim that the Bible Codes can be used to accurately predict future events. As mentioned earlier in this chapter, one of his major claims is that he personally discovered the coded word "Yitzchak Rabin," the first letter of his name, beginning in Deuteronomy 2:33 and the second letter 4772 letters forward, in the text of Deuteronomy 4:42 where the letter appears in the Hebrew surface text which reads "will be assassinated." In the King James Bible this phrase is translated "kill his neighbour unawares." Drosnin makes an extraordinary declaration. He claims that he flew to Israel and warned Prime Minister Rabin of imminent danger based on this code discovery. Although I read Israeli newspapers regularly and follow Israeli events daily on the Internet, I have not yet seen any of the prime minister's staff confirm that this warning was actually given to Rabin. Therefore it is difficult to evaluate his claim.

Nevertheless, if Drosnin actually flew to Israel to warn the prime minister, based solely on the fact that he found the second letter of Rabin's name in the phrase "will be assassinated" in Deuteronomy 4:42, he simply made an astonishing guess. How could Drosnin "know" that this code actually meant that Rabin would be assassinated in advance of the event? I don't deny that the code is significant. That is why I wrote about the "Rabin" code in my earlier book. However, in advance of the tragic event, it was impossible to know that the encoded word meant that the assassination would definitely occur. The most Drosnin could do was make a guess. He was certainly aware of the growing public threats to Rabin's life that appeared in letters to newspapers and on signs held up at political rallies in the year proceeding the assassination.

Why would Drosnin become convinced to the point of flying to Israel to warn Rabin simply because one of the eight letters of Rabin's name occurred in the surface text in the phrase "will be assassinated"? How could anyone *know*, in advance of the assassination, that the particular phrase "will be assassinated" was significant as opposed to the other phrases containing the other letters of Rabin's name stretched out every 4772 letters throughout the book of Deuteronomy. For example, the first letter of "Yitzchak Rabin" name in code is spelled out in Hebrew beginning in the first word of Deuteronomy 2:33 which reads: "And the Lord our God delivered him." The second last letter of Rabin's name, the letter yud, י appears in the words "sons of Levi." Before the assassination, how could Drosnin or anyone else know absolutely which of these phrases, if any, related to Rabin's future: "And the Lord our God delivered him," or "will be assassinated," or the words "sons of Levi?" Logically, at best Drosnin could only guess which, if any, of these phrases would turn out to be significant. Drosnin has already been proven wrong in his book's false prophecy that there would be a world war in 1996.

In his press release criticizing Drosnin's attempts to prophesy future events, Eli Rips, one of the major Israeli code researchers, pointed out a place in the Bible where you can find the words "Winston Churchill" encoded close to the phrase "will be murdered." If Drosnin had found this code years earlier when Churchill was still alive, would he have flown to Britain to warn Winston that his life was in imminent danger? However, this guess would have proven to be mistaken because Winston Churchill died peacefully. Therefore, the placement of Winston Churchill's name close to the phrase "will be murdered" was not a code foretelling the future. This illustrates the truth that we cannot and should not attempt to use the Bible Codes to predict future events. Significantly, the Israeli researchers, especially Eli Rips, who Drosnin quotes extensively, have publically repudiated Drosnin's sensational conclusions that the codes can be used to predict future events such as earthquakes or the next world war.

God forbids fortune telling and divination of any kind. The point is that the Bible Codes can only be interpreted accurately and confidently after an event has occurred to determine if the Bible contained encoded words that reveal God's supernatural prophetic knowledge thousands of years in advance. When the codes are interpreted after an event, we can verify that the codes are prophetically accurate. These discoveries support the Bible's claim to be supernatural in its origin, and God receives the glory, not the researcher. We need to remember the words of the prophet Isaiah: "For mine own sake, even for mine own sake, will I do it: for how should my name be polluted? and I will not give my glory unto another" (Isaiah 48:1).

An article recently appeared on the Internet, entitled *A Caution Concerning the Torah Codes*, that raises several concerns about the discovery of the Bible Codes. In the article, the writer found it surprising that the particular study of Genesis discovered the names and dates of death of numerous prominent Jewish rabbis and sages over the last two thousand years. Some critics have asked why God would encode within the Bible the names of rabbis who rejected the revelation Jesus Christ in the New Testament. We need to understand that the presence of a particular name in the Bible Codes, such as Anwar Sadat, Rabin, or the rabbis, does not imply an endorsement of their lives and teachings. It simply indicates that God must be the true author of the Bible because no one else could have encoded these names of people centuries before they were born. However, the presence of a particular name or group of names in the codes does not imply God's stamp of approval on their lives or teachings. Obviously, the discovery of the Holocaust codes, including the names *Hitler, Eichmann, Fuehrer, Genocide, Holocaust, Mein Kampf, Auschwitz, Belsen,* and *King of the Nazis* within Deuteronomy 10:17–22 and the surrounding verses does not suggest God's approval of the evil deeds associated with the tragedy of the Holocaust. Both the Bible surface text and the embedded codes contain the names and descriptions of many people, from the most noble to the most evil.

The critical article asked, "Why not [discover the encoded] apostles, or at least the prophets?" However, Yacov Rambsel and I independently discovered a series of fascinating ELS codes

revealing the names of Jesus, His disciples, Passover, the Nazarene, and much more that will be discussed in the next chapter.
Surely, the discovery of the name of Jesus *Yeshua* in dozens of
messianic passages throughout the Old Testament provides
powerful evidence to any unbiased reader that Jesus of Nazareth
is the promised Messiah of God. I personally believe that the
Yeshua codes glorifying Jesus Christ provide strong evidence that
the Bible Codes are genuine and that they were created by God to
speak to this skeptical generation.

The Yeshua codes examined in *The Signature of God* and *Yeshua*
glorify Jesus and reveal His divine nature as our Lord and Savior.
These codes (especially the Messiah codes in the next chapter)
reveal that it is Jesus of Nazareth who came in the flesh to fulfill
the messianic prophecies. The apostle John wrote, "Hereby know
ye the Spirit of God: Every spirit that confesseth that Jesus Christ is
come in the flesh is of God: And every spirit that confesseth not
that Jesus Christ is come in the flesh is not of God: and this is that
spirit of antichrist, whereof ye have heard that it should come; and
even now already is it in the world" (1 John 4:2–3). Both Yacov and
I feel that the hundreds of coded words that glorify Jesus Christ as
the Messiah and the Son of God are the Lord's seal of approval on
the code phenomenon. These codes were placed in the text of the
Hebrew Scriptures by the Lord Himself thousands of years ago to
provide evidence of the supernatural origin of the Bible to this
generation of skeptics.

Some critics point out that these codes are used by the orthodox Jewish community in seminars as evidence to convince
assimilated and agnostic Jews that the Bible is authentic. However, the critics complain that these seminars try to convince
participants through the use of the codes that the Jewish rabbinic
authorities hold a monopoly on unlocking the hidden truths of the
Bible. While it is true to some extent that they use these codes for
these purposes, it does not change the fact that the Bible Codes
were created by God. No human could have created such an
incredibly complex series of coded words as we have reported in
The Signature of God and *Yeshua*. In effect, some critics suggest that
the phenomenon of the codes (even though it is genuine) should
be rejected simply because the orthodox rabbis use it for their
purposes. However, this is foolish because the same argument
would demand that Christians refuse to teach from Old

Testament passages because the rabbis use the Hebrew Bible to teach against Christian beliefs.

Some have suggested that Christians should reject the Bible Codes because some orthodox rabbis relate these codes to their teaching of Kabbalah, Jewish mysticism, and gematria. Some rabbis use the Kabbalah to find guidance, uncover secrets, and attempt to foretell the future. This is fallacious reasoning. The fact that the some people misuse the Bible Codes as other groups misuse the Scriptures to teach false doctrines does not provide a valid reason to reject either the codes or the Bible.

The Bible Codes Do Not Allow Anyone To Predict the Future

The codes do not permit anyone to become a prophet and predict future events accurately. In my earlier book I reminded readers that God forbids fortune telling. The Bible warns, "For there shall be no more any vain vision nor flattering divination within the house of Israel" (Ezekiel 12:24). I have received more written questions and radio call-in questions asking whether we can use the codes to foretell the future than any other question asked. Let me explain why you cannot use the codes to accurately predict future events.

How Do We Actually Find Bible Codes?

First of all you need to understand how we actually use the computer program to discover a particular code. A researcher such as myself will ask the program to search the text of the Hebrew Bible to find a target word, such as "Hitler." The computer then begins with the first letter of the Hebrew word "Hitler" היטלר, which is the letter heh ה (Hebrew reads right to left). Then the program will search forward by skipping 2 letters, 3 letters, 4 letters, et cetera, (skipping up to 500 letters forward, for example) searching for the second letter in Hitler's name, the letter yud י. When the computer finds the second letter י in the target word "Hitler," after skipping, for example, 22 letters, the program will automatically skip forward an equal number of letters (22), looking for the third, fourth, and fifth letters. When the program fails to find the next letter in the target word at an equal spaced interval, it abandons that search and examines the next occurrence of the letter heh ה in the text and begins the process again.

There are more than 45,000 Hebrew heh ה letters in the first

five books of the Bible alone and the program will search up to 500
letters forward and 500 letters in reverse from each of the 45,000
heh ה letters. in the experiment. That means the computer will
compete 45 million calculations or searches just to find if the word
"Hitler" is encoded anywhere in the Torah. This is why serious
research could only be done after scientists had created high
speed computers in the last two decades.

To return to the question of predicting future events with the
codes, the answer is that it is simply impossible. Until a historical
event occurs, such as Anwar Sadat's assassination, you would not
know what target words to ask the computer program to search
for. It is only after an event has occurred that you can ask the
computer program to search a given area of the Hebrew text and
determine if a target word such as "Sadat" exists at any particular
interval (such as every 5th, 20th letter, etc.). To illustrate this:
imagine that you know about the Bible Codes and that you had a
computer with this program back in 1920. Could you have used
the codes back in 1920 to find "Adolph Hitler"? The answer is
clearly no! Adolph Hitler's real family name was Schicklgruber
until they changed it. He was an obscure demobilized Austrian
army soldier, a failed painter who lived in flop houses in Vienna.
Could you have found "Auschwitz" in 1920? No. Auschwitz was
an equally obscure Polish village with no importance at that time.
It is only after the evil historical events of the Holocaust had
occurred that you could ask the computer program to search for a
particular target word that may or may not be encoded.

No one can use the Bible Codes to discover the name of
Antichrist or anything else about the future. Even if a researcher
found a particular name of a current public person, the presence of
their name or other words would not tell you anything meaningful. The only prophecies that reveal anything meaningful about
future end-time events are found in the surface text of the Bible,
such as the Matthew 24 predictions of the signs of the Second
Coming of the Messiah.

Some critics ask whether the discovery of the encoded name
"Rabin" in the Bible means that God ordered the assassination?
Absolutely not! As I mentioned earlier, the fact that a name or
event is encoded does not mean that God is thereby endorsing that
person or event. The Bible records many events, good and bad, in
both the codes and the surface text. Secondly, the cowardly

assassin Yigal Amir was tragically and sinfully motivated by his irrational hatred of the prime minister's peace policies. The Bible Codes had nothing to do with his motivation for his despicable act. The discovery of these fascinating Bible Codes has caused many people to accept the supernatural origin of the Bible as the Word of God. It is illogical and ill-conceived to condemn the codes on the grounds that someone discovered that one of the letters of the encoded name "Rabin" appeared in a surface text of the Bible in the phrase "will be assassinated."

Let's examine the real issue. Are the Bible Codes valid? The answer is *yes*. Do these coded words appear in the biblical text in a manner that is beyond the statistical possibility that this is simply a random-chance occurrence? Anyone who spends a few hours studying the scholarly articles in *Statistical Science* journal (Aug. 1994), and *Bible Review* magazine (Nov. 1995), will conclude that the phenomenon is real. Dr. David Kazhdan, head of the mathematics department of Harvard University confirmed, "This is serious research carried out by serious investigators."

Answering Claims That the Codes Reveal That Yeshua Is A False Messiah

Some of the critics of the Yeshua codes discovered by Yacov Rambsel have claimed that they have discovered a hidden code in a messianic prophecy that spelled *yeshua mashiach sheker* "Jesus is a false messiah." First of all, we need to recognize that the name *Yeshua*, as the name of God's Messiah, naturally appears many times throughout the Old Testament. Therefore, the name *Yeshua* will inevitably be found in texts close to many other words. The claim that someone has found a text where the encoded word *Yeshua* occasionally appears within a few verses of the word *sheker* "false messiah" does not mean that the codes teach that Jesus is the false messiah, as some anti-Christians would like to suggest.

In conclusion, I have studied the phenomenon of the Bible Codes for the last ten years. In the last six years, I have used the computer programs to find new codes as well as to verify the discoveries by the scientists at Hebrew University and my friend Yacov Rambsel. I believe that the Bible contains a number of significant proofs that it is inspired by God. The Bible Codes are simply one additional proof that is especially meaningful to our generation in that they could not have been discovered or analyzed until the development of high-speed computers in our lifetime.

Why would God have placed hidden codes in the Bible that would not be discovered until the final generation of this millennium? Only God knows. However, I would suggest that God knew that our generation would be filled with skepticism and doubt more than any other generation in history. The Bible has suffered relentless attacks in the last eighty years that have caused many pastors and laymen to abandon their confidence in the authority and inspiration of the Scriptures. If these codes are genuine, and I believe they are, they were placed there by God to speak to this generation, to those who deny the supernatural inspiration of the Scriptures.

No human could have produced these incredibly complex codes. In addition, they glorify and lift up the name of Jesus Christ. Therefore, I conclude that they are powerful evidence of the inspiration and authority of the Bible. Together with the standard apologetic evidences, including the archeological and historical evidence, the advanced scientific and medical statements in the Bible, and the evidence from fulfilled prophecy, the Bible Codes will motivate many in our generation to consider the claims of the Bible about Jesus Christ. If we use this material wisely and carefully, in conjunction with these other evidences, we will fulfill God's command to us as revealed in 1 Peter 3:15: "But sanctify the Lord God in your hearts: and be ready always to give an answer to every man that asketh you a reason of the hope that is in you with meekness and fear."

In the following chapters we will examine the most fascinating codes I have ever seen — the Messiah Codes. These codes reveal the names of "Jesus," the "Nazarene," and the names of Christ's disciples encoded 740 years before the birth of Jesus.

Note

1. M. Margalioth, ed., *Encylclopedia of Great Men in Israel* (Tel Aviv: Joshua Chachik, 1961).

8

New Bible Code Discoveries

Since the publication of my book *The Signature of God*, numerous new Bible Codes have been discovered by various researchers in Israel and North America. In this chapter, I will share a number of the most fascinating codes that provide evidence of the supernatural origin of the Bible as the Word of God.

The Peace Process Between Israel and the PLO

For the last few years the eyes of the world have watched the dangerous peace negotiations between the PLO and Israel and their desperate search for an elusive peace in the Middle East. It is fascinating to discover that a series of encoded words in Deuteronomy, written by Moses over three and a half thousand years ago, reveal the names of the major participants in these negotiations. In a passage of only thirteen verses, beginning at Deuteronomy 8:16 through to 9:8, we find the following key words encoded: Israel ישראל; Arafat ערפאת; PLO אשׁף; Peace Treaty חוזה שלום; and the names of both of Israel's former prime ministers who were intensely involved in the peace process, Yitzchak יצחק (Rabin), and Shimon Peres שׁמעון פרס. These words are encoded as follows:

Word	Hebrew	Interval	Reference begins at
Israel	ישראל	(1)	Deut. 9:1
Arafat	ערפאת	(1)	Deut. 9:6
PLO	אשפ	(−15)	Deut. 9:4
Teaty	חוזה	(32)	Deut. 9:7
Peace	שלום	(−14)	Deut. 9:4
Yitzchak	יצחק	(1)	Deut. 9:5
Shimon	שמעון	(92)	Deut. 8:20
Peres	פרס	(−283)	Deut. 8:16

It is interesting that these coded words appear in a passage of the Word of God that deals with Israel's rebellion against God in provoking Him to wrath because they did not trust that He would enable them to possess the whole of the Promised Land. Perhaps significantly, the name of *Arafat* appears encoded in the surface text in Deuteronomy 8:6: "For thou art a stiff necked people." It is very hard to understand the decision of the political leaders of Israel to enter into negotiations to surrender portions of the Promised Land to the enemies of Israel, who have dedicated themselves, in their proclamations in the PLO Covenant, to destroying the Jewish people. At the time of the beginning of the Madrid peace negotiations, the PLO was at the weakest point they had ever been, yet Prime Minister Rabin surrendered vital areas of Israel to this fierce enemy when the PLO was on its last legs. Even Senator Jesse Helms, the Chairman of the United States Committee on Foreign Relations, was profoundly disturbed by Israel's surrender of land to her deadliest enemies. Senator Helms wrote at the time, "I mistrust Arafat profoundly. . . . "I will never completely understand how the leaders of Israel reached the decision to enter into negotiations with Yasser Arafat. . . ." (A letter to Alice Novick dated March 12, 1996).

The Assassination of Prime Minister Yitzchak Rabin

The tragic assassination of Yitzchak Rabin stunned the people of Israel and millions of Christians and Jews throughout the world who love the Promised Land and her people. In the days after the assassination code researchers in Israel and North America naturally checked with their computer code search programs to examine every instance where the name of the late prime minister appeared at ELS intervals in the biblical text. In an earlier chapter of this book I examine the claim of the author Michael Drosnin, who states that he sent a warning to the prime minister based on the occurrence of the coded words "Yitzchak Rabin" and a phrase in Deuteronomy 4:42 that suggested the possibility of assassination.

However, another passage of the Torah contains encoded information about the assassination that is even more extensive. When we examine the passage Genesis 48:13 through 48:19 we find the encoded names of Yitzchak Rabin, Israel, the day and year of Rabin's birth, the month and year of his tragic assassination, the name of his assassin, Yigal Amir, the phrase "will be murdered," and the word "Oslo." It is incredible to see that these eleven significant words are encoded together in only eight verses of the book of Genesis. The year 5682 in the Hebrew calendar corresponds to 1922, the year Yitzchak Rabin was born, while the first day of the Jewish month Adar occurred on our March 1. The month Heshvan in the Hebrew calendar year 5682 corresponds to November, 1995.

Prime Minister Yitzchak Rabin's Assassination

Word	Hebrew	Interval	Reference begins at
Yitzchak	יצחק	(1)	Gen. 48:15
Rabin	רבין	(138)	Gen. 48:15
Will be murdered	ירצח	(85)	Gen. 48:13
Yigal	יגאל	(−241)	Gen. 48:16
Amir	עמיר	(15)	Gen. 48:15
Israel	ישראל	(1)	Gen. 48:14
5682 — Year of Rabin's Birth	התרפב	(−225)	Gen. 48:14
1st Adar — Rabin's Birthday	אאדר	(−177)	Gen. 48:15
5756 — Year of Rabin's Death	תשנו	(118)	Gen. 48:19
Heshvan — Month of Rabin's Death	חשון	(−285)	Gen. 48:13
Oslo	אוסלו	(182)	Gen. 49:3

Bible Codes Relating to The War in the Gulf

It is astonishing to find codes in the Bible that reveal the names of the major participants in the War in the Gulf. During that war President Saddam Hussein of Iraq attempted to destroy many of the Jews living in Israel through his unprovoked missile attack on Israeli cities. The codes reveal an astonishing series of encoded words that reveal the names of key players in that recent conflict in which God manifested His power to save both the Jews of Israel and the Christian soldiers of America and its allies fighting against the armies of Iraq. The eleven encoded words located by computer programs in the Bible include the following key words: President Saddam Hussein of Iraq: *Saddam* סאדאם; *in Iraq* בעירק; the name of the thirty-nine Russian missiles fired against Israel: *Russian* רוסי; *Scud-B* סקאר בי; a description of the effect of the Scud-B missiles on those attacked:*the missile will terrify* יבהל טיל. In addition, an astonishing code actually named the day in the Israeli Hebrew calendar when Iraq's first missile attack began: *the 3rd of Shevat*, which fell on January 18, 1991. In Genesis 19:10 they discovered the phrase *they shut the door*, which may refer to the sealing of rooms by Israelis to protect against chemical weapons.

Within the same biblical passage, we find significant additional encoded names describing America's involvement in that conflict against Saddam Hussein: *George Bush* גורג בוש; *America* אמריקה; *and also in Iraq* והנ בעירק; and the name of the general who led the allied armies: *Schwarzkopf* שורצקופ.

The Gulf War Codes

Word	Hebrew	Interval	Reference begins at
Saddam (Hussein)	סאדאם	(6)	Gen. 8:12
And also in Iraq	והנ בעירק	(6)	Gen. 29:9
America	אמריקה	(100)	Gen. 29:2
George Bush	גורג בוש	(−3129)	Gen. 33:8
Schwarzkopf	שורצקופ	(6777)	Gen. 29:24
the Missile will terrify	יבהל טיל	(2)	Gen. 19:29
They shut the door	ואת הדלת סגרו	(1)	Gen. 19:10
Russian	רוסי	(−1)	Gen. 19:2
Scud-B	סקאר בי	(15)	Gen. 19:1
the 3rd of Shevat	בני בשבט	(−258)	Gen. 20:14

One of the greatest miracles during the War in the Gulf occurred when thirty-nine Russian designed Scud-B missiles rained down on Tel Aviv, the largest populated area of Israel, where the vast majority of the Jewish state's five million citizens live. Although the American Patriot anti-missile system proved of some use in destroying Iraq's Scud-B missiles launched against U.S. troops in Saudi Arabia, the same anti-missile system did nothing to protect the Jews against these thirty-nine missiles. Several times the Patriot managed to break up the incoming Scud-B missile in the air, but it did not destroy the weapon as hoped. The huge destructive explosives in the warheads of each of these thirty-nine missiles destroyed over 15,000 Israeli apartments and homes. However, not one single Jew was killed by this devastating attack! The odds against this miracle of protection occurring by chance are astronomical. Surely this was a demonstration of the supernatural protection of God to preserve His Chosen People from their enemies.

However, another miracle also occurred during those terrifying missile attacks that went almost unreported in the Western news. One of the powerful Scud-B missiles managed to hit its intended target precisely. Although launched from more than five hundred miles away, the Iraqi missile made a direct hit with its warhead on the Gush Dan main gas-line terminal in Tel Aviv that supplied hundreds of thousands of homes and apartments with gas. These gas lines, which connected every home in the area to the main terminal, would normally be filled with extremely flammable and explosive gas. Normally, a missile explosion on a main gas terminal would have created a chain reaction of exploding gas below every street in Tel Aviv, creating a fire storm holocaust that would have killed tens of thousands of innocent Israeli citizens or more.

However, to the astonishment of the Israeli military, there was no secondary explosion when the missile warhead detonated. The fires were immediately extinguished with no loss of life whatsoever and no chain reaction of exploding gas lines. Just days before the missile attack, technicians working for the utility detected a minor malfunction in the gas lines that forced the management to shut off and empty the entire gas-line system by draining off all of the gas to allow for a safe inspection and repairs. This miracle reminds me of the tremendous promises of God to protect His people so they can dwell in safety: "But when ye go over Jordan, and dwell in the land which the Lord your God giveth you to inherit, and when he giveth you rest from all your enemies round about, so that ye dwell in safety" (Deuteronomy 12:10).

Dr. Moshe Katz has reported in his excellent book, *Compu-Torah*, that another group of encoded words relate to the War in the Gulf was found in the book of Numbers. The worldwide television network CNN and its star reporter Peter Arnet were watched virtually every day of the conflict by millions around the world. In the book of Numbers, researchers in Israel found the names of CNN and Peter Arnet encoded. Interestingly, the reporter Peter Arnet's full name appeared in code in one single verse of Numbers. The name "Peter" פיטר was encoded left to right every four letters while his last name "Arnet" ארנט was encoded right to left every two letters in Numbers 36:5.

War in the Gulf — CNN Codes

Encoded Name	Hebrew	Interval	Begins at
CNN	סי-אנ-אנ	(–780)	Num. 33:28
Peter	פיטר	(–4)	Num. 36:5
Arnet	ארנט	(2)	Num. 36:5

The Oklahoma City Bombing

On April 19, 1995, the worst terrorist attack in the history of North America destroyed the U. S. federal Murrah Building and killed 169 innocent people. For the first time, the heartland of America felt itself to be vulnerable to the terrorism and madness that has afflicted so many other countries of the world during the last few decades. This tragic event destroyed forever the feeling of security that had been known by generations of Americans who felt they were immune from the random terrorist violence experienced by other nations throughout the modern world. The trial of the accused bomber has concluded with the conviction and death sentence of Timothy McVeigh who was found guilty by a jury for intentionally killing these innocent civilians who happened to work in a federal government building. The evidence put forward at the trial suggests that Timothy McVeigh was motivated by an intense hatred of the U. S. government as a result of the disastrous attack two years earlier on the Waco, Texas compound of the Branch Davidians, a strange messianic cult led by David Koresh, that led to the tragic death of many innocent lives, the greatest massacre of civilians in U. S. history.

Apparently, according to testimony given at his trial, Timothy McVeigh was filled with hatred against the American government as a result of his view of the injustice of the FBI attack on the Branch Davidians in Waco, Texas. As a result, McVeigh decided to exact his revenge against the government on the second anniversary of the April 19th, 1993 destruction of the Branch Davidian compound by the FBI, and U. S. military support units. Tragically, McVeigh was successful in destroying the building and hundreds of citizens. Serious questions remain unanswered as to possible foreknowledge of this terrorist event by agencies of the U. S. government who may have infiltrated the group but somehow failed to stop the attack in time to avert disaster. This event remains the single most destructive terrorist attack to date in the history of North America.

It is fascinating to discover encoded words that describe detailed aspects of this frightening event described in the pages of the Scriptures that were written three and a half thousand years ago by the prophet Moses. An extensive examination of the Bible Codes that relate to this tragic event reveals that there are ten specific codes that describe the tragic events that occurred on April 19, 1995 in Oklahoma City in precise detail. The codes discovered in the book of Genesis record the following words that appear to relate to the tragic Oklahoma bombing: *Oklahoma* אוקלהומה; *terror* חתת; *Murrah* מרה; *desolated, slaughtered* שממזבח; *death* מורת; *his name is Timothy* שמר טימותי; *McVeigh* מקוורי; *Day 19* יומיט; *on the 9th hour* שעהט; *in the morning* בבקר. This is an incredible listing of key words describing a tragic event that will effect the world for many years. The following list includes the information revealing where these ten encoded words are found within the text of the Hebrew Bible. Anyone with a Hebrew-English Interlinear Bible or the Torah Codes software program (available from our company through the order form at the end of the book) will be able to verify these encoded words in the text of the book of Genesis.

The presence of these codes in the text of the Holy Scriptures written by Moses more than thirty-five centuries ago is powerful evidence to all who will examine the data that the Bible is truly inspired by a supernatural God. There is no natural explanation to explain the existence of these encoded words describing detailed events in our generation found in the pages of the Bible, written by Moses thousands of years before the event occurred.

The Oklahoma City Bombing

Encoded Name	Hebrew	Interval	Begins at
Oklahoma	אוקלהומה	(–1445)	Gen. 35:5
Terror	חתת	(1)	Gen. 35:5
Murrah	מורה	(–5)	Gen. 36:8
Building	בירין	(96)	Gen. 36:24
desolated,			
slaughtered	שממזבח	(1)	Gen. 35:7
death	מות	(19)	Gen. 35:7
His Name is			
Timothy	שמו טימותי	(–377)	Gen.44:4
McVeigh	מקוריי	(389)	Gen. 34:21
Day 19	יומיט	(191)	Gen. 32:13
On the 9th hour	שעהט	(–126)	Gen. 34:18
In the morning	בבקר	(47)	Gen. 36:10

The Terrorist Assassination of the Israeli Policeman Nissim Toledano

One of the most extraordinary of the Bible Codes relates to a relatively little-known event that occurred in Israel several years ago involving the terrorist assassination of an Israeli border policeman, First Sergeant Nissim Toledano. He was assassinated by Arab terrorists from the Hamas Islamic organization that refuses to accept the existence of the state of Israel. At the end of 1992 the Israeli government exiled four hundred notorious Hamas terrorists to the northern Lebanese border who were previously convicted of various terrorist crimes against Israeli citizens.While the United Nations condemned Israel's mild actions against her worst enemies, the Hamas organization decided to launch a retaliatory attack against Israel. The leadership of Hamas sent a three-man team of Palestinian Arabs into Israel with the goal of assassinating an Israeli soldier or police officer. Three Arab terrorists infiltrated into Israel, stole a car, and searched for a target of opportunity. As the three-man terrorist team approached the Ben Guerion airport outside the city of Lod, they drove by an Israeli border policeman, First Sergeant Nissan Toledano, who was waiting for a bus.

The terrorists decided to kill their innocent target by running him down with their stolen car. However, after hitting him, they noticed he was still alive. They backed up and pulled their victim into their car and sped away. Some Israelis who were approaching the bus stop saw the kidnapping and alerted the authorities. After the reports of the kidnapping became public knowledge on the Israeli radio network that night, the whole nation realized the extreme threat to the Jewish population from random terrorist attacks. Dr. Moshe Katz, one of the most brilliant of the Israeli Bible Code researchers who has examined the code phenomenon for a decade, immediately went to his computer and asked the program to search for the name of the kidnapped victim, border policeman First Sergeant Nissim Toledano. Immediately, Dr. Katz found that names of the victim, *Toledano*, together with the words *captivity*, *Lod*, *First Sergent*, and *Border Policeman*. His incredible code discovery is described in his book *Compu Torah*.

The Captivity of Toledano

Encoded Name	Hebrew	Interval	Begins at
the captivity of Toledano	לשביית טולינו	(3191)	Gen. 21:23
first sergeant	רב סמל	(5)	Gen. 48:8
border police	מג"ב	(2)	Gen. 31:39
Lod	לוד	(-1)	Gen. 39:14

Immediately after the kidnapping, the terrorists had an argument in the car regarding what they should do with their captive. One argued for his immediate murder with a dagger, while two of his companions suggested that Toledano be kept alive as a ransom for their imprisoned terrorist comrades. Finally, the three terrorists decided to kill their captive, but they disagreed as to whether they should kill him with a knife or smother him. One terrorist suggested that they should "shed no blood." Another suggested that they smother him to death. Finally, after failing to smother Todedano, one said, "Lets kill him." The terrorists used a knife to kill their victim and cast his body into a pit in the desert. Three days later, the body of Toledano was found in a pit, and the Israeli security forces succeeded in capturing the three terrorists.

Following the capture of the terrorists, the captured men recounted to the police their assassination plans and the argument they had in the car about how to kill their victim. Incredibly, the reported conversations of the terrorists corresponded to the information revealed in the encoded words, as discovered by the Israeli researcher Dr. Moshe Katz, who used the minimal interval code technique on the night of the kidnapping. Incredibly, the surface text of the Genesis passage, approxiamately where the encoded words "Lod," and "border police" appeared is the story of Joseph being thrown into a pit in the desert by his brothers. In this Genesis account, we find these phrases that were uttered thousands of years ago by Joseph's brothers and were also uttered by the three terrorists during this kidnapping and assassination: "lets kill him"; "shed no blood"; "cast him"; "in the desert"; "lay no hand upon him"; "cried in a loud voice."

"lets kill him"	Gen. 37:21
"shed no blood"	Gen. 37:22
"cast him"	Gen. 37:22
"in the desert"	Gen. 37:22
"lay no hand upon him"	Gen. 37:22
"cried in a loud voice"	Gen. 39:14
"he will die"	Gen. 32:14

After the Israeli security forces captured the three terrorists their names were published in the Israeli newspapers, allowing Dr. Katz to confirm that the actual statements of the murderers were exactly as found in the text in Genesis. However, Dr. Katz went back to his computer and input the names of the three terrorists: *Atun; Abu Katish; and Isa.* To his amazement, all three of their names were found encoded at minimal ELS intervals in the surrounding biblical text.

The Names of the Three Terrorists Who Killed Toledano

Encoded Name	Hebrew	Interval	Begins at
Atun	עטרן	(19)	Gen. 41:45
Abu Katish	אבו קתיש	(−1584)	Gen. 37:22
Isa	עיסא	(2)	Gen. 41:16

The Hebron Massacre

The discovery of the precise details of the death of Nissim Toledano encoded in the text of Genesis is very thought provoking. If the history of this private man is encoded, it is possible that the Bible Codes may contain information of an astonishing number of topics. It is important to remember that this research of the Bible Codes has only begun in the last few years. Much more remains to be discovered. One of the saddest events in the history of modern Israel occurred when an American-born Jewish doctor, Baruch Goldstein, went insane and mercilessly attacked a group of Moslem worshipers who were peaceably worshipping within the ancient Cave of the Patriarchs in Hebron. This ancient building was built by Herod the Great two thousand years ago to surround the cave containing the revered tombs of Abraham, Sarah, and other patriarchs who are honored ancestors to both the Muslims, Christians, and Jews. This site is sacred to both the Jews and Muslims containing both a synagogue and a mosque. Both groups accept the ancient tradition that this site is the ancient burial place of the patriarchs of both the ancient Israelis as well as the Arab Muslims.

Baruch Goldstein was descended from a Jewish family who had lived through a brutal Arab massacre and riot that killed most of the Jews living in Hebron in 1929 during the British Mandate. He came to the Hebron area to help the Jewish nation rebuild in the Promised Land. However, as a doctor, he was constantly dealing with the violent results of Arab PLO terrorism against both innocent Jews and Palestinians. When one of his friends was killed, he became insane. Goldstein took an assault rifle and attacked a group of Muslim worshippers, killing and wounding many in a mad act of revenge. Significantly, the last letter in the encoded word *Goldstein* forms the first letter of the word *revenge.* The following encoded words appear to relate to this tragic event.

The Hebron Massacre

Encoded Name	Hebrew	Interval	Begins at
Cave of the Patriarchs	מערת המכפלה	(1)	Gen. 25:9
Baruch	ברוך	(-1)	Ex. 13:15
Goldstein	גלדשטין	(9193)	Ex. 31:10

Revenge	נקמה	(-1)	Lev. 25:16
Year 5689 = 1929	ה"תרפט	(18)	Lev. 19:21
Al Fatah			
(Arafat's PLO)	אל-כתח	(1)	Lev. 19:21

Twenty-five Trees Encoded in Genesis 2

In my book *The Signature of God* I pointed out that the Israeli code researchers had discovered the encoded names of twenty-five trees within the Hebrew text of Genesis 2, which contains the story of God's creation of Adam and Eve as well as the plants and animals in the Garden of Eden. Every one of the twenty-five trees that are mentioned by name in the rest of the Old Testament appear encoded within this short chapter (635 words in English). Obviously, this encoding of the Hebrew names of the trees is not prophetic. However, it is an incredibly complicated thing for any human to attempt to write a short story about any topic while, at the same time, encoding twenty-five names of trees at ELS intervals within the text. My estimate is that it would take the better part of one year for someone to accomplish this in Hebrew or English. In addition, the researchers found that the name of the garden "Eden" was also encoded sixteen times in this same chapter.

The Names of Twenty-five Trees Encoded in Genesis 2

Encoded Name	*Hebrew*
vine	גפן
grape	ענב
chestnut	ערמן
dense forest	עבת
date	תמר
accacia	שטה
bramble	אטד
cedar	ארז
nut	בטן
fig	תאנה
willow	ערבה
pomegranate	רמון
aloe	אהלים
tamarisk	אשל
oak	אלון

poplar	לבנה
cassia	קדה
almond	שקד
mastic	אלה
thorn bush	סנה
hazel	לוז
olive	זית
citron	הדר
fir	גפר
wheat (related to	חטה
tree of knowledge)	חטה

In my own recent computer code research on this fascinating portion of the Bible, I found that God had also encoded in this same chapter, Genesis 2, the Hebrew names of seventeen animals that are named throughout the balance of the Old Testament. Furthermore, the name *Torah* is encoded five times, and the name *Yeshua* is found ten times in this same chapter. These incredibly complex codes appear embedded in a text that flows quite naturally in the Hebrew and English language. In other words, there appears to be nothing artificial or contrived in the choice of words that the author has used to express the story of God's creation of mankind in the Garden of Eden. I believe that it would be virtually impossible for a human or a computer program to produce a short passage such as Genesis 2 and place as many encoded words hidden at ELS intervals within the text.

Among the most fascinating code discoveries made in recent years is the discovery that God has encoded the names of Jesus and His disciples, together with numerous other individuals involved in the life and ministry of our Lord, in two different portions of the Old Testament. In the following chapter that deals with the Messiah Codes, you will find overwhelming evidence that these codes describe virtually every significant person in the life of Christ in the Old Testament, written many centuries before Jesus of Nazareth was born. The following chapter will reveal Bible Code discoveries about Jesus Christ that will provide powerful evidence of the supernatural origin of the Scriptures as well as the identification of Jesus as the true Messiah.

The Hebrew Aleph-bet
Sefardi Pronunciation

Numerical Value	Phonetics	Letters Form	Final Form
1	aleph	א	
2	bet, vet	ב	ב
3	gimmel	ג	
4	dalet	ד	
5	hey	ה	
6	vav	ו	
7	zayin	ז	
8	chet	ח	
9	tet	ט	
10	yod	י	
20	kaf	כ	ך
30	lamed	ל	
40	mem	מ	ם
50	nun	נ	ן
60	samek	ס	
70	ayin	ע	
80	pey, feh	פ	ף
90	tzadi	צ	ץ
100	qof	ק	
200	resh	ר	
300	shin, sin	ש	ש
400	tav	ת	

Note: Hebrew is written and read from right to left.

9

The Messiah Codes

The Names of Jesus the Nazarene and His Disciples
Encoded in Isaiah 53

The central theme of the prophecies of both the Old Testament and the New Testament is God's inspired revelation of Jesus of Nazareth as the Messiah and the Son of God.

Special Note

While we cannot use the codes to predict future events, once a historical event such as the life, death, or resurrection of Jesus has occurred, we can examine the text of the Bible to see whether or not there are ELS-encoded words that reveal God's foreknowledge of that event. In this manner, only God receives the glory from our examination of these fascinating codes.

A powerful indication of the validity of these encoded insights is found in the fact that these codes truly glorify Jesus of Nazareth in His divine roles as the Messiah, Adonai, Jehovah, and Lord. The First Epistle of John teaches us that one important spiritual test is that those who declare that Jesus Christ has come in the flesh are speaking in the Spirit of God: "Hereby know ye the Spirit of God: Every spirit that confesseth that Jesus Christ is come in the flesh is of God" (1 John 4:2). I believe that the fact that these coded words glorify Jesus Christ as the Son of God who came in the flesh to die for our sins on the Cross, provides irrefutable evidence that God placed these codes into the ancient scriptural text to glorify Jesus Christ.

After my book *The Signature of God* and Yacov Rambsel's book *YESHUA* were released last year, they quickly became international bestsellers. However, some scholars challenged the significance of Yacov's discovery of the name *Yeshua* encoded in virtually every major messianic prophecy in the Old Testament, as presented in our books. Some critics claimed that since the name "Jesus" *Yeshua* יֵשׁוּעַ was a relatively short name with only four Hebrew letters, it could be found by random chance almost anywhere in Hebrew literature. However, they could not explain why the name *Yeshua* would appear encoded at small ELS intervals within so many major messianic prophecies throughout the Old Testament. We have not found any other significant names of historical individuals appearing repeatedly in small ELS intervals within these major messianic passages. These particular messianic prophecies where we found the name Yeshua encoded are considered significant messianic prophetic passages by most Christian students of the Bible. In addition, many of these same prophecies are identified as messianic by the Jewish sages in their writings.

Do the Yeshua Codes Point to Jesus of Nazareth?

However, the skeptics dismissed Yacov's discovery of the Yeshua Codes and declared that the encoded word *Yeshua* did not refer to Jesus of Nazareth. While they acknowledge that the word *Yeshua* appears repeatedly within these messianic passages, as our books claimed, they reject our claim that these codes are significant and meaningful. The skeptics claim that you can find *Yeshua* encoded in ELS intervals in almost any Hebrew literature, including the Israeli phone book or Woody Allens's writings translated into the Hebrew language. While you can find random or accidental ELS letters showing the name *Yeshua* and other names in Hebrew literature, the skeptics have not explained why the name Yeshua appears repeatedly in virtually every significant messianic prophecy. Our research indicates that no other name of any other historical personality turns up repeatedly in these messianic verses. However, the real question to be determined is this: Do the ELS codes showing the name *Yeshua* in messianic passages actually refer to the historic Jesus of Nazareth, or is this just a coincidence as the skeptics suggest? After thinking about this question for a while, I thought of an experiment that should settle the issue.

A few months ago I asked Yacov to complete an exhaustive analysis of the famous "Suffering Servant" messianic prophecy in Isaiah 52:13 through Isaiah 53 to search for other codes that would identify Jesus of Nazareth. This well-known messianic prophecy predicts many incredible details about Jesus Christ's death on the Cross that were precisely fulfilled seven centuries later. If there was any particular passage in the Old Testament that one might anticipate that God would place ELS codes about Jesus Christ and His disciples, most Christians would assume that Isaiah 53 would be the logical place to look.

Yacov made an astonishing discovery that God has encoded the names of Jesus Christ and virtually everyone that was involved in His tragic crucifixion two thousand years ago. He found the encoded names of Jesus, the Nazarene, Messiah, the three Marys, the two High Priests, Herod, Pilate, and many of Christ's disciples in one prophetic passage — Isaiah 53. Furthermore, these names were encoded in Isaiah's prophecy written in 740 B.C., more than seven centuries before Jesus was born. Can any unbiased observer of this evidence honestly claim that these codes refer to anyone other than Jesus of Nazareth?

The prophet Isaiah wrote a powerful passage known as the "Suffering Servant" prophecy that depicts Israel's Messiah suffering and dying for our sins. This famous passage is found in the messianic chapters of Isaiah — Isaiah 52–53. Isaiah 52 reveals God's promise of blessing. Isaiah 53 depicts the sacrificial price of the blessing. These two chapters in Isaiah should be read together as a complete passage. Beginning with Isaiah 52:13 and continuing through Isaiah 53:12, the prophet Isaiah provides a powerful description of the Messiah as the Lamb of God, as prophesied by His death, His burial, and His resurrection to life.

Throughout these vital chapters, God has hidden many astonishing ELS codes that reveal historic events and names of key individuals. Every one of these events and the role of the named people were fulfilled in the life of Jesus as recorded in the New Testament precisely seven centuries after the prophecy of Isaiah was written. Within these prophetic Scriptures, God encoded the name of His Messiah, Jesus *Yeshua*, together with the names of almost every single person involved in the crucifixion of Jesus the Messiah. In addition, Isaiah 53 reveals the names of both of the chief priests at the time of the crucifixion, as well as the names of Herod, Caesar, and many others involved in the crucifixion of Jesus of Nazareth.

God is perfect in all of His works. The Lord has meticulously placed every single word and letter in the whole Bible in its proper location. Jesus Christ affirmed the unerring accuracy of the Scriptures in these inspired words: "For verily I say unto you, Till heaven and earth pass, one jot or one tittle shall in no wise pass from the law, till all be fulfilled" (Matthew 5:18). The Lord declared that not "one jot or tittle" (the smallest letter and grammatical mark) is out of place. God has inspired every word of the Scriptures, allowing us to believe that every part of His revelation will be fulfilled to the letter.

First Thessalonians 5:21 declares, "Prove all things; hold fast that which is good," while 1 Peter 3:15 affirms, "But sanctify the Lord God in your hearts: and be ready always to give an answer to every man that asketh you a reason of the hope that is in you with meekness and fear." After the crucifixion, Thomas the disciple required more proof of Jesus' resurrection. Despite the fact that Jesus had been predicting His crucifixion and resurrection on the third day for three and one half years, Thomas would not believe the reports of the women that Jesus had indeed risen from the dead. However, the Lord personally appeared to Thomas in the Upper Room to give him the visual proof he needed. Many people today are like Thomas; they require additional verification of the truth of the Bible and the deeper things of God. In our generation, I believe God is using the discovery of the Bible Codes, including the astonishing insights recorded in this book about Jesus, to provide overwhelming scientific proof of the claims of Jesus Christ to be the Son of God. In addition, these Bible Codes provide a unique proof of the authority and inspiration of the infallible Word of God to our skeptical generation.

"Yeshua is My Name" ישוע שמי

One of the most astonishing discoveries mentioned in my book *The Signature of God* was the fact that the name of Jesus *Yeshua* was found encoded within the Hebrew text of the messianic passages of the Old Testament. Yacov Rambsel wrote an extraordinary book, *YESHUA,* that documented his incredible discovery of the name of *Yeshua* Jesus encoded in the major messianic prophetic passages throughout the Old Testament from Genesis to Malachi. The name "Jesus" in Hebrew is *Yeshua* יֵשׁוּעַ. *Yeshua* is spelled with four Hebrew letters (right to left) as follows: yod (יֵ); shin (שׁ); vav (וּ) and ayin (עַ). I was delighted when I verified by computer and through manual examination of my Hebrew-English Interlinear Bible that my friend Yacov Rambsel had found the name *Yeshua* encoded in Isaiah 53:10. This famous prophecy foretold the grief of the suffering Messiah and His atoning sacrifice when He offered Himself as the Lamb of God, a perfect sacrifice for our sins by His death on the Cross: "Yet it pleased the Lord to bruise him; he hath put him to grief: when thou shalt make his soul an offering for sin, he shall see his seed, he shall prolong his days, and the pleasure of the Lord shall prosper in his hand" (Isaiah 53:10).

The words *Yeshua Shmi* "Yeshua [Jesus] is My Name" יֵשׁוּעַ שְׁמִי are encoded in this messianic verse beginning with the second Hebrew letter yod (י) in the phrase "He shall prolong" *ya'arik* יַאֲרִיךְ and counting every 20th letter left to right. Yacov's discovery of the name *Yeshua* encoded in Isaiah 53 and in dozens of other well-known messianic prophecies has thrilled hundreds of thousands of readers of the books *The Signature of God* and *YESHUA.*

However, I challenged Yacov to continue his research and complete an in-depth investigation of additional codes related to the life of Jesus of Nazareth in Isaiah 53. As a result of hundreds of hours of detailed research, I would like to share Yacov's incredible new discovery. Over forty names of individuals and places associated with the crucifixion of Jesus of Nazareth are encoded in Isaiah's Suffering Servant passage, which was written seven centuries before the birth of Jesus. I hope that you will be as thrilled with this astonishing discovery as I am. Yacov's complete research on this project is documented in his latest book entitled *His Name Is Jesus,* published recently by our ministry, Frontier Research Publications, Inc. I highly recommend his book to anyone who is fascinated by the phenomenon of the Bible Codes. With Yacov's permission, I will share a portion of his research on the incredible codes found in Isaiah 53 together with my own discovery of a similar code in Exodus 30:16.

The Names of Jesus and His Disciples

Within these key chapters of Isaiah, God has secretly encoded the names of the people, the actual locations, and events in the life of Jesus Christ that are recorded in the New Testament. Incredibly, the precise details of the people, the places, and the precise history of Christ's crucifixion were encoded in the Old Testament Scriptures seven centuries before the events took place. God clearly is in charge of human history. The Lord has revealed His supernatural prophetic knowledge of future events to our generation through the extraordinary discovery of the Bible Codes. This unprecedented phenomenon is a forceful reminder of the words recorded by Moses thousands of years ago: "The secret things belong unto the Lord our God: but those things which are revealed belong unto us and to our children for ever, that we may do all the words of this law" (Deuteronomy 29:29). Let us examine the details of this remarkable series of Bible Codes about Jesus Christ and His crucifixion.

First, we need to review the words of Isaiah's remarkable prophecy about the Messiah who would suffer for the sins of mankind. The full passage from Isaiah 52:13 through chapter 53 reads as follows:

Isaiah's Suffering Servant Prophecy
Isaiah 52:13–53:12

Behold, My Servant shall deal prudently, He shall be exalted and extolled, and be very high. As many were astonied at Thee; His visage was so marred more than any man, and His form more than the sons of men: So shall He sprinkle many nations; the kings shall shut their mouths at Him: for that which had not been told them shall they see; and that which they had not heard shall they consider.

(Isaiah 52:13–15)

Who hath believed our report? and to whom is the arm of the Lord revealed? For he shall grow up before him as a tender plant, and as a root out of a dry ground: he hath no form nor comeliness; and when we shall see him, there is no beauty that we should desire him. He is despised and rejected of men; a man of sorrows, and acquainted with grief: and we hid as it were our faces from him; he was despised, and we esteemed him not. Surely he hath borne our griefs, and carried our sorrows: yet we did esteem him stricken, smitten of God, and afflicted. But he was wounded for our transgressions, he was bruised for our iniquities: the chastisement of our peace was upon him; and with his stripes we are healed. All we like sheep have gone astray; we have turned every one to his own way; and the Lord hath laid on him the iniquity of us all. He was oppressed, and he was afflicted, yet he opened not his mouth: he is brought as a lamb to the slaughter, and as a sheep before her shearers is dumb, so he openeth not his mouth. He was taken from prison and from judgment: and who shall declare his generation? for he was cut off out of the land of the living: for the transgression of my people was he stricken. And he made his grave with the wicked, and with the rich in his death; because he had done no violence, neither was any deceit in his mouth. Yet it pleased the Lord to bruise him; he hath put him to grief: when thou shalt make his soul an offering for sin, he shall see his seed, he shall prolong his days, and the pleasure of the Lord shall prosper in his hand. He shall see of the travail of his soul, and shall be satisfied: by his knowledge shall my righteous servant justify many; for he shall bear their iniquites. Therefore will I divide him a portion with the great, and he shall divide the spoil with the strong; because he hath poured out his soul unto death: and he was numbered with the transgressors; and he bare the sin of many, and made intercession for the transgressors.

(Isaiah 53:1–12)

Isaiah 52:13–15

13. הנה ישכיל עברי ירום ונשא וגבה מאד.

14. כאשר שממו עליך רבים כן-משחת
מאיש מראהו ותארו מבני אדם:

15. כן יזה גוים רבים עליו יקפצו מלכים פיהם כי אשר
לא-ספר להם ראו ואשר לא-שמעו התבוננו.

Isaiah 53:1–12

1. מי האמין לשמעתנו וזרוע יהוה על-מי נגלתה.

2. כיונק לפניו וכשרש מארץ ציה לא-תאר
ויעל לו ולא הדר ונראהו ולא-מראה ונחמרהו.

3. נבזה וחדל אישים איש מכאבות וידוע
חלי וכמסתר פנים ממנו נבזה ולא חשבנהו.

4. אכן חלינו הוא נשא ומכאבינו סבלם
ואנחנו חשבנהו נגוע מכה אלהים ומענה.

5. והוא מחלל מפשעינו מדכא מעונתינו
מוסר שלומנו עליו ובחברתו נרפא-לנו.

6. כלנו כצאן תעינו איש לדרכו
פנינו ויהוה הפגיע בו את עון כלנו.

7. נגש והוא נענה ולא יפתח-פיו כשה לטבח
יובל וכרחל לפני גזזיה נאלמה ולא יפתח פיו.

8. מעצר וממשפט לקח ואת-דורו מי ישוחח
כי נגזר מארץ חיים מפשע עמי נגע למר.

9. ויתן את-רשעים קברו ואת-עשיר במתיו
על לא-חמס עשה ולא מרמה בפיו.

10. ויהוה חפץ דכאו החלי אם-תשים אשם נפשו
יראה זרע יאריך ימים וחפץ יהוה בירו יצלח.

11. מעמל נפשו יראה ישבע בדעתו יצדיק
צדיק עברי לרבים ועונתם הו יסבל.

12. לכן אחלק-לו ברבים ואת-עצומים יחלק
שלל תחת אשר הערה למות נפשו ואת-
פשעים נמנה והוא חטא-רבים נשא ולפשעים יפגיע.

Jesus of Nazareth

Christ was called Jesus of Nazareth because He was raised in the city of Nazareth with His family until commencing His public ministry when He was thirty years of age: "And He [Jesus] came and dwelt in a city called Nazareth: that it might be fulfilled which was spoken by the prophets, He shall be called a Nazarene" (Matthew 2:23). Some of the critics of the Yeshua Codes have challenged our conclusion that the name *Yeshua* found encoded in

Isaiah 53 and other passages actually refers to the historical Jesus of Nazareth. However, if the critics examine the encoded words we have discovered in this messianic prophecy, they will find over forty encoded names identifying virtually everyone who was present at the crucifixion of Jesus Christ. The odds against finding these precise words naming each of these important people, places, and events in the life of Jesus of Nazareth by random chance in a similar sized non-biblical Hebrew text are simply astronomical.

Yeshua The Nazarene

In Isaiah 53:6, starting with the third letter in the eleventh word and counting every forty-seventh letter from right to left, we find the word *Nazarene* נזיר. Throughout Isaiah's messianic passage, the word Nazarene is encoded several times. This discovery of the encoded name *Nazarene* נזיר near the name *Yeshua* ישוע in the same messianic prophecy, together with the names of many of His disciples, is overwhelming evidence that these Bible codes refer to the historical Jesus of Nazareth. This identification was primarily based on the fact that Jesus lived with his family for most of His life in the town of Nazareth in northern Galilee where Joseph, the husband of Jesus' mother Mary, pursued the occupation of a carpenter. The word "Nazarene" was also used to describe a special person who was chosen for a sacred purpose and dedicated to the service of God. A Nazarite was totally dedicated to the worship of the Lord and was willing to take the serious vow of the Nazarene. Jesus is often called the Nazarene because of His total commitment to His sacred calling to fulfill the will of God to redeem mankind from the curse of sin. The prophet Samuel was dedicated to the Lord by his mother Hanna when she pledged her unborn son to the service of the Tabernacle under the terms of the vow of the Nazarene. The book of Samuel states, "And she vowed a vow, and said, O Lord of hosts, if Thou wilt indeed look on the affliction of thine handmaid, and remember me, and not forget Thine handmaid, but wilt give unto Thine handmaid a man child, then I will give him unto the Lord all the days of his life, and there shall no razor come upon his head" (I Samuel 1:11). Another identification with the Nazarene name in the life of Jesus, the Messiah, as described in the Gospel of Matthew: "And [Jesus] came and dwelt in a city called Nazareth:

153

that it might be fulfilled which was spoken by the prophets, He shall be called a Nazarene נזיר" (Matthew 2:23).

The Nazarene

Nazarene נזיר   (every 47 letters forward) ◯

6.   כלנו כצאן תעינו איש לדרכו

פנינו ויהוה הפגיע בו את עון כלנו.

7.   נגש והוא נענה ולא יפתח-פיו כשה לטבח

יובל וכרחל לפני גזזיה נאלמה ולא יפתח פיו.

8.   מעצר וממשפט לקח ואת-דורו מי ישוחח

כן נגזר מארץ חיים מפשע עמי נגע למו.

9.   ויתן את-רשעים קברו ואת-עשיר במתיו

על לא-חמס עשה ולא מרמה בפיו.

Isaiah 53:6-9

Galilee

In addition, the codes reveal the place where Jesus lived for most of his life — Galilee. In Isaiah 53:7, starting with the second letter in the first word and counting every thirty-second letter from left to right spells "Galilee" גליל. There are two ways in Hebrew to spell "Galilee." The first is with the hen ה at the end of the word, and the second is without the hen letter. Jesus was raised in Nazareth, in a region of northern Israel called Galilee, as confirmed in Matthew 21:11: "And the multitude said, this is Jesus [Yeshua] the prophet of Nazareth of Galilee." In addition, much of His ministry was conducted at various locations surrounding the beautiful Sea of Galilee.

The Three Marys Who Witnessed the Crucifixion

The Gospel of John records that three women named Mary
Miryam מרים were present at the crucifixion of Jesus, together
with His beloved disciple, John *Yochanan* יוחנן. John 19:25–27
says, "Now there stood by the cross of Jesus His mother, and His
mother's sister, Mary the wife of Cleophas, and Mary Magdalene.
When Jesus therefore saw His mother, and the disciple [John]
standing by, whom He loved, He saith unto His mother, Woman,
behold thy son! Then saith He to the disciple [John], Behold thy
mother! And from that hour that disciple took her unto his own
home." This moving passage reveals the profound love of Jesus
for His mother Mary and His loyal friend John.

Three Marys and the Disciple John at the Cross

When we analyse this prophecy in the Hebrew text, we find
that the names of the three Marys and the disciple John are also
encoded beside the name "Jesus"*Yeshua* ישוע, which is spelled
out at a twenty letter interval reading left to right beginning in
Isaiah 53:10. These phenomenal codes were fulfilled precisely
over seven hundred years after Isaiah recorded his prophecy.

In Isaiah 53:11, starting with the fifth letter in the ninth word
and counting every twentieth letter from left to right spells *Ma 'al
Yeshua Shmee ohz* מעל ישוע שמי עז, which means "exceedingly
high, Yeshua is my strong name." From the yod (י) in Yeshua's
name, counting in reverse every twenty-eighth letter spells "John"
יוחנן. Isaiah 52:13 says, "Behold, my Servant [Yeshua] shall deal
prudently, He shall be exalted and extolled, and be very high." In
Isaiah 53:11, starting with the first letter in the first word and
counting every forty-second letter from left to right spells
"Messiah" *Mashiach* משיח. From the mem (מ) in the word
"Messiah," counting every twenty-third letter from left to right
spells "Mary" מרים.

In Isaiah 53:10, all three of the names of Mary use the letter yod
(י) in the word, *ya'arik* יאריך. This is the same letter yod (י) that
forms the first letter in the encoded names "Yeshua" and "John."
In Isaiah 53:10, starting with the third letter in the seventh word
and counting every sixth letter from right to left spells "Mary"
Miryam מרים. In Isaiah 53:12, starting with the fifth letter in the
fourth word and counting every forty-fourth letter from left to

right again spells "Mary" *Miryam* מרים. It is incredible to find the names of three Marys encoded in these verses beside the encoded names "Yeshua" and "John" when we remember that John's Gospel records that these four individuals were present at the crucifixion of Jesus Christ. In addition to naming Mary, the mother of Jesus, we find in Isaiah 53:2, starting with the second letter in the first word and counting every 210th letter from right to left spells "Joseph" *Yoseph* יוסף, the name of Mary's husband.

In the following illustration, we show the text of Isaiah's prophecy that reveals three encoded words: the name of the disciple John *Yochanan* יוחנן and two appearances of the name "Mary" *Miryam* מרים. To simplify the illustration, I have included only two of the three occurrences of the name "Mary."

The Name of the Disciple John and Two of the Marys

John יוחנן (every 28 letters in reverse)

[note: the final two letters נן both represent the letter N]

Two Marys מרים (every 6th letter in reverse and every 44th letter forward)

8. מעצר וממשפט לקח ואת-דורו מי ישוחח
    כי נגזר מארץ חיים מפשע עמי נגע למו.

9. ויתן את-רשעים קברו ואת-עשיר במתיו
    על לא-חמס עשה ולא מרמה בפיו.

10. ויהוה חפץ דכאו החלי אם-תשים אשם נפשו
    יראה זרע יאריך ימים וחפץ יהוה בידו יצלח.

11. מעמל נפשו יראה ישבע בדעתו יצדיק
    צדיק עבדי לרבים ועונתם הוא יסבל.

12. לכן אחלק-לו ברבים ואת- עצומים יחלק
    שלל תחת אשר הערה למות נפשו ואת-פשעים
    נמנה והוא חטא-רבים נשא ולפשעים יפגיע.

Isaiah 53:9-12

The Name "Disciples" Found in Isaiah 53

In Isaiah 53:12, starting with the third letter of the second word and counting every fifty-fifth letter from left to right spells *limmudim ahnan* אנן למדים, which means "the disciples mourn." Sometimes, the letter tav (ת) precedes this word. In this same count of fifty-five, but adjacent to "disciples," we find the word "priest." In Isaiah 53:5, starting with the second letter in the first word and counting every fifty-fifth letter from left to right spells "the Kohanim" (the priestly tribe) *ha'kohain* הכהן. It is astonishing to discover that the names of almost every one of Jesus' disciples (Judas Iscariot is excluded, for example) are encoded within this famous messianic prophecy of Isaiah, written seven centuries before Jesus was born.

The Names of the Disciples Encoded before Jesus was Born

The disciple's names are encoded as follows:
1. *PETER. Kepha* כפה.

In Isaiah 53:3, we find the name "Simon Peter," starting with the second letter in the fifth word and counting every nineteenth letter from right to left, the code spells "Peter" *Kepha* כפה.

2. *JAMES*, the son of Zabbadai. *Ya'akov* יעקב.

In Isaiah 52:2, starting with the third letter in the ninth word and counting every thirty-fourth letter from left to right, the code spells "James" *Ya'akov* יעקב.

3. *JOHN*. The brother of the disciple James is known as "John" *Yochanan* יוחנן.

In Isaiah 53:10, starting with the fourth letter in the eleventh word and counting every twenty-eighth letter from left to right, the code spells "John" *Yochanan* יוחנן.

4. *ANDREW. And'drai* אנדרי.

In Isaiah 53:4, starting with the first letter in the eleventh word, which is "God" *Elohim* אלהים, and counting every forty-eighth letter from left to right, we find the encoded word "Andrew" *And'drai* אנדרי.

5. *PHILIP. Pilip* פילף.

In Isaiah 53:5, starting with the third letter in the tenth word and counting every 133rd letter from left to right spells "Philip" *Pilip* פילף.

6. THOMAS. *Toma* תומא.
In Isaiah 53:2, starting with the first letter in the eighth word and counting every thirty-fifth letter from right to left the encoded word spells "Thomas" *Toma* תומא.

7. MATTHEW. There are three ways to spell the name of the disciple Matthew: *Mati* מתי, *Mattai* מתתי, *Mattiyahu* מתתיהו. The encoded word *Mattai* מתתי is an accepted abbreviated form of Mattiyahu מתתיהו. In Isaiah 53:8, starting with the first letter in the twelfth word and counting every 295th letter from left to right we find the encoded word "Matthew" *Mattai* מתתי.

8. JAMES, son of Alphaeus. *Ben Chalipi Ya'akov* בן חלפי יעקב.
      In Isaiah 52:2, starting with the fourth letter in the third word and counting every twentieth letter from left to right the encoded word spells the word *Ya'akov* יעקב. Two of Christ's disciples were known by the name "James" *Ya'akov* יעקב. It is fascinating that we have found the name "James" *Ya'akov* יעקב encoded twice within Isaiah 53, in recognition that there were two disciples of Christ who were named James.

9. SIMON, (Zelotes) the Canaanite. *Shimon hakanai* שמעון הקני.
      In Isaiah 52:14, starting with the first letter in the second word and counting every forty-seventh letter from right to left we find the encoded word "Simon" *Shimon* שמעון.

10. THADDAEUS. *Taddai* תדי.
      In Isaiah 53:12, starting with the first letter of the eighth word and counting every fiftieth letter from left to right the encoded word spells the name "Thaddaeus" *Taddai* תדי.

11. MATTHIAS. *Mattiyah* מתיה.
      In Isaiah 53:5, starting with the fourth letter in the seventh word and counting every eleventh letter from left to right spells "Matthias" *Mattiyah* מתיה. It is fascinating to note that this name "Matthias" is the name of the last disciple who was chosen by lot by the elders of the early Church to replace the dead traitor Judas Iscariot, whose guilt in betraying Jesus Christ caused him to commit suicide. Luke, the writer of the book of Acts, records how Matthias, the replacement disciple, was actually chosen: "And they gave forth their lots; and the lot fell upon Matthias מתיה; and he was numbered with the eleven apostles" (Acts 1:26). It is note-

worthy that in the early Church an essential qualification for choosing a disciple to replace the deceased Judas Iscariot was that he had to have personally witnessed the three and one half year ministry of Jesus Christ and His supernatural resurrection (Acts 1:21–26). This eyewitness requirement was established so that Matthias could also personally testify to everyone about his personal, eyewitness experience of the life of Christ from His baptism to His death and resurrection from the dead, and finally, His ascension to heaven. It is fascinating to note that the names of virtually all of Christ's disciples are encoded near the name *Yeshua* within Isaiah's prophecy. However, the name of Judas Iscariot, the Lord's betrayer, is not found encoded in this passage.

The Names of Three of Christ's Disciples
Thomas, Peter and Andrew

Thomas *Toma* תומא (every 35 letters in reverse)

Peter *Kepha* כפה (every 19 letters)

Andrew And'drahi אנדרי (every 48 letters)

1. מן האמין לשמעתנו וזרוע יהוה על-מי נגלתה.

2. ויעל כיונק לפניו וכשרש מארץ ציה לא-תאר
לו ולא הדר ונראהו ולא-מראה ונחמדהו.

3. נבזה וחדל אישים איש מכאבות וידוע
חלי וכמסתר פנים ממנו נבזה ולא חשבנהו.

4. אכן חלינו הוא נשא ומכאבינו סבלם
ואנחנו חשבנהו נגוע מכה אלהים ומענה.

Isaiah 53:1-4

Jesus' Trial and the Names of the Two High Priests

When we examine the encoded information about those in power at the time of the crucifixion, we discover the names of the key participants. The codes reveal the names of Israel's two high priests at that time. Starting with the third letter in the seventh word in Isaiah 52:15, and counting every forty-first letter from right to left spells "Caiaphas" *Kayafa* כיפה, the name of the high priest of Israel named in the Gospel account of the trial of Jesus. In 1991, Israeli archeologists discovered the tomb of Caiaphas the High Priest. In Isaiah 53:3, starting with the fifth letter in the sixth word and counting every forty-fifth letter from right to left spells "Annas" *Ahnan* ענן, who was the former high priest and the uncle of Caiaphas. The New Testament reveals the names of these high priests in Luke 3:2: "Annas and Caiaphas being the high priests, the word of God came unto John the son of Zacharias in the wilderness." The high (chief) priests were leaders in the Sanhedrin trial in the Temple that lead to the crucifixion, according to John 19:15: "But they cried out, Away with Him, away with Him, crucify Him. Pilate saith unto them, Shall I crucify your King? The chief priests answered, We have no king but Caesar [the Roman]."

The Names of Israel's Two High Priests

The Names of Israel's Two High Priests

Caiaphas *Kayafa* כיפה (every 41 letters forward)

Annas *Ahnan* ענן (every 42 letters forward)

15. כן יזה גוים רבים עליו יקפצו מלכים פיהם כי אשר

לא-ספר להם ראו ואשר לא-שמעו התבוננו.

1. מי האמין לשמעתנו וזרוע יהוה על-מי נגלתה.

2. ויעל כיונק לפניו וכשרש מארץ ציה לא-תאר

לו ולא הדר ונראהו ולא-מראה ונחמדהו.

3. נבזה וחדל אישים איש מכאבות וידוע

חלי וכמסתר פנים ממנו נבזה ולא חשבנהו.

4. אכן חלינו הוא נשא ומכאבינו סבלם

ואנחנו חשבנהו נגוע מכה אלהים ומענה.

Isaiah 52:15 to 53:4

The Pharasees, the Levites, King Herod, Rome, and Caesar

The Pharisees and King Herod were also involved in the crucifixion, and we see their names encoded in Isaiah 53. In verse 9, starting with the second letter in the fourteenth word and counting every sixty-fourth letter from left to right we find the word "Pharisee" *pahrush* פרוש. These Jewish religious leaders were a strong force in both the Temple and in the broader Israeli society. They encouraged people to follow the strict religious laws of the Scriptures and the written and oral traditions based on the teachings of their rabbis over the centuries. It is amazing to note that in Isaiah 53:6, starting with the first letter in the fourth word and counting every twenty-ninth letter from left to right, we find the encoded words "the man Herod" *ish Herod* איש הורד. The fact that both the names "Pharisees" and "Herod" are encoded in this messianic prophecy in Isaiah is remarkable.

In Isaiah 53:11, starting with the first letter of the second word and counting every fourteenth letter from left to right spells the Hebrew word "Levis" *Levim* לוים, clearly identifying the Temple priests, chosen from the Jewish tribe of Levi, who joined in the attack on Jesus. In addition, starting with the second letter in the thirteenth word, in Isaiah 53:9, and counting every seventh letter from left to right the encoded letters spell "the evil Roman city" *rah eer Romi* רע עיר רומי, which identifies the Roman Empire, the political power ruling the known world at that time that actually ordered the death of Jesus. The Jewish authorities did not possess the legal power to inflict a death sentence upon any offender found guilty in their Sanhedrin Court in the Temple. The only way a death sentence could be carried out in Judea at that time was to find a Roman law that the prisoner had also broken and to then appeal to the Roman governor to sentence the person to death under the laws of Rome.

The Gentile soldiers of the Roman Empire who were present at the crucifixion clearly represented the Roman Emperor Caesar and the entire Gentile world who rejected the claims of Jesus as the Son of God and thus spiritually joined in the execution of God's Messiah. In this sense, all of humanity was represented at the crucifixion of the Lamb of God, Jesus Christ. In Isaiah 53:11, starting with the fourth letter in the seventh word and counting every 194th letter from left to right, we find the encoded words

Kaisar ahmail ovaid קיסר עמל אבד, which means "wicked, Caesar wretched (perish)," or alternatively phrased as "wicked Caesar, to perish." It is interesting to note that the Roman emperor Tiberius died within five years following the death of Jesus Christ.

Jesus Christ — The Atonement Lamb and the Light of the World

The gospel of John records that John the Baptist received a profound revelation of Christ as the Atonement Lamb of God when Jesus came to be baptized in the Jordan River. "The next day John seeth Jesus coming unto him, and saith, Behold the Lamb of God, which taketh away the sin of the world" (John 1:29). In Isaiah 52:12, starting with the second letter in the twelfth word and counting every nineteenth letter from left to right spells "from the Atonement Lamb" *me'kippur tela* מכפר טלא.

In Isaiah 53:5, starting with the seventh letter in the fifth word and counting every twentieth letter from right to left, "lamp of the Lord" *ner Adonai* נר יהוה is spelled out. This encoded word is adjacent to *Yeshua* ישוע at a twenty-letter interval. The gospel of John affirms repeatedly that Jesus Christ is the true light of the world. This is confirmed in the following quotation from John's gospel: "Then spake Jesus again unto them, saying, I am the Light of the world: he that followeth Me shall not walk in darkness, but shall have the Light of life" (John 8:12).

The Messianic Title "Shiloh"

In Isaiah 53:9, starting with the second letter in the eleventh word and counting every fifty-fourth letter from right to left spells *Shiloh* שילה. Both Jewish and Christian scholars acknowledge that the word *Shiloh* is a clear prophetic title of the coming Messiah. In Genesis 49:10, Moses recorded the deathbed prophecy of the patriarch Jacob: "The sceptre shall not depart from Judah, nor a lawgiver from between his feet, until Shiloh come; and unto Him [Yeshua] shall the gathering of the people be." This famous prophecy clearly identified the coming Messiah as "Shiloh." The discovery of the word *Shiloh* encoded beside the name *Yeshua* in the powerful messianic prophecy of Isaiah 53 provides powerful evidence of the identity of Jesus of Nazareth in this passage.

The Name of Jesus and His Messianic Title — Shiloh

Jesus - Yeshua ישוע (every 20 letters in reverse)

Shiloh שילה (every 54 letters forward)

9. ויתן את-רשעים קברו ואת-עשיר במתיו

עַל לא-חמס עָשָׂה ולא מרמה בפיו.

10. וַיהוה חפץ דכאו החלי אם-תשׂים אשם נפשו

יראה זרע יאריך יָמים וחפץ יהוה בידו יצלח.

11. מעמל נפשו יראה ישבע בדעתו יצדיק

צדיק עבדי לֲרבים ועונתם הוא יסבל.

12. לכן אחלק-לו ברבים ואת- עצומים יחלק

שלל תחת אשר הֶערה למות נפשו ואת-פשעים

נמנה והוא חטא-רבים נשא ולפשעים יפגיע.

Isaiah 53:9-12

In addition we have found the word *Yeshua* together with the word *Messiah* encoded in this key passage. In Isaiah 53:8, starting with the third letter in the second word and counting every sixty-fifth letter from left to right spells "Messiah" *Mashiach* משׁיח. In this same count, but starting with the third letter in the tenth word of verse 10, which is the ayin (ע), and counting every sixty-fifth letter from left to right spells *Yeshua* ישוע. It is fascinating that the words "Jesus" and "Messiah" are both encoded in this prophecy of Isaiah sharing the same 65-letter ELS interval. Also, the word "Passover" was found encoded in Isaiah 53:10. Beginning at the third letter of the thirteenth word at an interval of every sixty-two letters in reverse spells "Passover" *Peh'sakh* פסח.

Jesus the Messiah and the Feast of Passover

JESUS THE MESSIAH CRUCIFIED ON PASSOVER

Jesus   Yeshua   ישוע   (in reverse every 20 letters)

Passover   *Peh'sakh*   פסח   (In reverse every 62 letters)

Messiah   *Mashiach*   משיח   (In reverse every 42 letters)

8.   מעצר וממשפט לקח ואת-דורו מי ישוחח
כי נגזר מארץ חיים מפשע עמי נגע למו.

9.   ויתן את-רשעים קברו ואת-עשיר במתו
על לא-חמס עשה ולא מרמה בפיו.

10. ויהוה חפץ דכאו החלי אם-תשים אשם נפשו
יראה זרע יאריך ימים וחפץ יהוה בידו יצלח.

11. מעמל נפשו יראה ישבע בדעתו יצדיק
צדיק עבדי לרבים ועונתם הוא יסבל.

Isaiah 53:8-11

The Prophetic Symbols at the Passover Supper
The Bread and Wine

In Isaiah 53:1, starting with the fifth letter in the eighth word and counting every 210th letter from right to left spells "the bread" *ha'lachem* הלחם, which may refer to the powerful symbol of bread that Jesus used at the Last Supper to refer to His body, which was broken for our sins. Another group of Hebrew letters at the same 210-letter interval spells the word "wine" *yeyin* יין, which was the other symbol used by Jesus at His last Passover Supper in the Upper Room to symbolize His blood, which was shed for our sins. The word "wine" is spelled out in reverse at a 210-letter interval beginning with the second letter in the eleventh word and counting from right to left. The words "wine" and "bread" clearly represent the body and blood of Jesus, as revealed by Jesus to His disciples in the Upper Room.

It is interesting to find the names "Jonah" and "water"

encoded close together in this passage. In Isaiah 52:4, starting with
the fourth letter in the sixth word and counting every nineteenth
letter from left to right spells "Jonah" יונה. A few verses later, in
Isaiah 52:7, starting with the first letter in the ninth word and
counting every nineteenth letter from left to right spells "water"
מים. The prophet Jonah was placed in the water to awaken him to
God's command to preach to his enemies, the Ninevites. These
codes revealing "Jonah" and "water" remind us of the history of
the prophet Jonah, who was "three days and three nights in the
whale's belly." Jesus used Jonah's experience as a prophetic
symbol of His own death and resurrection.

Those Who Watched the Crucifixion from Afar

Mark 15:40 says, "There were also women looking on afar off:
among whom was Mary Magdalene, and Mary the mother of
James the less and of Joses, and Salome." In Isaiah 52:15, starting
with the third letter in the sixteenth word and counting every
113th letter from right to left spells "Salome" *Shalomit* שלמית. In
verse 13, starting with the fourth letter in the second word and
counting every 149th letter from right to left spells "Joses" *Yosai*
יוסי. The man Joses was apparently a son of Jesus' mother Mary,
and therefore His half-brother. According to Mark 15:40, both
Marys were weeping at the crucifixion of Jesus. Encoded in Isaiah
52:15, starting with the fifth letter in the eighteenth word and
counting every thirteenth letter from left to right spells the
words "the Marys weep bitterly" *na'ar Miryam be'ku abhor*
נאר מרים בכו. In Isaiah 53:9, starting with the first letter in the
third word and counting every twenty-eighth letter from right to
left spells "tremble Mary" *rahal Miryam* רעל מרים. The letters
adjacent to the above spell "the blessed" *habarucha* הברוכה.
Mary, the mother of Jesus, was called blessed in the Gospel of
Luke: "And the angel came in unto her [Mary], and said, Hail,
thou that art highly favoured, the Lord is with thee: blessed
(ברוכה) art thou among women" (Luke 1:28).

Thus far, we have found encoded words naming virtually
every one of the people involved with the crucifixion of Jesus, in
addition to many others who were present during His remarkable
life of ministry.

The Cross and the Passover Feast

In Isaiah 53:10, starting with the third letter in the second word and counting every fifty-second letter from right to left spells "cross" צלב. From the same word, taking the first letter and counting every 104th letter from right to left spells "Passover" פסח, as mentioned earlier. In Isaiah 52:14, starting with the third letter in the sixth word and counting every twenty-sixth letter from left to right spells "My Feast (my sacrifice)" *Chaggai* חגי. After sharing His last Passover Supper with His disciples in the Upper Room, Jesus was betrayed by Judas, and taken to a series of trials. His crucifixion took place the next afternoon on the day of the Passover Feast, known as *Chaggai* חגי.

The Ancestors of King David

The gospel of Luke records the genealogy of Jesus, proving that He was descended from the royal line of King David and therefore has the right to be called king. Luke 3:32 records a significant part of the royal lineage of Jesus, beginning with King David: "Which was the son of Jesse, which was the son of Obed, which was the son of Booz [Boaz]" It is intriguing to find these names encoded in Isaiah 53:7. Starting with the second letter in the third word for "was afflicted" נענה, and counting every nineteenth letter from left to right spells "Obed" *Ohved* עבד. The name Obed means "servant." It is significant that Obed was the son of Ruth and Boaz, the grandfather of King David. Jesus is called both "the Son of David" and "the suffering Servant [Obed]." In Isaiah 52:9, beginning with the first letter in the third word, which is "together" יחדו, and counting every nineteenth letter from left to right spells "Jesse" *Yishai* ישי, the son of Obed and the father of King David. The name Jesse means "wealthy" or "gift." Incredibly, these key ancestors of King David and Jesus of Nazareth are encoded in this messianic prophecy of Isaiah.

The Time and Place of Christ's Crucifixion

Jesus was crucified on the day of the Passover Feast, which took place annually on the 15th of the Jewish month Nisan (also known as the month of Aviv). Mount Moriah, the Temple Mount, is the place where God provided a ram as a substitute sacrifice in the place of Abraham's son Isaac. This was also the place where

God commanded King David to prepare for the building of the Temple, which was built by his son Solomon. However, Mount Moriah is a long mountain ridge that begins in the south of Jerusalem and continues northward past the northern city walls to the site of Golgotha, where Jesus was crucified outside the city walls, just north of the Damascus Gate. The book of Hebrews confirms the Gospel account that Christ's death took place outside the city walls: "Wherefore Jesus also, that he might sanctify the people with his own blood, suffered without the gate" (Hebrews 13:12). In Isaiah 52:1, starting with the third letter in the eighth word and counting every twenty-seventh letter from right to left spells *aviv ve'moriah* אביב ומריה, which means "Aviv of Mount Moriah." This is an astonishing code discovery naming the actual month, Aviv, and the place of Christ's sacrifice for our sins written by Isaiah centuries before the event. The adjacent letters spell *rosh* ראש, which means "the first" or "the head of the year" (the first month of the religious year was the month Nisan-Aviv, the month of Passover), when Jesus was crucified.

"Let Him Be Crucified"

Two thousand years ago, the Romans and the Jewish leaders joined together to crucify Jesus of Nazareth. Every human being on earth was morally represented by the Romans and the Jewish leadership because Jesus died on the cross for our sins. The gospel of Matthew records the terrible moment when the Roman governor decided on Christ's death. "Pilate saith unto them, What shall I do then with Jesus which is called Christ? They all say unto him, Let him be crucified" (Matthew 27:22). The prophet Isaiah foretold this tragic series of events seven centuries before they occurred. "He was taken from prison and from judgment: and who shall declare his generation? for he was cut off out of the land of the living: for the transgression of my people was he stricken" (Isaiah 53:8). Perhaps the most astonishing code discovery in this passage is the fact that this exact phrase was encoded in Isaiah's prophecy. Starting with the second letter in the sixth word of Isaiah 53:8 and counting every fifteenth letter right to left spells "let Him be crucified" *yitz'tzahlaiv* יצלב.

The Handwriting of God

"LET HIM BE CRUCIFIED"

Jesus Is My Name Yeshua Shmi ישוע שמי (every 20 letters in reverse)

Let Him Be Crucified Yitz'tzah'laiv יצלב (every 15 letters forward)

מעצר וממשפט לקח ואת-דורו מי ישוחח   8.

כי נגזר מארץ חיים מפשע עמי נגע למו.

ויתן את-רשעים קברו ואת-עשיר במתיו   9.

על לא-חמס עשה ולא מרמה בפיו.

וישוה חפץ דכאו החלי אם-תשים אשם נפשו   10.

יראה זרע יאריך ימים וחפץ יהוה בידו יצלח.

Isaiah 53:8-10

Over one thousand years before the birth of Jesus, the psalmist David wrote his prophetic Psalm that foretold the tragic crucifixion of Christ. David wrote of the future death of the Messiah: "The assembly of the wicked have enclosed me: they pierced my hands and my feet" (Psalm 22:16). Incredibly in Isaiah 52:10, we find the word "pierce" encoded. Starting with the third letter in the fifteenth word, which is "in His hands" בידו, and counting every ninety-two letters from left to right spells "pierce" *dahkar* דקר in reverse.

Can any unbiased reader have any remaining doubt that the Bible Codes identify Jesus of Nazareth as the Messiah who died for our sins as the Son of God?

The Signature of God

Last year, I wrote a book entitled *The Signature of God*, which explored the fascinating evidence from archeology, scientific and medical discoveries, fulfilled prophecy, and the incredible Bible Codes that prove the supernatural origin of the Bible. My thesis was that God had, in effect, written His authenticating signature on the inspired pages of His Holy Word through this supernatural evidence in the text, which no unaided human could have created. I was amazed when Yacov recently sent me a fax showing his latest discovery — a code that contained the words *me'chatimo* מחתימו, which means "His Signature." In Isaiah 52:7, starting with the fourth letter, the final mem ם, in the Hebrew word *shalom* שלום, the eighth word, and counting every forty-ninth letter from right to left spells "His Signature" *me'chatimo* מחתימו. The Hebrew letters ם and מ are variations of the same letter. These astonishing codes surely are the signature of God on the pages of the His word.

The final pages of this chapter contain a detailed summary of the major codes in Isaiah's prophecy that name virtually everyone associated with the crucifixion of Jesus. This list should be a convenience for the reader and an aid for those students of the Bible who wish to check out these Bible Codes for themselves.

A Challenge to the Critics of the Yeshua Code

When my book *The Signature of God* and Yacov Rambsel's book *Yeshua* were published in 1997, hundreds of thousands of readers rejoiced in this discovery about the Bible Codes. Many students of the Scriptures were especially fascinated with Yacov's research that revealed the encoded name of Jesus in well-known messianic prophecies. However, a number of Bible Code researchers in Israel and North America, as well as orthodox Jewish rabbis, have disputed the significance of this discovery of Yeshua's name. They have pointed out that the name *Yeshua* ישוע is a relatively small word with only four letters and two common vowels. Some of these critics have contemptuously challenged the significance of the Yeshua Codes and declared that one could find the name *Yeshua* ישוע in virtually any passage in Hebrew literature (from a novel to the Israeli phone book). However, the critics ignore the fact that the name *Yeshua* appears at very small ELS intervals (i.e., every 5th, 9th, or 20th letter, etc.) in dozens of familiar messianic prophecies. We have not found significant names of any other historic personalities encoded at small ELS intervals in dozens of messianic prophecies.

One critic claimed on the Internet that the name of the false messiah Rev. Sung Yung Moon appears frequently in these same messianic prophecies. However, this is false. While the short three letter Hebrew word for "moon" does appear frequently including some places near some of these messianic passages, the word "moon" does not identify the Rev. Sung Young Moon of South Korea, who formed the Unification Church. The encoded words do not reveal "Rev. Sung Young Moon" as the critics falsely imply; it is only the three letter word "moon" that appears frequently. This criticism is without merit.

Yacov's astonishing discovery of over forty names of individuals and places associated with the crucifixion of Jesus of Nazareth in this Isaiah Suffering Servant messianic passage is unprecedented. I would like to issue a challenge to the critics who reject the Yeshua Codes to find any other passage of similar length (fifteen sentences) in Hebrew literature outside the Bible that contains forty ELS codes, including the names of Jesus, the Nazarene, Messiah, Passover, Herod, Mary, and the names of Christ's disciples. A partial list of Yacov's code discoveries found in this prophecy from Isaiah 52:13 through Isaiah 53 is provided at the end of this chapter to help the reader realize the astonishing amount of detailed information encoded in this remarkable prophecy. The critics claim that these codes about *Yeshua* can be found by random chance in any Hebrew literature, and, therefore they reject the significance of this discovery.

Here is a challenge from Yacov and myself to the critics. Let them produce any other Hebrew literature of the same length as or shorter than this Isaiah passage that also contains all of the encoded names listed in the summary that follows. If they cannot discover these names encoded in any passage outside the Bible, and we believe it will be impossible, we will have additional evidence that these codes about *Yeshua* the Nazarene, and His disciples, are truly unprecedented.

Jesus and His Disciples Found Encoded in Isaiah 53

Name	Begins	Word	Letter	Interval
Yeshua Shmi	Isa. 53:10	11	4	(−20)
Nazarene	Isa. 53:6	11	3	(47)
Messiah	Isa. 53:11	1	1	(−42)
Shiloh	Isa. 53:12	21	4	(19)
Passover	Isa. 53:10	13	3	(−62)
Galilee	Isa. 53:7	1	2	(−32)

Herod	Isa. 53:6	4	1	(−29)
Caesar	Isa. 53:11	7	4	(−194)
The evil Roman city	Isa. 53:9	13	2	(−7)
Caiaphas — High Priest	Isa. 52:15	7	3	(41)
Annas — High Priest	Isa. 53:3	6	5	(−45)
Mary	Isa. 53:11	1	1	(−23)
Mary	Isa. 53:10	7	3	(6)
Mary	Isa. 53:9	13	3	(44)
The Disciples	Isa. 53:12	2	3	(−55)
Peter	Isa. 53:10	11	5	(−14)
Matthew	Isa. 53:8	12	1	(−295)
John	Isa. 53:10	11	4	(−28)
Andrew	Isa. 53:4	11	1	(−48)
Philip	Isa. 53:5	10	3	(−133)
Thomas	Isa. 53:2	8	1	(35)
James	Isa. 52:2	9	3	(−34)
James	Isa. 52:2	3	4	(−20)
Simon	Isa. 52:14	2	1	(47)
Thaddaeus	Isa. 53:12	9	1	(−50)
Matthias	Isa. 53:5	7	4	(−11)
Let Him Be Crucified	Isa. 53:8	6	2	(15)
His Cross	Isa. 53:6	2	2	(−8)
Pierce	Isa. 52:10	15	3	(−92)
Lamp of the Lord	Isa. 53:5	5	7	(20)
His Signature	Isa. 52:7	8	4	(49)
Bread	Isa. 53:12	2	3	(26)
Wine	Isa. 53:5	11	2	(210)
From Zion	Isa. 52:14	6	1	(45)
Moriah	Isa. 52:7	4	5	(153)
Obed	Isa. 53:7	3	2	(−19)
Jesse	Isa. 52:9	3	1	(−19)
Seed	Isa. 52:15	2	2	(−19)
Water	Isa. 52:7	9	1	(−19)
Levites	Isa. 54:3	3	6	(19)
From the Atonement Lamb	Isa. 52:12	12	2	(−19)
Joseph	Isa. 53:2	1	2	(210)

New Code Discoveries Revealing Jesus of Nazareth
in the Torah
Exodus 30:16

After the astonishing code discovery by Yacov Rambsel of the forty-one names related to the ministry and crucifixion of Jesus of Nazareth in Isaiah 53, I wondered if God had encoded this prophetic information confirming the identity of Jesus as His Messiah in any other place in the Bible. Using my Torah Codes computer program, I began a systematic search through the Hebrew Bible, focusing especially on the Torah to see if this information was encoded there as well. To my amazement, I found the following series of codes naming everyone who was significant in the ministry of Jesus Christ, including the three Marys, the names of every disciple, including the replacement for Judas Iscariot, the disciple Matthias, and much more. The following list of codes will enable anyone with a Hebrew-English Interlinear Bible to confirm my discovery.

Significantly, phenomenal codes were found in Exodus 30:16 that deal with God's commands to Moses regarding the atonement price for Israel's sins.

> And thou shalt take the atonement money of the children of Israel, and shalt appoint it for the service of the tabernacle of the congregation; that it may be a memorial unto the children of Israel before the Lord, to make an atonement for your souls.　　　　　(Exodus 30:16)

Jesus of Nazareth and His Disciples in Exodus 30

Name	Begins	Word	Ltr	Interval	Ends	Word	Ltr
Yeshua	Ex. 30:16	19	1	(12)	Ex. 30:18	1	2
Nazarene	Ex. 30:16	15	3	(8)	Ex. 30:16	20	4
Messiah	Ex. 30:13	12	3	(60)	Ex. 30:18	3	2
Shiloh	Ex. 30:14	7	1	(40)	Ex. 30:16	12	2
Passover	Ex. 30:9	7	4	(-9)	Ex. 30:10	1	3
Galilee	Ex. 29:19	7	3	(-39)	Ex. 29:21	8	3
Mary	Ex. 30:15	7	2	(60)	Ex. 30:18	11	1
Mary	Ex. 30:16	13	1	(61)	Ex. 30:20	8	2
Mary	Ex. 30:17	5	3	(92)	Ex. 30:23	14	2
Peter	Ex. 30:16	2	2	(32)	Ex. 30:17	1	2

Matthew	Ex. 30:20	8	2	(20)	Ex. 30:21	6	2
John	Ex. 29:19	9	1	(14)	Ex. 29:20	12	2
Andrew	Ex. 29:27	15	4	(115)	Ex. 29:36	7	4
Philip	Ex. 29:24	9	4	(50)	Ex. 29:27	4	5
Thomas	Ex. 30:18	14	4	(11)	Ex. 30:19	7	2
James	Ex. 30:7	6	2	(–59)	Ex. 30:10	14	5
Simon	Ex. 29:19	7	3	(–39)	Ex. 29:21	8	3
Nathanael	Ex. 30:4	8	2	(–100)	Ex. 30:12	8	2
Judas	Ex. 29:13	9	2	(24)	Ex. 29:15	2	1
Thaddaeus	Ex. 30:16	2	2	(32)	Ex. 30:17	1	2
Matthias	Ex. 30:20	8	2	(20)	Ex. 30:21	6	2
Let Him Be							
Crucified	Ex. 30:20	1	1	(8)	Ex. 30:20	8	1

In this passage, we find twenty-one signficant codes naming virtually every significant person in the minstry of Jesus of Nazareth. The fact that these codes were found in the Torah is especially important. The Bible established the principle that the truth was confirmed in the word of two witnesses. Moses wrote, "At the mouth of two witnesses, or at the mouth of three witnesses, shall the matter be established" (Deuteronomy 19:15). Therefore, it is extremely significant that this complex series of codes revealing the identity of Jesus of Nazareth as the Messiah has been located in two separate portions of the Bible by two independent researchers using two different search methods. I believe that these Messiah codes are the most important code discoveries that have been found to date.

10

The Heavenly Prince Melchisedec Scroll

In 1947, through the providence of God, an Arab shepherd boy discovered the greatest treasury of ancient Jewish manuscripts the world has ever seen. In one moment of time the world's confidence in the total accuracy of the transmission of the Old Testament by the Jewish scribes through the last two thousand years sky rocketed. The scholars were delighted to find that every one of the thirty-nine books of the Old Testament were hidden in these caves with the sole exception of the book of Esther. However, the discovery contained a manuscript that includes a commentary on the book of Esther. This precious library was owned by the Essenes, a somewhat monastic Jewish group that longed for the coming Messiah. This group of religious Jews had left the Temple in rejection of the increasing corruption in the religious life and practices of the Temple priesthood. They established their own religious center, Qumran, in the desert beside the Dead Sea. The Jewish historian Flavius Josephus wrote that the Essenes were the third largest sect practicing ancient Judaism during the time of Christ. With four thousand members, the Essenes were smaller than only the Pharisees and Sadducees.

When the scholars compared these two-thousand-year-old biblical texts against the oldest biblical manuscripts in the libraries of Europe, they were astonished to discover that there were almost no significant textual changes in any of the books of the Old Testament. The Jewish Masoretic scholars had carefully preserved the accuracy of the biblical text to such a remarkable degree that when the scholars examined the Torah, from Genesis to Deuteronomy, there were only 169 Hebrew letters that differed in the Dead Sea Scrolls text from the biblical texts that were used by the King James Bible translators in 1611. Significantly, none of these 169 letter variations changed the meaning of a single word. In other words, 99.94% of the letters of the Torah were identical with the texts that had been copied over the centuries.

For thousands of years, God had preserved the accuracy of His Holy Scriptures through the careful reproduction of the manuscripts by these extraordinarily dedicated Jewish Masoretic scribes. When the scribe copied the manuscript of Genesis (which contains 76,064 Hebrew letters), he would literally count out the precise number of times each of the twenty-two letters in the Hebrew alphabet occurred in the text. He would also make notations on the margin of the page to assure that no letters were added or taken away. If even one letter was missed or added improperly, the master scribe would destroy the imperfect copy, lest an error creep into the holy text of the Word of God.

These Masoretic notes were originally placed in a separate text, but eventually they were added to the margins of the medieval Jewish Bibles. They included notes identifying the middle clause in each book of the Bible, together with notations of the exact number of times each of the twenty-two Hebrew letters appeared in that particular book of the whole of the Scriptures. As an example, the scribes calculated that there were 1534 verses or sentences in Genesis and that the middle clause was found in Genesis 27:40, "By thy sword shalt thou live." A researcher named Walton completed an exhaustive analysis of the Masoretic notes in the last century and produced the following table that illustrates the incredible precision of the dedicated labor involved in order to preserve the accuracy of the Bible.

The Masoretic Counting of the 815,140 Letters of the Hebrew Bible

Hebrew Letter		Times Found in the Bible	Hebrew Letter		Times Found in the Bible
א	Aleph	42,377	ל	Lamed	41,517
ב	Beth	38,218	מ	Mem	77,778
ג	Gimel	29,537	נ	Nun	41,696
ד	Daleth	32,530	ס	Samech	13,580
ה	He	47,554	ע	Ain	20,175
ו	Vau	76,922	פ	Pe	22,725
ז	Zain	22,867	צ	Tsaddi	21,882
ח	Cheth	23,447	ק	Koph	22,972
ט	Teth	11,052	ר	Resh	22,147
י	Yod	66,420	ש	Shin	32,148
כ	Caph	48,253	ת	Tau	59,343

Source: *A General and Critical Introduction to the Study of Holy Scripture* by A. E. Breen

One of the most incredible of the valuable scrolls found in the caves of Qumran was a little known scroll called *The Heavenly Prince Melchizedek*. This fascinating manuscript was found in thirteen fragments in the floor of Cave 11 near the village of Qumran by the Dead Sea. It was first published in Stduien, Leiden by A. S. Van der Woude under the title *Melchizedek als himmlishce Erlosergestalt. . . . 'Oudtestamentishche* (p. 354–73) as an Essene example of an eschatological Midrash, a Jewish prophetic commentary on a passage of the Old Testament. It also appeared in an article entitled "11Q Melchizedek and the New Testament" in *New Testament Studies* (p. 301–26), published in 1966.

This scroll includes an astonishing teaching of the ancient Jewish sages about the role of the most mysterious person in the Bible — Melchizedek. The Genesis account hints that Melchizedek is a theophany, a mysterious appearance of the second person of the Godhead on earth. Melchizedek appears in the biblical record as the king of Salem (Jerusalem) who encounters Abraham. This event followed Abraham's great victory over five kings of this region who had conquered Sodom and Gomorrah and had taken his nephew Lot and his property in their conquest. Before examining this remarkable scroll a review of the Bible's own teaching about the nature of the mysterious king of Salem will be helpful.

The Biblical Record of Melchizedek, King of Salem

And Melchizedek king of Salem brought forth bread and wine: and he was the priest of the most high God. And he blessed him, and said, Blessed be Abram of the most high God, possessor of heaven and earth: And blessed be the most high God, which hath delivered thine enemies into thy hand. And he gave him tithes of all.

(Genesis 14:18–20)

There is clearly a mystery about the nature of Melchizedek. Abraham receives the priestly blessing from the king of Salem, who is called "the priest of the most high God." Furthermore, Abraham gives "tithes of all" to Melchizedek as a sign of worship. Note that Melchizedek offers Abraham bread and wine, exactly as did Jesus to His disciples at the Last Supper at Passover.

The Psalmist David records the following significant declaration about who Melchizedek really is:

The Lord said unto my Lord, Sit thou at my right hand, until I make thine enemies thy footstool. The Lord shall send the rod of thy strength out of Zion: rule thou in the midst of thine enemies. Thy people shall be willing in the day of thy power, in the beauties of holiness from the womb of the morning: thou hast the dew of thy youth. The Lord hath sworn, and will not repent, Thou art a priest for ever after the order of Melchizedek. The Lord at thy right hand shall strike through kings in the day of his wrath. He shall judge among the heathen, he shall fill the places with the dead bodies; he shall wound the heads over many countries. He shall drink of the brook in the way: therefore shall he lift up the head. (Psalms 110:1–7)

This remarkable prophecy of King David reveals the future victory of Jesus the Messiah who is called David's Lord. When David wrote, "The Lord said unto my Lord, Sit thou at my right hand, until I make thine enemies thy footstool," he clearly referred to the mystery of the Trinity. However, while prophesying of the Messiah's final victory, David identifies Jesus the Messiah, our High Priest and Son of God, with Melchizedek: "Thou art a priest for ever after the order of Melchizedek." Therefore, the Bible teaches that God appeared to Abraham as a theophany in the person of Melchizedek.

In the book of Hebrews, the apostle Paul also wrote about the mysterious Melchizedek. Referring to Jesus of Nazareth, Paul declared, "As he saith also in another place, Thou art a priest for ever after the order of Melchisedec. . . . Called of God an high priest after the order of Melchizedek" (Hebrews 5:6, 10). Again, Paul affirms the connection between Melchizedek and Christ in these words, "Whither the forerunner is for us entered, even Jesus, made an high priest for ever after the order of Melchizedek" (Hebrews 6:20). The final New Testament passage about this subject is found in the book of Hebrews:

> For this Melchisedec, king of Salem, priest of the most high God, who met Abraham returning from the slaughter of the kings, and blessed him . . . For he was yet in the loins of his father, when Melchisedec met him. If therefore perfection were by the Levitical priesthood, (for under it the people received the law,) what further need was there that another priest should rise after the order of Melchisedec, and not be called after the order of Aaron? (Hebrews 7:1, 10–11).

> And it is yet far more evident: for that after the similitude of Melchisedec there ariseth another priest, . . . For he testifieth, Thou art a priest for ever after the order of Melchisedec. . . For those priests were made without an oath; but this with an oath by him that said unto him, The Lord sware and will not repent, Thou art a priest for ever after the order of Melchisedec (Hebrews 7:15, 17, 21).

The Heavenly Prince Melchizedek Scroll

The Melchizedek scroll, found in 1947 by the scholars who first examined the Dead Sea caves surrounding Qumran, has received little attention in the last fifty years since its discovery. However, I believe that this scroll reveals an astonishing teaching about Melchizedek that parallels exactly the teaching of the New Testament, in which the king of Salem is identified with the Messiah, the Son of God. We know that to this day Judaism has continued to vehemently reject the Christian teaching that Jesus is the true Messiah and that He is also the Son of God, equal with the Father and Holy Spirit. However, as I discussed earlier in the chapter on the mystery of the Trinity, remarkable Jewish teachings about the Trinity existed during the time of Christ in the first century. The existence of these amazing Jewish texts detailing the nature of the triune God — One in Three and Three in One — helps answer the question of how someone like the apostle Paul and many other Jews, including rabbis, could accept the claims of Jesus to be the true Son of God, while still remaining true to their monotheistic Jewish teaching that there is only one God.

This Heavenly Prince Melchizedek scroll provides us with fascinating insights into the beliefs of at least some of the Jewish Essenes living during the first century. I believe that these teachings prepared some of the Essenes to accept the claims that Jesus of Nazareth was the Son of God. In my last book, *The Signature of God*, I quoted from a number of scrolls found in the Qumran caves that refer to the Messiah as the Son of God. One five-line scroll identifies the Messiah as the leader of the community who was "pierced" and "wounded" (crucified) for the sins of the people, as the prophet Isaiah had predicted in the Old Testament. This scroll must refer to Jesus because He is the only person who claimed to be the Messiah who was crucified. Although these scrolls were discovered fifty years ago, they were not well known outside the small circle of scroll scholars until today. During the last half century, the liberal scroll scholars denied that any of the scrolls found in the Dead Sea caves referred to Jesus or to Christianity. Now that the scrolls are more widely available, evidence exists to prove that, not only do these manuscripts refer to Jesus, they even contain remarkable quotations from portions of the New Testament. These facts suggest that some members of the Essenes, a group strongly committed to holiness and the Jewish Scriptures, might have responded positively to the message of John the Baptist and the teachings of Jesus of Nazareth.

The following excerpts are from the English translation of *The Heavenly Prince Melchizedek* scroll. Note the incredible parallels between the nature, titles, and actions of Melchizedek and Jesus Christ. I have included in brackets the biblical references for Scriptures that the writer of this scroll refers to in his manuscript.

The Heavenly Prince Melchizedek

And concerning that which He said, In this year of Jubilee each of you shall return to his property (Leviticus 25:13) and likewise, And this is the manner of release: every creditor shall release that which he has lent to his neighbour. He shall not exact it of his neighbour and his brother, for God's release has been proclaimed (Deuteronomy 15:2) And it will be proclaimed at the end of days concerning the captives as He said: To proclaim liberty to the captives (Isaiah 61:1). Its interpretation is that He will assign them to the Sons of Heaven and to the inheritance of Melchizedek; for He will cast their lot amid the portions of Melchizedek who will return them there and will proclaim to them liberty, forgiving them the wrongdoings of all their iniquities.

And this thing will occur in the first week of the Jubilee that follows the nine Jubilees. And the Day of Atonement is the end of the tenth Jubilee, when all the Sons of Light and the men of the lot of Melchizedek will be atoned for. And a statute concerns them to provide them with their rewards. For this is the moment of the Year of Grace for Melchizedek. And he will, by his strength, judge the holy ones of God, executing judgment as it is written concerning him in the songs of David, who said Elohim has taken his place in the divine council; in the midst of the gods he holds judgment (Psalms 82:1). And it was concerning him that he said; Let the assembly of the peoples return to the height above them; El (God) will judge the peoples (Psalms 7:7–8). As for that which he said How long will you judge unjustly and show partiality to the wicked? Selah (Psalms 82:2). Its interpretation concerns Satan and the spirits of his lot who rebelled by turning away from the precepts of God to . . .

And Melchizedek will avenge the vengeance of the judgments of God . . . and he will drag them from the hand of Satan and from the hand of all the spirits of his lot. And all the gods of Justice will come to his aid to attend to the destruction of Satan. And the height is all the sons of God

... this ... This is the day of Peace/Salvation concerning which God spoke through Isaiah the prophet, who said, How beautiful upon the mountains are the feet of the messenger who proclaims peace, who brings good news, who proclaims salvation, who says to Zion: Your Elohim reigns (Isaiah 52:7).

Its interpretation; the mountains are the prophets ... and the messenger is the Anointed one of the spirit, concerning whom Daniel said, Until an anointed one, a prince (Daniel 9:25) ... And he who brings good news, who proclaims salvation: it is concerning him that it is written ... To comfort all who mourn, to grant to those who mourn in Zion (Isaiah 61:2–3). To comfort those who mourn; its interpretation, to make them understand all the ages of time ... In truth ... will turn away from Satan ... by the judgment(s) of God, as it is written concerning him, (who says to Zion); your Elohim reigns. Zion is ..., those who uphold the Covenant, who turn from walking in the way of the people. And your Elohim is Melchizedek, who will save them from the hand of Satan.

As for that which He said, Then you shall send abroad the loud trumpets in the seventh month.   (Leviticus 25:9)

The Parallel Views of Melchizedec Prefiguring Jesus Christ

1. **Timing**: This fascinating text, describing Melchizedek as the key figure in the final judgment of mankind and the angels, uses a number of phrases that remind us clearly of Old and New Testament prophecies about the return of Jesus Christ. These phrases include "the end of days," "the year of Jubilee," "the Day of Trumpets in 7th month," "the Day of Atonement," "the Year of Grace," "the Day of Vengeance," "the day of Peace/Salvation," and "the day when Elohim reigns."

2. **Jubilee**: The scroll refers repeatedly to the "redemption of the land" and "redemption of the captives," reminding us of the New Testament teaching of Christ's role as our Redeemer. "And grieve not the holy Spirit of God, whereby ye are sealed unto the day of redemption" (Ephesians 4:30).

3. **Judgment**: We read in the scroll about Melchizedek

"executing judgment." Further, he will judge the "Sons of Heaven" and "the Holy Ones" and give "vengeance," exactly as the Bible teaches that all judgment is in the hands of Jesus Christ. In the book of Jude we read, "And Enoch also, the seventh from Adam, prophesied of these, saying, Behold, the Lord cometh with ten thousands of his saints, To execute judgment upon all" (Jude 14–15).

4. *Forgiveness of sins*: It is astonishing to discover that the scroll teaches of Melchizedek "forgiving them the wrongdoings of all their iniquities," exactly as Christ forgives our sins if we repent. The writer also describes Melchizedek's role in atonement for the righteous: "Sons of Light and the men of the lot of Melchizedek will be atoned for." The New Testament teaches us that Christ atones for our sins. We know that only God can forgive sin. Therefore, the scroll's author is declaring the divinity of Melchizedek.

5. *Divinity*: Although most ancient Jewish writings describe the Messiah as a man with a divine mission, this Melchizedek scroll, as well as the *Targums*, describes the Messiah as God. The scroll says that "He takes His place in the Divine Council." The scroll also declares that Melchizedek will judge Satan and destroy him. In addition, the author of this scroll calls Melchizedek "Elohim" (the plural name for God), four times in this manuscript.

6. *Melchizedek's Identification*: A careful reading of this scroll reveals that the author identified Melchizedek as both the Messiah and as Elohim (God) in several passages. This is a remarkable indication that some of the Jews truly understood the mystery of the divine nature of God's Messiah. Consider the following titles that the author of the scroll ascribes to the Heavenly Prince Melchizedek:

The Messiah, the Prince
The Anointed One who proclaims salvation
The Prince
The Judge
The Avenger
Elohim
The High Priest of the Year of Jubilee
The Messenger of God

This extraordinary scroll, hidden in a cave for two thousand years, throws an entirely new light on the religious views of some of the Jewish people during the critical years of the first century, when the new Christian faith was presented to Israel in the life, death, and resurrection of Jesus Christ. It appears that at least some of the Jews were prepared to accept the claims of Jesus to be the Son of God, due to the teachings they received from these texts.

11

The Mystery of the Jews: God's Hand in Human History

But, whether you abandon it or whether you follow it, Israel will journey on to the end of days.

Edmond Fleg, *Why I Am A Jew*

And I will make my covenant between me and thee, and will multiply thee exceedingly. And Abram fell on his face: and God talked with him, saying, As for me, behold, my covenant is with thee, and thou shalt be a father of many nations. Neither shall thy name any more be called Abram, but thy name shall be Abraham; for a father of many nations have I made thee. (Genesis 17:2–5)

As the host of heaven cannot be numbered, neither the sand of the sea measured: so will I multiply the seed of David my servant, and the Levites that minister unto me.

(Jeremiah 33:22)

Centuries ago a skeptical and agnostic king of France was discussing philosophy and religion with his royal court counsellor. After numerous arguments were presented by the Christian advisor in favor of the position that God had revealed Himself in the Holy Scriptures, the king finally demanded that his counsellor prove to him that God existed in an argument using only two words. After careful deliberation the counsellor replied, "The Jews!" In those two words the counsellor summed up one of the most miraculous demonstations of God's supernatural intervention in the history of humanity. The survival and prospering of the Jewish people during thousands of years of brutal persecution, pogroms, and the tragedy of five and one-half million Jews massacred in Hitler's Holocaust is a mysterious miracle unparalled in the history of the human race.

Each of the mighty empires of the past — Assyria, Egypt, Babylon, Media-Persia, Greece, and Rome — who conquered Israel and carried her Jewish citizens into slavery have themselves turned to dust. Their powerful armies and huge treasuries did not stop the relentless march of history. Their time of power and grandeur came and went, leaving their great cities and monuments in ruins to be covered by the sands of the deserts. Where is mighty Rome or Babylon today? Yet the Jewish people, the least among the ancient nations of the Middle East, have survived throughout centuries, despite the overwhelming persecution and opposition against them. No other people in history have ever lost their national homeland for thousands of years, survived dispersed in over seventy different nations for twenty centuries, and then returned to their ancient homeland to rebuild their national life atop the desolate ruins of the cities and fortifications of its many conquerors.

What other nation lost its national language for twenty centuries, only to recover it and teach its ancient language to millions of its returning exiles? Today, five million Jews in Israel speak Hebrew, the language of her ancient prophets and kings. The miracle of the survival of the Jewish people is unprecedented. In fact, throughout the world, the only peoples who can claim to trace their continued existence as a race as far back as the Jews are the Chinese people. The Bible's declaration that God made an eternal, unbreakable covenant with the Jews, through their father Abraham, has remained the guiding principle and focus of the Jewish people's survival against overwhelming odds for the last thirty-five hundred years. God's covenant with Israel was the motivating force behind the Jews remarkable survival as a distinct people, even when surrounded by Gentile cultures.

In addition to the miracle of Israel's survival in a cruel world, we must add the remarkable history of the astonishing Jewish contribution to the arts, philosophy, writing, science, and medicine. Consider the difficulty placed in the paths of most Jews in a world of Gentiles throughout most of the last two thousand years. While the influence of ancient Rome and Greece on Western society is as great as that of the Jewish people, these nations were much more powerful and conquered huge areas of the ancient world for many centuries. Despite the small size of the Jewish population, the Jewish contribution to Western and Eastern society is unparalled by any other comparably sized group. There are approximately six billion people alive in the world today. Of these, only eighteen million (less than one-half of 1 percent of the world's population) are Jews. There are hundreds of equally small population groups throughout the planet that are absolutely unknown to anyone but their closest neighbours.

However, the contributions of the Jewish people to modern culture is overwhelming. A recent estimate calculated that more than 12 percent of the Nobel prizes have been awarded to Jews in the fields of medicine, mathematics, chemistry, and physics. The contribution of the Jewish people to the fields of arts, music, literature, and religious writing is outstanding in its quality and quantity. The influence of Jews on the history and the thinking of the Western world, as represented by the communist Karl Marx, the mathematician Albert Einstein, the psychologist Sigmund Freud, and the philosopher Baruch Spinoza, is staggering. The success of the Jewish people in the areas of business and finance is far beyond what one would expect, considering their small numbers and the opposition they face from people with anti-Semitic attitudes. However, the greatest Jewish influence on the history of mankind came from the lives, teachings, and actions of two Jews — Moses and Jesus of Nazareth. The Jews are finally looking at the life and teachings of Jesus and acknowledging that His influence on the nations has been both powerful and beneficial. They realize that the terrible atrocities and persecutions of the medieval period and the Holocaust were not based on genuine Christianity but were a perversion of evil produced by sinful men who, by their evil actions, rejected the teachings of Jesus.

In light of the great tragedy to the Jews, few people realize that the Nazi Holocaust was an attack on Christianity just as much as it was an attempt to annihilate the Jewish people. While five and one-half million Jews were savagely killed in the evil Nazi concentration camps, the Nazis also murdered seven million Europeans of the Christian faith in those same death camps. Captives from thirty European nations were taken in trains to those terrible death camps to be worked to death or immediately executed. A fascinating book by the brilliant author Max I. Dimont, entitled *Jews, God, and History* reveals startling information that most Christians have never been told:

> We must recognize the fact that Nazism was not anti-Semitic but anti-human. Because Nazi beliefs of racial superiority had no basis in fact, Nazism was like a nightmare, unfolding without a past or future in an ever-moving present. Because none but German Aryans were qualified to live in the Nazi view, it stood to reason that everyone else would be exterminated. The chilling reality is that when the Russians overran the concentration camps in Poland they found enough Zvklon B crystals to kill 20 million people. Yet there were no more than 3 million Jews left in Europe. The ratio of contemplated mass killing was no longer 1.4 Christians for every Jew, but 5.3 Christians for every Jew. Nazi future plans called for the killing of ten million non-German people every year.
>
> If the Christian reader dismisses what happened in Germany as something which affected a few million Jews only, he has not merely shown his contempt for the seven million Christians murdered by the Nazis but has betrayed his Christian heritage as well. And, if the Jewish reader forgets the seven million Christians murdered by the Nazis, then he has not merely let five million Jews die in vain but has betrayed his Jewish heritage of passion and justice. It is no longer a question of the survival of the Jews only. It is the question of the survival of man.

The greatest evidence of the influence and importance of the Jewish people is the fact that God chose the Jews to receive and carefully preserve His written commandments to man in the inspired Holy Scriptures. Both the Old and New Testaments were written by Jews who were obeying the command of God to record His words for all of mankind. The Bible is the inspired and authoritative record of God's progressive revelation of Jesus Christ, His divine and human nature, His marvellous character, and His perfect revealed will for our lives. The Scriptures are a special revelation given to a distinct people, the Jews, who were chosen by God to be both the guardians of this precious treasure and the sharers of this divine revelation with the rest of humanity. The Lord commanded the Jewish people to communicate this written revelation of the will of God to all mankind. It is significant that God's blueprint for the Temple included a Court of the Gentiles. However, the Jewish people, by and large, chose to hold this revelation as their national possession. With very few exceptions, including the prophet Jonah's reluctant mission of prophetic warning to the Assyrian capital of Nineveh, the Jews generally did not preach the revealed message of God to the nations.

The Scriptures contain a written revelation of God's plan to redeem all who repent that was ultimately consummated in the unique person, life, and message of Jesus Christ. Despite the fact that the Jewish race has never constituted more than a small fraction of 1 percent of the world's population, the profound religious influence of the Jews upon the rest of mankind over the last four thousand years is incalculable. Today, almost one third of the six billion humans throughout the planet acknowledge that God revealed Himself in an astonishing and unique way to the prophets and patriarchs of the ancient Jews. Today almost two billion people, including Jews, Muslims, and Christians, have accepted that portions of the Jewish Bible are a sure guide through time to eternity. The Bible deserves constant and careful study. This study will be richly repaid by an ever-growing appreciation in the spirit of the follower of Jesus Christ who will see Him afresh in every page.

The Phenomenon of Biblical Anniversaries

When we examine the biblical and historical records concerning the nation of Israel we encounter a phenomenon that is unprecedented in the history of the nations. I refer to my discovery that God has displayed His sovereign control over the destiny of the Jewish people by His influence over the events surrounding the nation of Israel. God has caused an incredible series of eight major historical events to occur on a single day in the ancient Jewish calendar. If we closely examine the history of the nations of Europe or Asia, we discover that these nations have experienced their victories, defeats, and natural disasters on random days that occur on various days of the calendar. Since there are 365 days in the solar calendar, the odds are obviously 365 to 1 against any nation experiencing two defeats or two victories in war on the exact same day of the calendar. This is why so few nations in history have ever experienced parallel events occurring on the very same day of the year as an earlier victory or defeat.

However, when I began to examine the remarkable history of the Jewish people, I discovered an extraordinary phenomenon of biblical anniversaries in which every one of over forty major events in the history of the nation of Israel had occurred on one of the major feast or fast days of the biblical calendar. This calendar of religious feasts and fast days was established thirty-five hundred years ago by God when the Jews where still wandering in the Sinai during the forty-year Exodus from their slavery in Egypt. A detailed study of these amazing anniversaries can be found in my book *Armageddon — Appointment With Destiny*. However, in this book I would like to explore eight major events in the history of Israel that have occurred on one single day in the ancient Hebrew calendar. This will illustrate the awesome pattern of God's sovereign control of the destiny of the nations. In the following pages we will witness the unprecedented phenomenon in which Israel experienced a series of eight national disasters — the most devastating in her history — every one of which occurred on the same day of the calendar. The odds against these eight disasters occurring on the same day is staggering. At the conclusion of this section, I will share with you the awesome mathematical odds against any nation experiencing these eight disasters on one single day of the calendar.

The Appointed Feast Days: "A Shadow of Things to Come"

The apostle Paul spoke of the importance of these special feast days in his epistle to the church at Colosse. "Let no man therefore judge you in meat, or in drink, or in respect of an holy day, or of the new moon, or of the sabbath days: Which are a shadow of things to come; but the body is of Christ" (Colossians 2:16–17). In these verses, Paul was primarily admonishing the church to free itself of legalisms. However, he also clearly revealed that the holy-day feast, the new moon celebration, and the Sabbath day were intended by the Lord as prophetic signs of future events.

As we contemplate the sovereignty of God revealed in this precise alignment of feast days and significant anniversary events in Israel's history and future, we should feel a profound sense of wonder. God is truly in charge of the events in the lives of individuals as well as nations, such as Israel. God knows the end from the beginning, and He is concerned that we seek to understand His will as He unfolds His plan of redemption in human history.

The Ninth Day of Av: A Fast of Mourning

The prophet Zechariah referred to this fast day as follows: "When ye fasted and mourned in the fifth [Av] and seventh month" (Zechariah 7:5). This day of fasting, known to the Jewish people as Tisha Be-Av, became a day of national mourning and remembrance of Israel's loss of both of their sacred Temples. It is one of the most historically significant anniversaries in the life of their nation and is commemorated by Jews throughout the world as the tragic day when God withdrew His Presence and divine protection. The children of Israel wept as their precious Temple burned to the ground on the ninth day of Av, not once but twice in history. The Jewish historian, an eyewitness to the Roman destruction of the Temple, in A.D. 70, pointed to the burning of both Temples on the same day as proof of the Hand of God in these tragic events.

Tisha Be-Av, Israel's fast of mourning, which occurs on the ninth of the month of Av (our month of August), has witnessed eight of the greatest disasters in Israel's history. In fact, this date has seen more national disasters than any other date in world history. The ninth of Av has become a day when Jews not only mourn their loss but also look forward to that great day when their Messiah will finally appear to end their centuries of suffering. The prophet Zechariah declared that when the Messiah and the long promised Kingdom comes, all of their fasts, including this one, "shall be to the house of Judah joy and gladness, and cheerful feasts" (Zechariah 8:19). Let us examine the biblical and secular history of the Jewish people which contains the record of the tragic events which occurred on this day.

Eight National Disasters that Fell on the Ninth of Av

1. *The Twelve Spies Return with their Evil Report*

Moses sent out the twelve tribal leaders to spy out the Promised Land for forty days prior to entering the Promised Land of Canaan. However, due to their unbelief, ten of the twelve spies returned with pessimistic reports about how impossible it would be to conquer the inhabitants of the land, even though God had promised them victory. The ancient Jewish commentary, the *Mishna*, records that the people believed the evil report and mourned all night in fear. They turned against Moses and the two faithful spies (Joshua and Caleb) on the ninth day of the month Av *(Ta'anit* 29a). The result, according to Numbers 14:1–10, was a mutiny and led to an attempt to stone Moses. The rebels planned a return to the bondage of Egypt on the ninth of Av, 1490 B.C.

If this rebellion had been successful, this violation of God's covenant with Abraham would have led to the death and final assimilation of the Jewish people in Egypt. God destroyed the rebel leaders and warned Israel that their sinful rebellion would result in the death of that whole generation of Jews while wandering in the wilderness of Sinai over the next forty years, even as the spies had searched out the land for forty days. The result of this awful rebellion and their lack of belief in God's promises was the loss of the Promised Land for that entire generation, save for the two faithful spies, Joshua and Caleb. The Bible records that "Moses told these sayings unto all the children of Israel: and the people mourned greatly" (Numbers 14: 39).

Thus, from the time of this rebellion on the ninth of Av, this day became a fast of mourning as Israel wept over their lack of obedience to God and the tragedies that followed repeatedly during the next thirty-five centuries.

2. *The Destruction of Solomon's Temple by the Babylonian Army*

The Babylonian army under Nebuchadnezzar besieged Jerusalem in 589 B.C. After a two-year siege, on the seventeenth of Tammuz, they breached the walls and forced the ending of the daily sacrifice in the Temple. Twenty-one days later, on the ninth of Av, 587 B.C., the Babylonian army broke through the walls of

Jerusalem to directly attack the Jews' final defenses on the massive Temple Mount.

According to the Jewish commentary, *Me'am Lo'ez*, by Rabbi Yaakov Culi and Rabbi Aguiti, and other historical sources, including *Ta'anit* 29a from the *Jerusalem Talmud*, the Babylonian army fought their way into the Temple courtyard on the seventh day of Av. "His men ate, drank and caroused there until the ninth of Av. Toward evening, they set the Temple on fire. It burned all night and through the next day, the tenth day of Av." The prophet Jeremiah, who was an eyewitness to the terrible destruction of Jerusalem, recorded that the Babylonian captain of the guard, Nebuzaradan, conquered the city, captured King Zedekiah, and burned the Temple. With no one attempting to fight the enormous fire, the huge Temple complex burned throughout the next day as well, the tenth of Av (Jeremiah 52:5–14).

This tragedy of the loss of their beloved Temple has been commemorated by the Jews ever since. This commemoration has been held on the solemn fast on the ninth of Av, known as Tisha Be Av. For twenty-five hundred years, on this day, the Jews have read the book of Lamentations in which Jeremiah laments the Babylonian destruction of Jerusalem and the great Temple of Solomon. "The Lord hath cast off His altar, He hath abhorred His sanctuary, He hath given up into the hand of the enemy the walls of the palaces; they have made a noise in the House of the Lord, as in the day of a solemn feast" (Lamentations 2:7; Zechariah 8:9).

3. *The Destruction of the Second Temple by the Roman Legions*

The Roman Empire had been at war with the Jews for three and one-half years since their initial revolt in A.D. 66. The Roman legions were finally ready to crush the Jewish revolt by destroying their capital, Jerusalem, in A.D. 70. Over 1,250,000 people were surrounded inside the city by the encircling wall built by the Roman legions to prevent escape or supplies reaching the city. The original Roman attack occurred on the Feast of Passover. A huge number of Jewish pilgrims had arrived in Jerusalem to celebrate the Passover Feast and were trapped there, along with the rest of the population. Since the Passover Feast attracted up to five times the normal population of the city, the Romans were glad to seize the opportunity to seal off the city in hopes of starving the rebels into submission.

The daily sacrifice in the Temple ceased again on the same day, the seventeenth of Tammuz, due to the Roman attacks. Twenty-one days later, on the ninth day of the month of Av, the Roman army reached the edge of the Temple compound. The Roman general, Titus, gave strict orders that the beautiful Temple, the most magnificent building in the whole Roman Empire, should not be destroyed. He implored the Jewish defenders to surrender, so that their city and their beloved Temple would not have to be destroyed. However, the judgment of God had been delivered almost forty years earlier by Jesus Christ. Jesus had warned the population of Jerusalem what awaited her because they had chosen to reject God's Messiah:

> And when he was come near, he beheld the city, and wept over it, Saying, If thou hadst known, even thou, at least in this thy day, the things which belong unto thy peace! but now they are hid from thine eyes. For the days shall come upon thee, that thine enemies shall cast a trench about thee, and compass thee round, and keep thee in on every side, And shall lay thee even with the ground, and thy children within thee; and they shall not leave in thee one stone upon another; because thou knewest not the time of thy visitation. (Luke 19:41–44).

This terrible appointment with destiny could not be avoided. The Jewish rebel leaders rejected the offers of General Titus. The last desparate pitched battle for the Temple Mount began.

Despite his firm orders to the Roman centurions to preserve the Temple intact, the enraged soldiers, who had endured two years of Jewish attacks from the Temple walls, threw torches into the Temple. Within minutes, the holy Temple became an inferno. An eyewitness, Flavius Josephus, reported that General Titus stood in the great entrance to the Holy Place of the burning Temple and beat back his soldiers with his sword in a vain attempt to save at least the Inner Temple from their cruel act of destruction. It is also reported that when Titus saw that the flames had reached the inner sanctuary, he fell to his knees and cried out, "As God is my witness, this was not done by my order."

Neither General Titus nor his soldiers realized that they were unconsciously fulfilling two very specific scriptural prophecies. First, the prophet Daniel, more than six hundred years earlier, had predicted in his great prophecy of the Seventy Weeks that "after threescore and two weeks shall Messiah be cut off, but not for himself: and the people of the prince that shall come shall destroy the city and the sanctuary; and the end thereof shall be with a flood, and unto the end of the war desolations are determined" (Daniel 9:26).

This strange phrase reveals two facts: (1) the people (the Roman soldiers), would be responsible for the destruction, not their leader, "the prince"; and (2) "the prince that shall come" refers to the "prince" of the Roman Empire. When General Titus initially began the Jewish War, he was not of royal blood. However, his father, the General Vespasian (a commoner), became Emperor of Rome in A.D. 69. When the final siege was undertaken in A.D. 70, Titus, Vespasian's son, had, therefore, become the "prince," and thus initially fulfilled the ancient prophecy. The final fulfillment of Daniel's prophecy of the "prince that shall come" will occur in the rise of the future Antichrist, when the Antichrist and his revived Roman Empire again attack the city of Jerusalem and the rebuilt Temple during the last days.

The second major prophecy regarding the destruction of the Temple was given by Jesus Christ in Luke 19:41–44. After the Pharisees had told Jesus to restrain His disciples from their joyful praise of God, "He answered and said unto them, I tell you that, if these should hold their peace, the stones would immediately cry out" (Luke 19:40). As the crowd drew near to Jerusalem, Jesus looked at the city and its Temple and wept over it. He warned them in these words: "For the days shall come upon thee, that shine enemies shall cast a trench about thee, and compass thee round, and keep thee in on every side, and shall lay thee even with the ground, and thy children within thee; and they shall not leave in thee one stone upon another; because thou knewest not the time of thy visitation" (verses 43–44).

This prophecy was fulfilled to the smallest detail in A.D. 70. As the Romans burned the Temple to the ground, the tremendous heat of the fire melted the sheets of gold that covered much of the Temple building. The molten gold ran down into every crack between the foundation stones. When the fire finally died down, the Roman soldiers used wedges and crowbars to overturn every stone to search for this gold, thus fulfilling Christ's words.

4. *The Romans Plowed Jerusalem and the Temple with Salt in A.D. 71*

In A.D. 71, one year after the destruction of the city of Jerusalem and the burning of the Temple, on the ninth of Av, the Roman army plowed the Temple Mount and the city of Jerusalem with salt to destroy any vegetation necessary to support a population. This was a complete fulfillment of the prophecy of Micah: "Therefore shall Zion for your sakes be plowed as a field, and Jerusalem shall become heaps, and the mountain of the house as the high places of the forest" (Micah 3:12). A rabbinical source, *Ta'anit* 26b, records that this was done to turn the city into a Roman colony totally dependent on Rome for survival.

5. *The Destruction of Bar Kochba's Army in A.D. 135*

After the fall of Jerusalem in A.D. 70, there was a period of enforced peace for six decades. In Matthew 24, Jesus spoke about Daniel's prophecy of the destruction of the Temple: "If any man shall say unto you, Lo, here is Christ, or there; believe it not. For there shall arise false Christs, and false prophets, and shall shew great signs and wonders; insomuch that, if it were possible, they shall deceive the very elect" (Matthew 24: 23–24). There were no false messiahs before the life of Jesus of Nazareth. Following His death and resurrection, a number of false messiahs arose to bring religious confusion to the Jewish people.

Among those false prophets was a dynamic Jewish leader named Simon Bar Kochba. As Jesus had predicted, many people, including the famous Jewish scholar Rabbi Akiba, proclaimed Simon Bar Kochba as the Messiah. Jesus had prophesied this event before His rejection: "I am come in my Father's name, and ye receive me not; if another shall come in his own name, him ye will receive" (John 5:43). How sad that after rejecting the true Messiah the Jewish people would now accept a counterfeit messiah who led them to national disaster.

For two years, despite overwhelming odds against them, Simon Bar Kochba and his followers succeeded in defeating the Roman legions. Finally, Emperor Hadrian and his enormous Roman army with six legions attacked and destroyed the Jewish rebels at Beitar, a few miles southwest of Jerusalem. On that tragic ninth of Av, A.D. 135, the last great army of an independent Israel was slaughtered without mercy.

Dio Cassius, the Roman historian, says that 580,000 Jewish soldiers fell by the sword alone, not counting those who fell by fire and famine. The horses of the Romans, he says, were wading in blood up to their girths in the mud and mire of the valley battleground. Sixty-five years to the day after the city of Jerusalem and the Temple were destroyed in A.D. 70, this final rebellion against Rome ended in terrible tragedy for the Jews with the destruction of Israel's army in A.D. 135, the ninth day of Av.

The prophet Isaiah may have referred to this event when he prophesied, "For the head of Syria is Damascus, and the head of Damascus is Rezin; and within threescore and five years shall Ephraim [Israel] be broken, that it be not a people" (Isaiah 7:8). In 721 B.C., sixty-five years after Isaiah spoke these words, the Assyrian exile of the northern tribes of Israel fulfilled Isaiah's prophecy. However, it appears that the prophet Isaiah may also have been alluding to the final shattering of the nation of Israel in 135 A.D., which also occurred on the sixty-fifth anniversary of the Roman burning of the Temple, the ninth of Av.

6. *England Expelled All Jews in A.D. 1290*

On July 18, 1290, the ninth of Av in the Jewish calendar, King Edward I ordered the expulsion of all Jews from England. For the next four centuries, England did not prosper as a nation beyond her own small island. Almost four hundred years later, Oliver Cromwell, Lord Protector of England, a strong Bible believing Christian, granted the Jews the legal right of settlement throughout England in 1657. It is interesting to note that the British Empire's prosperity and world power can be traced to its beginnings during the reign of Lord Cromwell. The Jews returned and prospered in England and in all her colonies throughout the British Empire. The history of England's rise and fall can be traced to this ancient prophecy in the book of Genesis: "And I will bless them that bless thee, and curse him that curseth thee: and in thee shall all the families of the earth be blessed" (Genesis 12:3). As England blessed the Jews, God blessed the British Empire until it ruled one-quarter of the globe.

On November 2, 1917, Lord Balfour, the British Foreign Secretary, wrote his historic declaration endorsing the setting up of a national homeland for the Jews in Palestine. This was partly in response to the tremendous scientific contribution by Chaim

Weizmann (who later became Israel's first president), a Jew who produced explosives to aid England's war effort. At the end of World War I, a victorious England held power through its British Empire over one-quarter of the world. Tragically, at the very same time as England was promising the Jews a national homeland in Palestine, Lawrence of Arabia was promising the Arabs that England would give them the lands that were occupied by the Turkish Empire in return for their help in defeating Germany and Turkey in the war. However, in these intense negotiations, the territory of Israel itself was never demanded by the Arabs. The reason for this lack of interest was that few Arabs lived in the barren and empty land of Palestine. Ultimately, the Arabs received five hundred times as much territory as Israel, over five million square miles of land which now comprise twenty-one Arab countries. Meanwhile, the Jews received only eight thousand square miles of land in a strip along the Mediterranean Sea (less than one-fifth of 1 percent of what the Arabs received).

In the 1920s and throughout the period until 1948, England repeatedly reversed its promises to the League of Nations to facilitate Jewish immigration and failed to provide the promised national homeland for the Jews. Israel ultimately received only 17.5 percent of the territory promised her by the Balfour Declaration and the British Mandate, as endorsed by the League of Nations (the predecessor to the United Nations). Britain prevented most Jewish immigration from Europe to Palestine throughout that thirty-year period. This illegal and immoral reversal of her solemn obligation to allow the Jews to return to the Promised Land contributed tragically and immeasurably to the magnitude of the Holocaust. The Jews of Europe had no homeland to flee to when the savage persecution of Adolf Hitler began. The five and one-half million Jews who died in the Nazi death camps might have fled to Palestine if the British had not broken their word and stopped Jewish immigration to Palestine.

It is not improbable that the decline of Britain from its exalted status as the preeminent superpower that "ruled the seas" to the position of a second-level power is connected to her betrayal of the Jews and her opposition to a Jewish national homeland in Israel. In this same period, 1917–1948, England lost her vast empire, spanning one-quarter of the globe, including the southern part of Ireland. Over four thousand years ago, God gave us a profound insight into the reasons behind the history of the rise and fall of many nations and His divine intervention in history: "I will bless them that bless thee, and curse him that curseth thee" (Genesis 12:3). This lesson of history from both the Bible and the events of this century should stand as a severe warning to our national leaders to stand with the Jewish people in their right to live in Israel in peace with secure borders.

7. *Spain Expelled All Jews in A.D. 1492*

On August 2, 1492, the ninth of Av, the Spanish government ordered the expulsion of 800,000 Jews, despite the fact that these Jews had lived in Spain for more than fifteen hundred years. The New Testament records that the apostle Paul travelled to Spain to preach to the Jews and Gentiles in that country. This tragic expulsion of the Jews marked a watershed in the rise of the Spanish Empire. From that point on, the Spanish Empire's fortunes began to decrease, in fulfillment of God's promise to Abraham that "I will bless them that bless thee, and curse him that curseth thee" (Genesis 12:3).

It is interesting also to note that the ninth of Av, 1492 was the very same day that the Italian explorer Christopher Columbus left Spain to discover the New World. This pivotal event was of tremendous importance to the Jews because America ultimately became a place of refuge for the Jewish people. In addition, there is some evidence to suggest that Columbus may have been of Jewish ancestry. Therefore, the ninth of Av, 1492 was a propitious day for him to leave Spain to avoid the persecution. Significantly, when the new nation of Israel was reborn in 1948, the United States of America became Israel's strongest protector and supporter.

8. *Russia Mobilized for World War I and Launched Persecutions against the Jews*

On the ninth of Av, August 1, 1914, as the Jews fasted and mourned, Russia and Germany declared war, beginning World War I, one of the major disasters in human history. This four-year war involved the greatest military struggle in history to that point, in fulfillment of Christ's prophecy that in the last days, "nation shall rise against nation and kingdom against kingdom" (Matthew 24:7). As Russia mobilized its huge army on the ninth day of Av, the local governors triggered persecutions and attacks against the Jews in the Pale of Settlement in eastern Russia including Poland (then part of Russia), killing as many as one hundred thousand Jews. These persecutions forced many Jews to emigrate to either America or the Holy Land. These Russian and eastern European Jewish immigrants joined the native-born Jewish "Sabras" in building the agricultural settlements and infrastructure of the embryonic Jewish state. This wave of Jewish immigration set the stage for the dramatic events leading to the creation of Israel in 1948.

As mentioned earlier, the phenomenon of eight major historical disasters affecting one nation over a period of thirty-five centuries occurring on a single day of the year is unprecedented in human history. As a student of history over the last thirty-five years, I can assure you that no other nation has experienced any such pattern of historical anniversaries or "coincidences."

In fact, if any of my readers are mathematically inclined, I would suggest that they check the probability that these eight historical tragedies could have occurred by random chance rather than by God's foreknowledge and sovereignty. Because there are 365 days in a year, the chance that even a second significant historical tragedy would occur by chance alone on the anniversary date of a previous tragedy on a given day, say, the ninth day of Av (August), is only one chance in 365. The odds against a third similar event occurring on exactly the same day, the ninth day of Av, can be calculated as follows:

$$1 \times 365 \times 365 = \text{one chance in } 133,225$$

In other words, the odds against even three national disasters occurring by chance alone on a particular anniversary day, such as the ninth day of Av, is only 1 chance in 133,225!

This mathematical reality is why the historical records of the nations do not reveal any other nation, except for Israel, that has sustained repeated victories or defeats on particular anniversary dates of the calendar.

The odds that all eight disastrous events for Israel would occur by chance alone on the ninth day of Av, rather than by God's design, is equal to:

$$1 \times 365 \times 365 \times 365 \times 365 \times 365 \times 365 \times 365 \times 365 =$$
Only 1 chance in 863,078,009,300,000,000
or
1 chance in 863 Million Times a Billion!

It is important to remember that the above probability analysis only considers eight of Israel's anniversary events, only those that occurred on the ninth day of the biblical month Av.

In all, there are more than forty major anniversary events that have occurred throughout Israel's history. I examine these events in my book *Armageddon — Appointment With Destiny*. If we were to add these additional thirty-two anniversary dates to our probability figures, the numbers would be so astronomically high that no rational person could conclude that these events had happened on their respective dates by chance alone.

The consideration of these astonishing historical records will lead many to believe, along with this author, that the only rational explanation for this phenomenon is that God has had His hand upon the Jewish people and the nation of Israel. Furthermore, this evidence provides strong proof that the Bible, which reveals these staggering, historically verified events, is truly the inspired Word of God.

12

The Rocks Cry Out: The Historical Evidence For the Bible

The last one hundred and fifty years of archeological exploration in the Middle East has provided students of the Bible with an unparalleled abundance of evidence confirming thousands of detailed historical statements found in both the Old and New Testaments. In this chapter, we will explore a small fraction of the powerful historical and archeological evidence that has been discovered in Israel and throughout the Middle East that throws new light on the pivotal events that have shaped our modern Western culture. It is important that we place this evidence in its proper context. Archeology and historical documents can never prove that the Bible is inspired. Rather, the confirmation of the statements of the Bible through archeological and historical investigations provides us with powerful evidence of the historical truthfulness of the Word of God and indicates that its statements were accurately transmitted over thousands of years.

One of the greatest of these pioneer archeologists is the Jewish scholar Dr. Nelson Glueck, considered by many to be the greatest Jewish archeologist in history. Professor Glueck has written, "It is worth emphasizing that in all this work no archaeological discovery has ever controverted a single, properly understood biblical statement."[1] Professor Glueck's statement is a powerful antidote to the pervasive skepticism and unbelief of so many of the liberal theologians who inhabit the seminaries and universities of the West. Despite the cynicism and skepticism of many liberal theologians to the accuracy of the biblical account the scientific evidence of archeology continues to confirm the accuracy of the Bible's statements. Meanwhile, liberal theologians continue to ignore this overwhelming evidence in favor of their presuppositions and strongly held prejudice against the authority, inspiration, and accuracy of the Word of God.

Dr. Glueck wrote about the wonder of exploring the ancient ruins of the Promised Land and finding confirmation after confirmation of the truthfulness of this incomparable book, the Holy Scriptures.

> Acquaint yourself with the needs and fears, the moods and manners, of the broken array of peoples and civilizations that appeared at intervals along the horizon of time and, in a general way, you will know in advance where to look for the clues they left behind in the course of their passage. . . . And above all, read the Bible, morning, noon and night, with a positive attitude, reading to accept its historical references. . . . And then go forth into the wilderness of the Negev and discover, trite as it may sound, that everything you touch turns into the gold of history, and that it is almost impossible not to stumble across the treasures of a robust past, whose existence becomes as real and as full of content and color and sound and fury and the thrill of progress and the pity of failure as the transient present, which is always ticking away so furiously to join the throng of those that need no longer hurry.[2]

Jerusalem, The City of David

Modern liberal scholars who reject the biblical evidence about the monarchies of King David and his son Solomon in the tenth century before Christ also dismiss the Bible's claims about Jerusalem being the capital city of a united Israel. Many of these biblically minimalist scholars, including Professor Thomas

Thompson of the University of Copenhagen, totally reject the Bible's description of Jerusalem as Israel's capital city during the reigns of King David and Solomon in the period 1000 B.C. to 930 B.C. In an article in *Biblical Archeological Review*, Thompson stated, "We don't have a tenth-century Jerusalem ... The last point is that Jerusalem becomes a really major town only after the destruction of Lachish in 701 B.C. . . . Its very difficult to talk about a united monarchy [under David and Solomon] in the tenth century B.C.E."[3] [*Note:* academic scholars use B.C.E. (before common era) rather than the normal designation B.C. (before Christ) for fairly obvious reasons].

In other words, Professor Thompson and his many liberal colleagues totally deny the detailed biblical record of the reigns of Israel's greatest kings and Solomon's Temple. From their skeptical standpoint, they automatically reject every biblical statement unless it is verified by multiple pagan historical or archeological sources. However, a logical question arises. How could such a detailed historical tradition and national memory of King David's and King Solomon's deeds, their conquests, and their Temple have arisen in Israel if these events never occurred?

Modern anthropologists admit that nearly always there is some historical event behind every tradition. The biblical minimalist scholars reject the historical and archeological evidence, as well as the biblical evidence, that attests to Jerusalem's existence as a significant city in Palestine during the time of Israel's conquest of Canaan, which occurred several centuries before the rise of King Saul and then King David to rule Jerusalem as Israel's capital. A fascinating article entitled "Cow Town or Royal Capital" by Nadav Na'aman appeared in the July/August 1997 issue of the respected *Biblical Archeological Review* magazine. This article contained interesting archeological evidence about ancient Jerusalem including a reference to the Tell el Amarna Letters. Although I had read a summary of these letters years ago, I was delighted to acquire an excellent copy and translation of these vital ancient documents from a rare-book dealer several weeks ago. It was fascinating to read these letters by the pagan king of Jerusalem during the time of the conquest of the Promised Land.

Evidence about Jerusalem From the Tell el-Amarna Tablets

The famous Amarna letters were discovered at Tell el-Amarna in Egypt more than a century ago. These thirty-five hundred-year-old clay tablets included diplomatic letters that were written in the 14th century B.C. in Akkadian cuneiform characters, the common official language at the time. This valuable library of government documents includes more than three hundred diplomatic letters written by the governors or kings of Canaan to the Egyptian pharaoh who ruled Canaan as a province of the Egyptian-controlled territory in Palestine and Syria. This extensive correspondence includes hundreds of letters written by two well-known Egyptian pharaohs (Amenophis III [1391–1353 B.C.] and Amenophis IV, popularly known as Akhenaten [1353–1337 B.C.]). The dates when these Egyptian pharaohs ruled are widely accepted.

The most important portion of the letters for biblical scholars include six diplomatic messages sent from the King of Jerusalem, who ruled Canaan (present-day Israel and the West Bank). These letters are incredibly valuable for the detailed historical evidence they provide about the situation in Canaan at the approximate time of the conquest of the Promised Land under the leadership of Joshua and Gideon, according to the biblical record found in Joshua and Judges. The Tell el-Amarna Tablets provide invaluable independent information about historical conditions in Canaan. Written by several kings who ruled their provinces and cities under the rule of Egypt, these letters are of vital importance to scholars because they describe conditions in Canaan only one or two generations after the Exodus at the very time the Bible tells us the conquest of the Promised Land was occurred.

All serious scholars who have examined the Tell el-Amarna letters agree that the name "Urusalim" found in the letters clearly refer to the city of Jerusalem, according to the detailed geographical descriptions about its location. The Amarna letters mention the city of "Urusalim" (Jerusalem) which appears repeatedly in this fascinating correspondence. At the time of this correspondence, Jerusalem and other cities of Canaan were ruled by local kings under ultimate Egyptian control. Jerusalem itself was ruled by a local dynasty which passed the crown from father to son. Other sources refer to these local rulers of city-states as kings. In most of these letters, the king of Jerusalem appeals desperately, and without success, for troops and archers from his overlord, the pharaoh of Egypt. Apparently at this time, the pharaoh ruling Egypt was distracted from defending his province of Canaan against the invaders who were attacking the cities under the control of the king of Jerusalem. This invasion of the foreign "Habiru" occurred during the reign of Pharaoh Amenophis IV, often called Akhenaten (1353–1337 B.C.). Apparently Akhenaten ignored military defense because he was focussed solely on creating a new religion in Egypt to worship the sun god.

Consider the powerful historical evidence provided in these six letters from the king of Jerusalem to his overlord, the king of Egypt, that prove Jerusalem existed as a capital city during this critical historical period. In addition, these letters provide evidence that the Promised Land was being invaded at this time by a victorious army of foreign people called "Habiru." Many scholars admit that the "Habiru" were most likely the conquering Israelites, who called themselves "Hebrews." For example, Abdi-Hiba, the king of Jerusalem, wrote to the pharaoh in desperation requesting Egyptian troops to defend his territory.

Letters From The Tell el-Amarna Tablets[4]

There is no garrison here.
So let the king care for his land.
Let the king care for his land.
The lands of the king, the lord,
have all deserted.
Ilimilku has devastated the whole land of the king.
(Letter of Abdi-Hiba, King of Jerusalem to
    the Pharaoh —Tell el Amarna Letter — Number 2)

No lands of the king remain.
The Habiru plunder all lands of the king.
If archers are here this year, then the lands of the king,
the lord, will remain; but if archers are not here,
then the lands of the king, my lord, are lost.
(Letter of Abdi-Hiba, King of Jerusalem to
    the Pharaoh — Tell el Amarna Letter — Number 3)

Verily, the king has set his name
upon the land of Urusalim for ever.
Therefore he cannot abandon
the lands of Urusalim.
(Letter of Abdi-Hiba, King of Jerusalem
to the Pharaoh — Tell el Amarna Letter — Number 3)

In his letters the king protested that the pharaoh's indifference to his desperate military request for additional troops indicated that he didn't want to fight the "Habiru."

As long as the king, my lord, lives
I will say to the deputy of the king, my lord:
"Why do you love the Habiru, and hate the regents ?"
(Letter of Abdi-Hiba, King of Jerusalem to
the Pharaoh — Tell el Amarna Letter — Number 2)

But if there are no archers
the land of the king will desert to the Hiabiru.
This will be the fate of the land.
(Letter of Abdi-Hiba, King of Jerusalem
to the Pharaoh — Tell el Amarna Letter — Number 6)

Could the reluctance to fight this group of invaders stem from the historical memory of the Egyptians' of God's supernatural deliverance of the Israelites and the destruction of Egypt's army at the Red Sea during the Exodus?

Abdi-Hiba, the king of Jerusalem, indicated the significance of his kingdom and capital in his description of his gift of over five thousand slaves to his Egyptian overlord. If Jerusalem was a small, insignificant town, its king would not have had a military victory that afforded him the opportunity to send a gift of five thousand prisoners captured from his enemies. The biblical minimalist scholars assert that during this period (three centuries before King David and Solomon), Jerusalem was only a tiny, insignificant town, but their assertions have been proven to be false by the Amarna Letters of the Egyptian government.

__ __ I have sent to the king, [my] lor[d]
__ __ prisoners, five thousand __ __ __ __ ,
[three hundr]ed and eigh[teen] bearers for
the caravans of the king;

they were taken in the fields (iati) near [Ialuna.
(Letter of Abdi-Hiba, King of Jerusalem to
   the Pharaoh — Tell el Amarna Letter — Number 3)

Finally, Abdi-Hiba reveals his personal fear of imminent defeat by these conquering "Habiru" (Hebrews), who are taking city after city throughout his weakly defended territory. The king of Jerusalem warns the pharaoh that his fellow regents (local kings under Egypt's rule) are succumbing to the Habiru attack. Lastly, he admits that because Egypt is indifferent ("yet the king holds himself back") that the soldiers of another Canaanite king, "Zimrida of Lakisi," have deserted to join the victorious Habiru army.

But now the Habiru are taking
the cities of the king.
No regent is (left)
to the king, my lord; all are lost.

Behold, Turbazu has been killed
in the gate of Zilu, yet the king holds himself back.
Behold, Zimrida of Lakisi — servants,
who have joined with the Habiru, have smitten him.
(Letter of Abdi-Hiba, King of Jerusalem to
   the Pharaoh — Tell el Amarna Letter — Number 4)

Other correspondence in the series of Tell el Amarna Letters indicates that the territory ruled by the king of Jerusalem at that time (during the days of Joshua and Gideon) included land extending from Hebron in the south to the town of Bethel in the north. In addition, these letters indicate that the territory of the king of Jerusalem extended from the midpoint of present-day West Bank to the Jordan River.

In conclusion, an analysis of the Tell el Amarna Letters clearly confirms that, in the 14th century B.C., the city of Jerusalem was a capital city ruling over a considerable amount of territory in Canaan under the oversight of the Egyptian pharaohs. The area encompassed a significant portion of the current West Bank as well as the areas to the west of Jerusalem. The letters confirm that the king of Jerusalem lived in a palace with a pagan temple and a full court of officials. Most importantly, these records confirm that Jerusalem was sophisticated enough to possess court scribes who carried on a continuing diplomatic correspondence with neighboring states, including its overlord, Egypt. In addition, the letters confirm that couriers from Egypt carried on regular correspondence with the court of Jerusalem.

In conclusion, the powerful historical evidence from these ancient Egyptian Tell el Amarna documents provides one more strong link in the chain of evidence from sources outside the Bible that tends to confirm the historical accuracy of these biblical accounts.

King Hezekiah's Tunnel Inscription

The ancient king of Judea, King Hezekiah ordered his workmen to carve a long tunnel through 1,749 feet of hard bedrock to bring in a safe supply of water from a spring that was located outside the walls of the City of David, ancient Jerusalem. This undertaking was a truly phenomenal engineering task, especially when we consider the limited mining and surveying knowledge as well as the primitive tools, available to Jewish engineers in the 8th century B.C. An inscription describing this undertaking reveals that the leader of the project ordered two groups of miners to begin digging toward each other from opposite ends of the tunnel. The reason for attempting the very difficult task of trying to bore through so much solid rock in the hope of meeting in the center rather than simply working from one end only, must have been the fear of an impending invasion of Jerusalem. Tourists visiting Jerusalem can now safely wade through the shallow waters of Hezekiah's Tunnel that lead to the Gihon Spring. Kaye and I have walked underground in this engineering marvel, and have witnessed proof of the incredible accuracy of the historical accounts recorded in the Holy Scriptures.

The tunnel inscription was written in ancient classical Hebrew on a plaque located near the pool. The inscription described the construction of this unusual tunnel: "Behold the tunnel. This is the story of its cutting. While the miners swung their picks, one towards the other, and when there remained only 3 cubits to cut, the voice of one calling his fellow was heard — for there was a resonance in the rock coming from both north and south . . . and the water flowed from the spring towards the pool, 1200 cubits. The height of the rock above the head of the miners was 100 cubits." This engraved inscription is enormously important to archeologists because it clearly confirms a very specific and unusual biblical account. The engraving was carved out of the base rock that formed the side of the ancient excavated tunnel. After its discovery, it was removed by the Turkish authorities to their capital of Istanbul in 1880. It was forgotten and laid aside as an unknown inscription until an Israeli archeologist visited the museum and recognized that the engraved stone was incredibly valuable, the long-forgotten Hezekiah Tunnel inscription. He alerted the museum curator to the fact. This priceless inscription from the past can now be seen in an exhibit in an archeological museum in Istanbul, Turkey.

It is interesting to look back in Church history to view the attitudes toward the authority of the Bible expressed by the great men of faith in past generations. In the fourth-century book *The City of God*, Saint Augustine declared, "Scripture, which proves the truth of its historical statements by the accomplishment of its prophecies, gives no false information.

Can We Trust the Historical Statements of the Bible?
The Testimony of Archaeologists and Classical Scholars

Professor Millar Burrows of Yale University discussed the findings of recent archeological digs and their impact on the views of the critics of biblical historical accuracy: "Archaeology has in many cases refuted the views of modern critics. It has shown in a number of instances that these views rest on false assumptions and unreal, artificial schemes of historical development"[5] Dr. Burrows explained the underlying assumptions that creates this climate of rejection of the Scriptures: "The excessive skepticism of many liberal theologians stems not from a careful evaluation of the available data, but from an enormous predisposition against the supernatural." His comments underline the fundamental role of presuppositions in the minds of all intellectuals as they approach any area of study. If you approach the Bible determined to reject any of the statements that reveal the prophetic and supernatural nature of God's revelation to man, then you have determined your negative conclusions before commencing your study.

As a leading archaeologist in the field of biblical Middle Eastern studies Burrows revealed that the results of modern archeological research have provided powerful new evidence in favor of the historical accuracy of the statements found in the Scriptures: "On the whole, however, archaeological work has unquestionably strengthened confidence in the reliability of the scriptural record. More than one archaeologist has found his respect for the Bible increased by the experience of excavation in Palestine"[6] In conclusion Burrows affirmed that the net result of the recent discoveries has actually increased our ability to categorize the Bible's statements as solid evidence by eyewitnesses to these ancient events: "Such evidence as archaeology has afforded thus far, especially by providing additional and older manuscripts of the books of the Bible, strengthens our confidence in the accuracy with which the text has been transmitted through the centuries."[7]

Sir Frederic Kenyon, a well-known archeologist in the earlier part of this century, has written that the results of modern research has profoundly increased our knowledge and understanding of the biblical world. Professor Kenyon wrote that Christians can welcome the results of continued archeological research because the continuing evidence produced from the digs in the Middle East has strengthened our confidence in the total accuracy of the Word of God.

> It is therefore legitimate to say that, in respect of that part of the Old Testament against which the disintegrating criticism of the last half of the nineteenth century was chiefly directed, the evidence of archaeology has been to re-establish its authority, and likewise to augment its value by rendering it more intelligible through a fuller knowledge of its background and setting. Archaeology has not yet said its last word; but the results already achieved confirm what faith would suggest, that the Bible can do nothing but gain from an increase of knowledge.[8]

F. F. Bruce is a leading researcher in the area of biblical studies. He has stated that, far from disproving the Bible, recent archeological finds have proven the truthfulness of the scriptural account: "Where Luke has been suspected of inaccuracy, and accuracy has been vindicated by some inscriptional evidence, it may be legitimate to say that archaeology has confirmed the New Testament record."[9] Professor Merrill Unger, the editor of the well respected *Unger Bible Dictionary* has pointed out the incomparable value from the results of modern archeology in enabling us to understand the ancient world of the kings and prophets of Israel: "Old Testament archaeology has rediscovered whole nations, resurrected important peoples, and in a most astonishing manner filled in historical gaps, adding immeasurably to the knowledge of biblical backgrounds."

The dismissive attitude toward the literal truth of the historical accounts in the Bible as displayed by liberal theologians such as Bishop Spong, the author of *Rescuing the Bible From Fundamentalism*, is in direct contradiction to the powerful evidence confirming the reliability of the Bible's history from the actual archeological digs. An underlying attitude and prejudice of the liberals is that they deny that the four Gospels were written by Matthew, Mark, Luke, and John, all eyewitnesses and contemporaries of Jesus and the people who were present during the life, death, and resurrection of Jesus of Nazareth. This attitude is displayed in the Jesus Seminar and its negative conclusions that any statement of Jesus that displays evidence of the supernatural, prophecy or His claim to be the Messiah and the Son of God, is "inauthentic." These liberals declare that the four Gospels were created by editors or redactors at least a century after the events they record. In denying the claims of the New Testament writers that they were actually recording events in which they participated, these liberal scholars suggest that the claims of the New Testament regarding the virgin birth, and the resurrection of Jesus, as well as His teachings and miracles, can be dismissed as imaginary creations of editors far removed from the historical events they describe.

The underlying assumption of the liberal scholars who reject the historicity of the Gospels is their belief that these documents were composed over one hundred years after the events of Jesus' life and death. The scholars call the period between the death of Christ and the writing of the Gospels the formative period. The popular German Tubingen school of thought or theory is that the Gospels were edited by unknown Christian redactors to create new theological statements that Jesus never uttered. They suggest that these Gospel accounts were mainly myths or religious legends that developed during the lengthy interval between the lifetime of Jesus and the time these accounts were set down in writing. While this attitude is extremely widespread in liberal universities and seminaries, the evidence produced in the last fifty years provides powerful proof that the Gospel writers were eyewitnesses and contemporaries of Jesus of Nazareth.

The continuing historical research provides overwhelming proof that the three Gospels of Matthew, Mark, and Luke were written within forty years of the Cross. The importance of this fact cannot be overestimated. Archeologists had discovered numerous early papyri manuscript portions of the four Gospels in Egypt and Syria that were written between A.D. 32 and the beginning of the second century. These early manuscripts closed the gap between the time of the Cross and the previously known Gospel manuscripts from the second century. Professor William F. Albright, an outstanding biblical archaeologist, concluded in 1955, "We can already say emphatically that there is no longer any solid basis for dating any book of the New Testament after circa A.D. 80, two full generations before the date between 130 and 150 given by the more radical New Testament critics of today."[10] Dr. Albright's personal assessment of the conclusions of the liberal critics who deny the authenticity of the New Testament is informative: "Only modern scholars who lack both historical method and perspective can spin such a web of speculation as that with which critics have surrounded the Gospel tradition."

Concerning the Old Testament, Professor William F. Albright has written, "There can be no doubt that archaeology has confirmed the substantial historicity of Old Testament tradition." In response to the question of widespread skepticism and outright contempt for the authority of the historical statements of the Bible Dr. Albright wrote the following:

> The excessive skepticism shown toward the Bible by important historical schools of the eighteenth and nine-teenth centuries, certain phases of which still appear peri-odically, has been progressively discredited. Discovery after discovery has established the accuracy of innumer-able details and has brought increased recognition to the value of the Bible as a source of history . . . As critical study of the Bible is more and more influenced by the rich new material from the ancient Near East we shall see a steady rise in respect for the historical significance of now

neglected or despised passages and details in the Old and New Testament.[11]

The importance of this proof of the early composition of the Gospel records cannot be overestimated. If the Gospels were written and widely distributed within the lifetime of thousands of people who personally saw the miracles of the feeding of the five thousand and the resurrected Jesus then they must be true historical accounts. In another interview with *Christianity Today* magazine in January 1963, Dr. Albright announced his professional conclusion that every one of the books of the New Testament were written "probably sometime between circa A.D. 50 and 75." Professor Albright correctly noted that this twenty-to forty-five-year interval between the actual historical event and the subsequent writing of the Gospels is "too slight to permit any appreciable corruption of the essential center and even of the specific wording of the sayings of Jesus." Many modern scholars suggest the hypothetical existence of a "Q" source manuscript, containing numerous traditions about Jesus's life and ministry, that they believe was used by Matthew and Mark. However, even these liberal scholars usually suggest this hypothetical (nonexistent) "Q document" was written by some follower of Jesus before A.D. 50. Therefore, even if this theory were correct, the Gospel tradition was still written by eyewitnesses and immediately read by people who personally knew Jesus and the apostles.

If the Gospels contained imaginary or false information then Christianity would never have prevailed in light of the massive persecution of its followers. Why would hundreds of thousands of Christians allow themselves and their beloved family members to die horribly in the Roman Coliseum when all they had to do to escape was to deny their faith that Jesus was God? It is inconceivable that these martyrs would die for their Christian faith if they held the slightest doubt as to the historical accuracy of the Gospel accounts that Jesus was the Son of God who had risen from the dead. The only possible way to explain the steadfast faith of these first-century believers is to acknowledge that they were totally persuaded of the truth of the Gospel account about Jesus of Nazareth.

Consider the confident faith represented by the apostle Paul in his inspired letter to the church at Rome, to people who lived in constant expectation of martyrdom.

> Who shall separate us from the love of Christ? shall tribulation, or distress, or persecution, or famine, or nakedness, or peril, or sword? As it is written, For thy sake we are killed all the day long; we are accounted as sheep for the slaughter. Nay, in all these things we are more than conquerors through him that loved us. For I am persuaded, that neither death, nor life, nor angels, nor principalities, nor powers, nor things present, nor things to come, Nor height, nor depth, nor any other creature, shall be able to separate us from the love of God, which is in Christ Jesus our Lord. I say the truth in Christ, I lie not, my conscience also bearing me witness in the Holy Ghost (Romans 8:35 –9:1).

During the last year, I completed a detailed study of the research on the dating of New Testament documents in *Redating the New Testament*, written by Dr. John A. T. Robinson, the well respected lecturer at Trinity College, Cambridge. Dr. Robinson is an eminent critic of the New Testament period. He concluded that the New Testament is the work of the actual disciples of Jesus and their contemporaries who worked in the early Church, and that, furthermore, every one of the New Testament books, including John, must have been written before A.D. 64.[12] Robinson also wrote about the reliability and early dating of the Gospel of Luke in his book *Luke the Historian in the Light of Research*. He concluded that both Luke and Mark were written at some point before A.D. 59 by the named authors. Furthermore, he wrote, "The early date of both Gospel and Acts gives a strong presumption in favor of the historical value of the books. There was less time for legends to grow. The author was nearer to his sources of information . . . But at any rate, since Luke the physician, the friend of Paul, wrote the two books, they cannot be thrown aside as second-century romances written to deify Jesus and to idealize Peter and Paul. The writer is so close to the facts of which he writes that he has to receive serious consideration to see if, after all, he has not drawn his characters to the life."[13]

Saint Peter's Fish

Some of my favorite passages in the Gospels tell us about the life, teachings, and miracles of Jesus that occurred during His ministry in His home region surrounding the Sea of Galilee. When my wife, Kaye, and I travel to Tiberias on the Sea of Galilee, we always stop at St. Peter's Restaurant to enjoy their main course of St. Peter's Fish, while watching the fishing boats on the usually quiet sea. This species of fish belongs to the Cichlidae family and flourishes in this warm freshwater sea. St. Peter's Fish is occasionally called the "mouth breeder." It is found naturally in only three places, all of which lie along the geological zone extending from the Sea of Galilee thousands of miles to the south in Lake Victoria, Uganda. This species of fish is found only in the Nile River, in Lake Victoria, and in the Sea of Galilee. The Gospel account recorded in Matthew 17:24–27 describes the disciple Peter catching a fish with a shekel coin in its mouth to provide the tribute money that the government officials demanded of Peter and Jesus of Nazareth. Jesus told Peter, "Notwithstanding, lest we should offend them, go thou to the sea, and cast an hook, and take up the fish that first cometh up; and when thou hast opened his mouth, thou shalt find a piece of money: that take, and give unto them for me and thee" (Matthew 17:27)

Dr. Jim Fleming, a professor of archaeology and historical geography at Hebrew University in Jerusalem, has taught about the unusual nature of this fish in connection with Matthew 17:24–27. The female St. Peter's Fish carries her eggs in her mouth to protect them against predators until they hatch. As the brood of minnows begins to grow, she opens her mouth to let them out to swim around her from time to time. However, the mother fish opens her mouth again and quickly scoops them up whenever danger is present. The mother will fast almost to the point of starvation to avoid the danger of inadvertently swallowing her young offspring. On account of her well-known maternal habits, the fishermen of Galilee call the female St. Peter's fish by the Hebrew name "The Mother-Fish." After the young mature to the point where they can survive independently, they swim away. However, the mother fish often keeps a substitute in her mouth to perpetuate her habit of carrying her young. St. Peter's Fish are sometimes caught by fishermen and when they examine their mouths they find pebbles or coke bottle caps inside. The popular name for the fish is "St. Peter's fish" because of the account in Matthew 17:24–27 about Peter catching a fish that carried a shekel coin in its mouth. This habit of the fish to pick up items from the lake bottom in no way minimizes the miracle of our Lord. Only the Son of God could have known that this particular fish would be carrying a shekel coin in its mouth.

In the last century, the writer H. L. Hastings wrote about the astonishing survival and success of the Bible, despite centuries of attacks on its authority and accuracy. The Scriptures have withstood the blistering attacks of skepticism. Hastings wrote, "Infidels of eighteen hundred years have been refuting and over-throwing this book, and yet it stands today as solid rock. Its circulation increases, and it is more loved and cherished and read today than ever before. Infidels, with all their assaults, make about as much impression on this book as a man with a tack hammer would on the Pyramids of Egypt."

Notes

1. John W. Montgomery, *Christianity for the Tough Minded* (Minneapolis: Bethany Fellowship Inc., 1973) 6.

2. Dr. Nelson Glueck, *Exploring Southern Palestine — The Negev* (1959).

3. *Biblical Archeological Review* July/August, 1997.

4. *The Tell el-Amarna Tablets.*

5. Millar Burrows, *What Mean These Stones?* (New York: Meridian Books, 1956) 29.

6. Millar Burrows, *What Mean These Stones?* (New York: Meridian Books, 1956) 1.

7. Millar Burrows, *What Mean These Stones?* (New York: Meridian Books, 1956) 42.

8. Sir Frederic Kenyon, *The Bible and Archeology* (New York: Harper & Row Publishers, 1940) 27.

9. F. F. Bruce, *Revelation and the Bible* (Grand Rapids: Baker Book House, 1969) 33.

10. Howard Frederick Vos, *Can I Trust My Bible?* (Chicago: Moody Press, 1963) 136.

11. William Albright, *The Archaeology of Palestine* (Middlesex: Pelican Books, 1960) 127–128.

12. John A. T. Robinson, *Redating the New Testament* (Philadelphia: Westminster Press, 1976) 351-353.

13. John A. T. Robinson, *Luke the Historian in the Light of Research* (New York: Charles Scribner's Sons, 1923) 39–40.

13

New Scientific Discoveries and the Scriptures

The Marvel of the Human Eye

Three thousand years ago, the wisest man in the world, King Solomon, wrote, "The hearing ear, and the seeing eye, the Lord hath made even both of them" (Proverbs 20:12).

The human eye is a marvel of God's creation. It astonishes the mind of anyone who begins to contemplate the scientific research that has been conducted on its amazing construction and activity. The degree of complexity displayed in the wondrous construction of the various parts of the eye make the theory that it "evolved over millions of years by tiny random-chance mutations" an absolute impossibility. The naturalist creator of the theory of evolution, Charles Darwin, actually admitted that the engineering of the human eye was so specialized and complex that he could not begin to image how it might have developed through the evolutionary processes of random mutation and natural selection.

> To suppose that the eye with all its inimitable contrivances for adjusting the focus to different distances, for admitting different amounts of light, and for the correction of spherical and chromatic aberration, could have been formed by

natural selection, seems, I freely confess, absurd in the highest degree.[1]

Another evolutionary scientist, Dr. Ernst Mayer, admitted the difficulty in imagining how the complex human eye could possibly form through chance mutations. It is a considerable strain on one's credulity to assume that finely balanced systems such as certain sense organs (the eye of vertebrates or the feathers of birds) could be improved by random mutations[2]. One of the great problems facing those who deny a Creator is to explain how natural selection or random mutation could evolve such a phenomenally complex organ as the human eye when none of the hundreds of thousands of imagined intermediate mutations could have any value until the entire system was in place to allow vision to take place. The only rational conclusion is that God created the fully developed human eye when He created Adam and Eve.

The eye is engineered far more precisely than a modern, sophisticated camera. However, recent research into its functions reveals that the human eye is vastly more complex and sophisticated than any camera ever made by man. In a manner similar to advanced cameras in the last decade, the human eye displays advanced auto-focus features with a remarkable ability to adjust the diaphragm of the iris automatically and at a phenomenal speed. The lens of your eye modifies its shape through tiny muscles that allow the eye to correctly focus on an object that is moving toward you or away from you. This act is not unlike the workings of a sophisticated, computer-controlled modern camera when it calculates distances and automatically adjusts to bring the object into focus. The lens of your eye is constructed of microscopic and transparent living cells. These cells allow light photons to enter through the cornea, pass through the fluid, and be analyzed by the phenomenal organ known as the retina.

To understand the complexity and sophistication of the engineering of the eye, we need to appreciate the retina. The retina lines the back of your eye and acts as a form of film which receives the actual image composed of light photons passing through the iris, cornea, and eye fluid. Your retina is thinner than paper yet its tiny surface (one inch square) contains 137 million light-sensitive cells. Approximately 95 percent of these cells are rods that can analyse black and white images, while the balance of

B &w   130 mil.   222
Color   7 mil

approximately seven million cone cells are used to analyze color images. Each of these millions of cells are separately connected to the optic nerve that transmits the signal to your brain at approximately three hundred miles per hour. The millions of specialized cells in your eye can analyze more than one million messages a second.

The retina in your eye is the most light-sensitive object in the universe. It is so much more sophisticated in its design than even the most powerful electron microscope or spy camera. For example, the most advanced film available today can differentiate between a range of one thousand to one. However, recent experiments have confirmed that the retina of the human eye can easily differentiate and analyze a range of ten billion to one. Experiments have revealed that the retina can actually detect one single photon of light in a dark room, something beyond the range of engineering instruments. Recently, scientists have determined that the specialized cells in the retina actually partially analyze the image in the eye before it is ever transmitted through the optic nerve to the brain. These retina cells perform up to ten billion calculations per second in determining the nature of the image transmitted to the eye by light photons. No computers on earth are capable of matching these virtually instantaneous calculations.

In an article in *Byte* computer magazine in April 1985, Dr. John Stevens made the following comparison:

> To simulate 10 milliseconds of the complete processing of even a single nerve cell from the retina would require the solution of about 500 simultaneous non-linear differential equations one hundred times and would take at least several minutes of processing time on a Cray super computer. Keeping in mind that there are 10 million or more such cells interacting with each other in complex ways it would take a minimum of a hundred years of Cray time to simulate what takes place in your eye many times every second.

In the article, Dr. Stevens wrote that if we were to attempt to duplicate the computing power of the human eye, we would have to build the world's most advanced computer with a single silicon chip (normally the size of a dime) that would cover 10,000 cubic inches and contain billions of transistors and hundreds of miles of circuit traces. The retina is so small that it fills only 0.0003 inches of space. If we could ever build the advanced device to mimic the human eye, the single computer chip would weigh at least 100 pounds, in comparison to the human retina that weighs less than a gram. The retina operates with less than 0.0001 watts of electrical charge. To duplicate the retina's abilities, the computer would need to consume 300 watts of power. In other words, the retina is 3,000,000 times more efficient in its power consumption.

When we consider the marvellous design of the smallest parts of our body, we are filled with wonder at the glory of God's creation. Anyone who suggests that these phenomenally complex and sophisticated organs have evolved without a designer, by random-chance mutations, is a fool or a liar. The Bible has only one answer to those who would deny the Creator: "The fool hath said in his heart, There is no God" (Psalms 14:1). The Psalmist David acknowledged the truth that we are created by God. "Know ye that the Lord he is God: it is he that hath made us, and not we ourselves; we are his people, and the sheep of his pasture" (Psalms 100:3).

The Function of the Eye

The light of the body is the eye: if therefore thine eye be single, thy whole body shall be full of light. But if thine eye be evil, thy whole body shall be full of darkness. If therefore the light that is in thee be darkness, how great is that darkness! (Matthew 6:22–23)

As mentioned above, the human eye functions like a modern camera. The light enters the eye through the iris — the "lamp of the body." The "light" we allow to enter into our eye affects our soul and our spirit. The cornea of the eye can become very painful if it is hurt or scratched. The prophet Zechariah warned those who would attack God's Chosen People: "For thus saith the Lord of hosts; After the glory hath He sent me unto the nations which spoiled you: for he that toucheth you toucheth the apple of his eye" (Zechariah 2:8). In other words, when men hurt the Jewish people, it is as if they have inflicted the same pain to God as we feel when our eye is injured.

A fascinating insight into the physiology of the human eye is demonstrated in the book of Judges. The passage describes the Israeli army's attack on their enemies. Led by their brilliant general, Gideon, the Jewish army waited to attack until the change of the guard, when "they had but newly set the watch," meaning that the general in charge of the enemy army had just placed newly awakened troops on watch to perform sentry duty. The book of Judges declares, "So Gideon, and the hundred men that were with him, came unto the outside of the camp in the beginning of the middle watch; and they had but newly set the watch: and they blew the trumpets, and brake the pitchers that were in their hands" (Judges 7:19). In other words, Gideon, as a wise general, delayed his attack until the moment the enemy soldiers, who had just awakened from sleep, were placed on guard duty. This meant that the pupils of their eyes would not yet have fully adapted to the darkness and would have had difficulty in seeing their enemy approaching in the dark.

The Seed of the Father Determines the Sex of the Child

"For the man is not of the woman; but the woman of the man."   (1 Corinthians 11:8)

This verse in the New Testament may refer to the fact that Genesis declares that God formed the woman Eve from the rib of the man Adam. However, another, more subtle scientific truth is revealed in this inspired statement by the apostle Paul. The apostle's statement "the woman of the man" reveals the scientific truth that "the woman comes out of the man." In other words, the determination that the child will be born female is dependent solely upon the genetic information contained in the sperm of the man. The sex of the child is not determined by genetic information from the ova from the woman's body. In a similar manner, Paul affirms "for the man is not of the woman." His statement confirms that the sex of the male child is not determined by the mother. In fact, the sex of the child is dependent solely on the sperm of the father. It is the father's sperm containing either the X or the Y chromosome that will determine the sex of the baby. Tragically, throughout history, many wives have been unjustly repudiated by their aristocratic or royal husbands because they bore female offspring rather than male children. However, science now knows that the sex of the baby is entirely determined by the sperm of the father, exactly as indicated by the Scriptures two thousand years ago.

The Virgin Birth of Jesus of Nazareth

Both the Old Testament prophecies and the New Testament histories agree in affirming the virgin birth of Jesus of Nazareth. Significantly, the first prophecy in the Bible predicted the miraculous virgin birth of the promised Messiah. The prophetic words of God revealed that the Messiah would be of the "seed" of the woman. Since all children are produced naturally by the "seed" of the man, this curious prophecy revealed the mystery of the virgin birth of our Lord. This unique expression "her seed" has no parallel in the rest of Hebrew literature, within or outside of the pages of the Bible. Since all of Hebrew literature and common sense affirm that a child is born of "his seed," the sperm of a man, it was unusual and unprecedented for the Bible to declare that the future Messiah, the victor over Satan, would be born supernaturally from a virgin as "her seed." "And I will put enmity between thee and the woman, and between thy seed and her seed; it shall bruise thy head, and thou shalt bruise his heel" (Genesis 3:15).

The prophet Isaiah also predicted the supernatural nature of the birth of Jesus 740 years before the event in the following verse, "Therefore the Lord himself shall give you a sign; Behold, a virgin shall conceive, and bear a son, and shall call his name Immanuel" (Isaiah 7:14). Some scholars have disputed this prophecy of the virgin birth of Christ. They have rejected the King James translators' choice of the word "virgin" to translate the Hebrew word העלמה *almah* that is used by Isaiah in this verse. However, the Hebrew word *almah* is normally translated as an "unmarried young woman." The question is this: Does העלמה *almah* refer to a young, moral, virginal, unmarried woman, or does the word refer to an immoral, sexually experienced, young, unmarried woman. As far as I can determine, the word *almah* always refers to a "an unmarried young woman" who is a virgin, as indicated in Strong's Concordance reference to a "damsel, maid, virgin."

Only an immoral society would suggest that "an unmarried young woman" does not refer to a virgin. Furthermore, the prophet Isaiah refers to the fact that this "almah" would "conceive, and bear a son" as a prophetic "sign" given by the Lord to the nation. If the skeptics were correct in their assertion that the word *almah* does not denote that the woman was a virgin when she gave birth to the son, then we must ask the question: Where is the prophetic "sign"? According to the critics, the prophet Isaiah simply predicted that an "almah," an "unmarried young woman," would have sexual relations with a man and give birth to an illegitimate son. If this was correct, where is the prophetic "sign?" Immoral young women give birth to sons everyday worldwide. There is nothing unusual about this that would qualify this event as a prophetic "sign" to Israel of the coming of their Messiah. Obviously, this refusal to accept the normal meaning of the word "almah" as a "young unmarried, virgin woman" is a vain attempt to evade the clear prophecy of Scripture that foretold the miracle of the virgin birth of the coming Messiah.

Finally, the Gospel records the historical fact that Jesus of Nazareth was supernaturally born to the virgin Mary (Matthew 1:23). This "virgin birth" of Jesus was essential to fulfill the ancient prophecies of the coming Messiah. If Jesus had been born as the result of the union of the natural seed of a man and woman, He would not have qualified as the perfectly innocent and sinless Son of Man. However, in addition to separating Jesus of Nazareth from all other humans born of a mother, the virgin birth of Christ ensured that His blood would be unique from all other human blood. He would therefore be the perfect sacrifice for the sins of mankind. The genetic information that produces the blood in the body of the unborn baby is produced solely from the genetic information in the sperm of the father. That is why there are paternity blood tests (as opposed to maternity blood tests) to determine the father of a child. Every person's blood is determined by the father. As a result of the virgin birth, Jesus of Nazareth was the first person in history who did not have within Him the sin-tainted blood of Adam that has been passed down to every human through every generation from Adam until today. Since Jesus had no biological father, it was essential for God to create His blood by means of a special miracle.

Jesus Was Supernaturally Conceived in the Womb of Mary

The New Testament writers referred clearly to the virgin birth of the Messiah. The Gospel writer Luke recorded the inspired message of the angel Gabriel to Mary, the mother of Jesus: "And, behold, thou shalt conceive in thy womb, and bring forth a son, and shalt call his name Jesus" (Luke 1:31).

The Holy Scriptures proclaim that Jesus was supernaturally

conceived by God within the womb of Mary (without the necessity of a male sperm) as God's true Messiah. Modern medicine
reveals that normal human conception (the union of the male
sperm and the female ova) takes place within the female body as
the sperm meets the ova in the fallopian tubes of a woman.
However, the Holy Scriptures declared that God caused the
conception of Jesus to supernaturally occur within the womb of
Mary, the chosen vessel to be the mother of our Lord. This biblical
statement confirms the true supernatural nature of the conception
and birth of Jesus.

The Value of PI Revealed in the Bible

An astonishing discovery was made by Shlomo Edward
G. Belaga that appeared in Boaz Tsaban's Rabbinical Math section
on the Internet. In addition, a number of other sources have
recently examined this interesting subject. The discovery indicates
that the scientific value of PI, which enables us to accurately
calculate the precise circumference of a circle, is contained in the
Bible.

The Bronze Laver in Solomon's Temple

And he made a molten sea, ten cubits from the one brim to
the other: it was round all about, and his height was five
cubits: and a line of thirty cubits did compass it round
about. And under the brim of it round about there were
knops compassing it, ten in a cubit, compassing the sea
round about: the knops were cast in two rows, when it was
cast. It stood upon twelve oxen, three looking toward the
north, and three looking toward the west, and three
looking toward the south, and three looking toward the
east: and the sea was set above upon them, and all their
hinder parts were inward. And it was an hand breadth
thick, and the brim thereof was wrought like the brim of a
cup, with flowers of lilies: it contained two thousand
baths.   (1 Kings 7:23–26)

This huge bronze laver was used by the priests to wash themselves and the rest of the Temple worship objects connected with
the Temple sacrifices.

A paraphrase of the key passage would read as follows:

"He [King Solomon] made the Sea of cast metal, circular in shape, measuring ten cubits from rim to rim [the diameter was 10 cubits] and five cubits high. It took a line of thirty cubits to measure around it. [The circumference was equal to 30 cubits]."

Everyone of us can remember our geometry classes in high school in which we learned that the formula to calculate the precise value of a circumference was the value of PI times the diameter of the object to be measured. The precise value of PI was extremely difficult to calculate until fairly recently.

The Declared Scientific Value of PI = 3.1415926

A casual reading of 1 Kings 7:23 appears to suggest that the Scriptures declared that the value of PI was only 3. The text says the huge cast metal basin was ten cubits wide (18 feet) and that its circumference was precisely thirty cubits around. In other words, it looks as though the biblical writer was mistaken and gave only a rough approximation of the value of PI as being equal to 3 by mistakenly stating that the circumference of the basin was only ten cubits.

However, a careful analysis of this passage by some Israeli scientists and rabbis has revealed a mysterious feature in the language of this Hebrew text that provides a startling revelation of the wisdom of God regarding the true scientific value of PI.

The normal Hebrew word for "line" or "circumference" ק ו is spelled with two letters: qof ק and vav ו.

But, in this particular verse, 1 Kings 7:23, the word for "circumference" is spelled with an extra letter heh ה. This unusual spelling of circumference with the additional letter is ק ו ה.

The ancient Jews did not have Arabic numerals so they used each of the 22 letters of their alphabet to stand for numbers. Thus they spelled out their numbers, such as the number 5, using the Hebrew letter heh ה. Similarly, the number 100 is indicated by the Hebrew letter qof ק, and the number 6 is indicated by the Hebrew letter vav ו.

Since the unusual spelling of "circumference" in 1 Kings 7:23 is ק ו ה the Israeli rabbis noted that this indicated a formula. The numerical value of ק ו ה is 111:

Qof ק = 100 + Vav ו = 6 + He ה = 5, which total 111.

However, the usual spelling of circumference is ק ו, whose whole letters add up to 106:

Qof ק = 100 + Vav ו = 6, which total 106.

Expressed as a mathematical formula, the unusual spelling of "circumference" would read as follows:

$$(111/106) = (3.14150943\ldots/3)$$

Remember, that the real scientific value of PI = 3.1415926 . . .

The difference between 3 × 111/106 [3.14150943 . . .] and the true value of pi (3.1415926 . . .) is only 0.0000832, which is only an error of 0.00026%.

Due to the inherent limitations of expressing numbers in the form of Hebrew letters, this revelation of the value of PI in 1 Kings 7:23 is as close as the biblical Hebrew language could come to expressing this extremely precise number.

This calculation indicates that the ancient Scriptures included this astonishingly accurate calculation of the value of PI indicating the tremendous engineering knowledge available to King Solomon, the wisest man in history according to the Scriptures.

Notes

1. Charles Darwin. *The Origin of Species.* (London: J.M. Dent & Sons Ltd., 1971) 167.

2. E. Mayer. *Systematics and the Origin of Species.* (Columbia: University Press, 1942) 296.

14

The Coming Collapse of Evolution

The main philosophical position that underlies much of the attack on the authority of the Bible as the inspired Word of God is based on an almost universal acceptance of the theory of evolution. This widely held evolutionary theory itself is based on an assumption of atheism — that there is no God and that everything in this universe, including mankind, has accidentally evolved from dead, inanimate matter by random chance over billions of years. This fundamental rejection of the existence of God and His role as the Designer of Creation provides the intellectual climate within which the educational and scientific communities espouse the theory of evolution. Moreover, the theory of evolution provides the only other possible alternative to Creation that can explain the amazing complexity of biological life on this planet.

I will not attempt an exhaustive refutation of the theory of evolution in this chapter. However, the fundamental importance of this topic demands that we examine the mounting evidence that evolution is about to collapse of its own weight. This topic is vital to all who wish to come to terms with the authority of the Bible because the Scriptures clearly teach us that God created the heavens and the earth by His marvellous design with a purpose to create man in His own image. This biblical doctrine that is taught from Genesis to Revelation is fundamentally contradicted by the theory of evolution which denies the existence of God and proclaims that man lives in an accidental universe without purpose, plan, or design. If evolution is true, then the Bible and the words of Jesus Christ are false. It is as clear as that. When the world abandoned the biblical teaching that God created the heavens and the earth, they substituted a theory of evolution that made man nothing more than a random accident in a meaningless universe with no absolutes of good or evil.

The reason this subject is so important is the powerful contradiction that exists between the paradigm of Christianity and the world view of evolution. They are so fundamentally opposite that there is no possibility that both can be true. Therefore, this inherent conflict produces a dangerous double-mindedness in the minds of millions of Christians who have been educated from elementary school to the university in the theory of evolution as if it was an absolute truth. At some point in their lives Christians enter into a personal relationship with Jesus Christ as their Lord and Savior, based on their acceptance of the teaching of the Bible about the nature of Jesus, His sacrifice on the Cross, and their hope for salvation and heaven. If they never receive adequate information that proves to them that evolution is flawed, they continue to hold within their mind the unchallenged teachings about evolution taught to them through their schools and television. On the one hand, they hold the belief, based on their education, that evolution is true and that logically the Bible's account of God's special creation of the universe must be false. On the other hand, they are trusting for their salvation, their peace of mind and their hope of heaven based on their belief that the Bible is absolutely true in all of its statements regarding the nature of Jesus Christ, salvation, and heaven.

Do you see the problem? If evolution is true then logically the Bible is fundamentally false in its teachings about the creation in its first book, Genesis. If evolution is true, then Jesus Christ would have to be mistaken when He spoke approvingly of the biblical account of the creation of the universe and Adam. If evolution is true, then it would be illogical to trust your very soul on the belief that the Scriptures are wrong about Creation but are absolutely trustworthy regarding the rest of the Bible's doctrines including salvation and hell. If the Bible is false about Creation, how can we know that it is true in its other doctrines. In other words, if a Christian simultaneously holds to a belief in evolution and his belief in the truthfulness of the Bible, then he is in serious danger of being a "double minded man." The apostle James wrote, "A double minded man is unstable in all his ways" (James 1:8).

I believe that a major reason for the weakness of the Church today, as well as the weakness of many Christians in their daily walk and in witnessing to others about their faith, is the fact that they have accepted the truthfulness of the theory of evolution without examination. As a result, they have a profound but often unrecognized weakness in their faith in Christ and in the teachings of the Bible because they have never come to terms with the contradictions between their biblically based faith and their acceptance of the theory of evolution. This contradiction is seldom thought about consciously, but it is so profound that it can not help but affect their general confidence in the truth of the Scriptures and, thus, weaken their daily faith.

When we examine the lives, deaths, and statements of faith of Christians in past centuries, we find evidence of an unshakable faith in Jesus and the truthfulness of the Scripture. This confidence motivated millions of believers to face torture and bloody martyrdom rather than deny their faith in Jesus Christ. Where did this faith come from? What motivated these believers to count their lives as insignificant in comparison to their utter confidence in the Lord Jesus Christ as taught in the beloved pages of Scripture? The evidence of history is overwhelming that Christians in past centuries were motivated by a profound love and trust in the absolute authority and inspiration in the Word of God. This faith in the trustworthiness of the Bible motivated the reformer Martin Luther to stand before the German authorities who held his life in their hands and say to them, "Here I stand. I can do no other." It was the firm confidence of the Reformers in the truth of the Holy Scriptures that motivated their rallying cry "Sola Scripture," an affirmation that their faith and doctrine were based solely on the divine revelation in the pages of the Bible.

The Theory of Evolution

The theory of evolution suggests that all living things on earth have come into being through accidental, natural processes that began with a primeval mass of subatomic particles and radiation billions of years ago. Evolution is taught as if it is a fact, not a theory, in the universities and schools throughout the world. Although the theory was popularized by Charles Darwin almost one hundred and fifty years ago, it remains just that — a theory — because the evidence to prove it has not been found.

In fact, the scientific problems and inconsistencies of evolution are so overwhelmingly obvious that it faces collapse on all fronts. The only thing holding the tattered theory of evolution together is the overwhelming desire of millions of people to hold on to evolution regardless of its weakness because the alternative is "unthinkable" to its practitioners. The only logical alternative to evolution to any thinking person is obviously the theory that a supernatural being — God — actually created the universe and man. The idea of God as Creator ruled Western society for almost nineteen hundred years. However, during the last one hundred years, the widespread rejection of the Bible's authority and its claim for God's special creation of life has produced a virtual monopoly for the evolutionary theory in our lifetime.

A fascinating book, entitled *The Intellectuals Speak Out About God*, was published a few years ago that astonished many readers with its revelations about the recent scientific discoveries that disprove evolution. These scientists discuss numerous scientific discoveries that support both special creation and the existence of God as the great Designer.

Professor Stephen D. Schwarz explained that many of the latest discoveries of science have illustrated the impossibility that this complex universe and life itself could have formed by random chance, no matter how old we assume the universe is.

> Until recently it was thought by many people that science supports atheism, that science is even the rational alternative to theism. It is now clear that science not only does not support atheism, but even lends rational support for theism. There is strong scientific evidence for God. Scientists, without presupposing God or creation, without trying to prove them, have come up with findings that strongly support God, His creation of the universe and man, and a supernatural purpose for the world we live in.[1]

Where Did the Universe Originate?

There are four fundamental scientific reasons why the universe and life itself could never have come into existence without a supernatural Creator. One of the most fundamental of all scientific observations is known as the Second Law of Thermodynamics. This law of science states that the total amount of usable energy throughout the universe is constantly decreasing. In other words the universe is running down, the constant loss of its original usable energy, which means the universe is ultimately running out of usable energy. This law is fundamental in science because scientists have never found a single exception to this observation. The obvious conclusion is that the universe must have been created at some point in time and has been running down ever since. This means the theory of some early evolutionary scientists that the universe has always existed is false.

In addition, since the universe is running down there must have been some point in the past when it began with the original totality of energy available — the moment of its beginning or creation. However, the question that must be faced is this: Where did the universe and its massive energy come from and when did it begin? It is illogical to believe that the universe came into existence out of nowhere accidentally, by random chance, without a designer or creator. The only logical conclusion is that the universe was created out of nothing by a Creator with an intelligent design and supernatural power. That Creator is God.

The Impossibility That a Prebiotic Soup Ever Existed on Earth

The second fundamental problem faced by evolutionary theory is the absolute impossibility that life was spontaneously generated from inanimate or nonliving elements. The evolutionist accounts for the chance development of life from nonliving matter by imagining that the earth's oceans in the distant past (in a universe without life) were an unusual chemical mixture they call "prebiotic soup." In other words they suppose that the oceans were accidently filled with all of the essential chemicals and that some energy source, possibly lightning, somehow stimulated these chemicals to bond together over billions of years by purely random chance to spontaneously generate life from nonliving material. Although it seems improbable that this spontaneous generation of life could occur by chance without a designer or purpose, the evolutionist is forced to imagine this actually occurred. Since he rejects the possibility of a supernatural God, he is forced to accept the only other rational alternative — random chance.

Professor Chandra Wickramasinghe, an eminent British scientist, describes the absolute impossibility of this prebiotic soup ever forming in the oceans of earth by random chance to create even the possibility of life being spontaneously generated over billions of years. The professor concluded:

> One of the earliest questions that was raised in connection with the primordial soup was deciding whether at any early stage in the earth's history, if there was a situation when the earth's atmosphere was not of its present character, that is, it was reducing rather than oxidizing. We looked at this rather carefully, and we decided that the earth's atmosphere was never of the right character to form an organic soup . . . we published this in a book under the title of *Lifecloud* . . . Geochemists and geologists have now come round; they now go on to say that the primordial soup had to be imported from outside . . . There's no way it could have developed upon the Earth . . . The organic soup itself is not such a marvellous thing. It is a prerequisite for any biological activity to start; that's certainly true. But it doesn't follow that if you have an organic soup it could get life started . . . And when we looked at the probabilities of the assembly of organic materials into a living system, it turns out that the improbabilities are really horrendous, horrific in extent and I concluded along with my colleague that (this) could not have happened spontaneously on the earth . . . There's not enough time, there's not enough resources and there's no way in which that could have happened on the earth.[2]

The Impossibility of Spontaneously Generating Life From Non-Life

Let's, for the sake of argument, imagine that the impossible occurred by chance, producing this prebiotic soup. But, then what are the actual odds against the spontaneous generation of life from this "prebiotic soup." Biologists have calculated that the odds against these chemicals spontaneously generating life by random chance are one chance in $10^{40,000}$. This number is 10 to the 40,000 power. The odds are equal to 10 followed by 40,000 zeros! It is a number so large that the human mind can scarcely conceive of it. To put this in perspective, scientists have calculated that the total number of atoms existing throughout the known universe of 50 billion galaxies (each containing 100 million stars like our Milky Way) is only 10^{74}. That is 10 followed by 74 zeros. However, the odds against life being generated by random chance from dead matter are inconceivably less than your chance of locating one single target atom in a whole universe of atoms by travelling blindfolded through the universe in a spaceship aimlessly hoping to find a particular target atom by chance. Theorizing how an incredibly complex biological system could evolve by random chance from these processes belongs in the realm of pure fantasy, not science.

The truth is that biologists know that the probability of life being generated by chance out of nonliving chemicals is a virtual impossibility. However, many evolutionary scientists argue that, no matter how statistically impossible it is, life must have formed from dead matter by chance. Given billions of years, they argue that even the most statistically unlikely event might have occurred. This is pure blind faith in the religion of evolution! The truth is that the odds against life occurring spontaneously by random chance are so large that it is more probable that you would win the one million dollar grand prize in the Lottery every single night for the next ten thousand years in a row!

Some of the evolutionary scientists who admit that life could never have spontaneously evolved on earth have made a novel suggestion that either the prebiotic soup or life itself was brought to earth from another universe! They call this novel and totally bizarre theory "Panspermia," as noted in a February 1992 article in the *Scientific American* magazine. This is not science; it is science fiction! If the mathematical odds make evolution impossible on earth then the same odds make evolution impossible anywhere else. This desperation of the scientists reveals two things. Evolution is finally collapsing due to the total absence of evidence in its favor and the insurmountable problems with the theory that life evolved by chance. Secondly, their desperation reveals their real motive for holding to this discredited theory — their desire to escape the consequences of the existence of God. A British academic journal made an interesting admission regarding creation. "By spreading out creation in time and space, there is no reduction in the mystery" (*The British Journal for the Philosophy of Science*, 1954).

What About Natural Selection?

The evolutionary scientists argue that natural selection provides the answer as to why random chance would result in the progressive evolution of life. Natural selection requires continuous progressive development at every successive step. However, random evolution cannot possess understanding and planning and thus produce a half-formed heart as a transition in order to ultimately form a final heart. How could the heart have been produced by evolution in stages as natural selection demands it to have been formed by step by step mutations in gradual stages? Obviously, until the heart was fully formed and functional it was of no use whatsoever. "It seems that evolutionists, whether consciously or unconsciously, have regarded the blind and inanimate forces of the environment, or nature, as having the ability to create and think."[3]

How Could the Hemoglobin in our Blood be Produced by Chance?

Dr. David Humphreys of McMaster University recently gave a speech called "Evidence for a Creator" in which he suggested that conventional science has produced substantial evidence that the universe, and hence life on Earth, was created by an intelligent rational being (a speech at the University of Waterloo, Canada on July 12, 1997). Dealing primarily with the evidence from chemistry and biology, Dr. Humphreys compared the theory of evolution which suggests everything was produced by random chance, against the theory that an intelligent being, namely God the Creator, created the universe.

Dr. Humphreys suggests that it is statistically improbable and unreasonable to assume that the universe was created by pure chance, given the statistical improbability of life occurring on earth, the complexity and diversity of biological life forms, and the current estimated age of the universe. For Humphreys, it is more logical and more consistent with current scientific evidence to conclude that the universe and life were produced as a result of intelligent design. Dr. Humphreys noted that hemoglobin molecules in our blood are composed of twenty amino acids that occur in nature. These twenty amino acids could be arranged by random chance into a total of 10^{650} possible chemical combinations. However, only one of those nearly infinite combination would produce the correct complex hemoglobin molecule that is essential for the blood system of billions of animals and human beings. "The simultaneous formation of two or more molecules of this complexity is so improbable as to be inconceivable . . . Some people argue that given enough time the improbable may become probable. Although five billion years for the age of the earth sounds like a long time, it is actually less than 10^{18} seconds. If the sequence of each protein molecule could be changed a thousand times per second, there could be only a total of 10^{67} sequences in five billion years."[4] In other words, even five billion years would not be enough time for evolution to form the haemoglobin in our blood by random chance.

Professor Chandra Wickramasinghe discussed his conclusions from his years of research on the possibility of life forming in this prebiotic soup in the earth's oceans by random chance.

> And from the point of view of geo-chemistry and terrestrial experiments, if you look at the early earth as a possible site for manufacturing life, it turns out that the case is non-existent, I would say, for such a thing happening on the earth . . . All that I am sure about is that life could not have happened on the earth spontaneously.[5]

Professor Chandra Wickramasinghe has written that years of laboratory research has provided powerful evidence that the evolutionary theory of the development of biological life on earth is simply impossible. The scientist concluded that complex biological life could not have formed by chance even if we supposed that the prebiotic soup existed on earth (the evidence shows that the prebiotic soup could not have formed on earth). Furthermore, even if we suppose that a simple form of micro-organism life actually formed by chance (which has been proven to be impossible) the evolution of that simple life into the complex forms as witnessed in millions of insect species, etc. is still impossible.

These scientists have shown that every one of the essential steps required by the evolutionary theory is fatally flawed.

Furthermore, even if every one of the these essential steps to evolve life by chance was possible (and they are not possible), the evolution of increasingly complex life forms from simple one-celled biological life forms by random mutations is still impossible. Professor Wickramasinghe summarizes the absurdity of this theory.

> If you start with a simple micro-organism no matter how it arose on the earth, primordial soup or otherwise, then if you just have that single organizational, informational unit and you said that you copied this sequentially time and time again, the question is does that accumulate enough copying errors, enough mistakes in copying, and do these accumulations of copying errors lead to the diversity of living forms that one sees on the earth. That's the general usual formulation of the Theory of Evolution . . . It's been claimed that the combination of the mistakes and the selection leads to the steady evolution of life. We looked at this quite systematically, quite carefully, in numerical terms. Checking all the numbers, rates of mutation and so on, we decided that there is no way in which that could even marginally approach the truth. On the contrary, any organized living system that developed or emerged say in the form of a microbe, 4 billion years ago, if it was allowed to copy itself time and time again, it would have destroyed itself essentially . . . For every favorable mutation there will be hundreds of unfavorable mutations.[6]

Aside from the obvious impossible odds against a particular species of life developing by random chance without design, we need to keep in mind that there are more than three million existing species of insects, together with thousands of species of mammals, reptiles, and birds. Remember, for evolution to be true, every one of these millions of individual species would have needed to beat the unimaginably large odds against the accidental evolution of its own species. To anyone who is willing to look at these odds, it is obvious that the origin of millions of separate species cannot be explained by the theory of evolution.

The Evidence of Design

The huge advances in genetic research in the last four decades have enabled scientists to unlock some of the vast mysteries of the DNA genetic code which determines the formation of every organ in your body, the color of your eyes and whether or not you will have black hair or blonde. The recent science called *Information Theory* allows us to analyse mathematically the information patterns of a written language such as English. Recently researchers studied the information patterns encoded in the double helix DNA of simple, one-celled bacteria. Incredibly, the scientists discovered that identical mathematical information patterns exist in human language as exists in DNA. The information patterns in a language such as English can be mathematically analyzed because the information forms a purposeful pattern. Obviously, by definition, information in a language is purposeful, not random. If words were thrown together by random chance, they would not convey information. When we find words in patterns of sentences expressing meaningful information, we naturally conclude that this information was created by an intelligent mind like our own.

All living biological organisms are incredibly complex. When we examine the simplest one-celled bacterial organism, we discover an almost unbelievable complexity of miniaturized design that make the technical specifications for a modern automobile look relatively simple. Biologists realize that the simplest cell is not simple at all. A cell is an enormously complex structure that is far more complicated than a computer. The smallest of cells is composed of over fifty billion atoms arranged into one hundred different proteins, together with the staggering amount of information encoded in the DNA and RNA that govern its activities, nutrition, repair, and replication. The problem for evolution is that it takes all of the above to function at all. You can't start with part of this material because everything is necessary to function as a whole.

Dr. A. E. Wilder-Smith wrote about the awesome complexity of the biological cells:

> When one considers that the entire chemical information to construct a man, elephant, frog, or an orchid was compressed into two minuscule reproductive cells [sperm

and egg nuclei], one can only be astounded. In addition to this, all the information is available on the genes to repair the body (not only to construct it) when it is injured. If one were to request an engineer to accomplish this feat of information miniaturization, one would be considered fit for the psychiatric clinic.[7]

Logically, the discovery of incredibly complex information patterns encoded within the double helix DNA genetic code governing all biological life provides overwhelming evidence that an intelligent designer must have created this DNA. Professor Geisler wrote about the significance of the DNA information patterns, "It is scientifically necessary to point to intelligence as the cause of the first living cell." The Bible reveals that this supernatural intelligence is God: "In the beginning God created the heaven and the earth" (Genesis 1:1).

When the evolutionary scientist examines fossils, he finds that very complex entities appear quite suddenly in the fossil record without any evidence of simpler forms existing before them. For example, the trilobites, which supposedly evolved in the far-distant past, are found with incredibly complex compound lens in their eyes. The only answer that fits the evidence is that each of these marvelously designed species was created in perfection by a supernatural designer.

However, when we consider the design of the human brain, we are filled with absolute awe. The human brain weighs only three pounds but this small organ is now known to be the most complicated and masterfully designed machine in the universe. The complex design of the brain is far in advance of the greatest computers ever designed or that man could ever design. Each of our brains contains up to fifty billion neurons, special communication cells, as well as an additional three hundred billion glial cells. Incredibly every one of the fifty billion neuron cells is connected with every other neuron cell. Each microscopically small neuron cell has thousands of slender dendrites which interconnect with other dendrites from other neurons. The point of connection between these dendrites is called a synapse. Some researches calculate that your brain contains up to a thousand trillion synapses. Astonishingly, recent research confirms that some neurons are communicating information to as many as

50,000 other neurons. This phenomenally complex design makes it possible for the brain to communicate amongst its billions of neurons instantaneously. As a result of this awesome design, our human brain can store and manipulate almost infinite amounts of data. The capabilities of the brain are staggering. Anyone who can declare that the marvelously complex brain evolved from a simple one-celled organism through random chance mutation is kidding.

The brilliant English astronomer Sir Fred Hoyle, the Professor of Astronomy at Cambridge University, wrote that it was virtually impossible that life has formed through evolutionary means. Professor Hoyle wrote this memorable phrase to describe the likelihood of evolution as a solution to the question of the origin of animals and man. "The chance that higher life forms might have emerged in this way is comparable with the chance that 'a tornado sweeping through a junk-yard might assemble a Boeing 747 from the materials therein.'"[8]

What About the Fossil Evidence — the Missing Links?

The theory of evolution declares that simple forms of life gradually mutated over long periods of time to produce successive and gradual changes in a species until it actually formed a new species. Charles Darwin was troubled by the fact that the new science of paleontology had failed to find a single fossil that provided any evidence of these transitional forms or "missing links." Darwin wrote, "I have asked myself whether I may not have devoted my life to a fantasy . . . I . . . am ready to cry with vexation at my blindness and presumption."[9] He also admitted, "If it could be demonstrated that any complex organism existed which could not possibly have been formed by numerous, successive, slight modifications, my theory would absolutely break down."

However, writing in 1850, Darwin optimistically predicted that, as more scientists joined the search, it was certain that thousands of these missing link fossils would show up in the fossil record and thereby prove the truth of his evolutionary theory.

Why then is not every geological formation and every stratum full of such intermediate links? Geology assuredly does not reveal any such finely graduated organic chain; and this, perhaps, is the most obvious and serious objection which can be urged against the theory. The explanation lies, as I believe, in the extreme imperfection of the geological record.[10]

In other words, Charles Darwin explained the total lack of missing links as a result of the fact that they had only begun in the 1850s to search for these transitional forms. These transitional forms are intermediate forms of life appearing in the fossils that would provide evidence of a stage between existing organisms and ones from the past. However, Charles Darwin was honest enough to admit that the absence of transitional forms or missing links would prove that his theory was false. Darwin wrote, "Why, if species have descended from other species by insensibly fine gradations, do we not everywhere see innumerable transitional forms? Why is not all nature in confusion instead of the species being, as we see them, well defined?" The obvious answer is that the well defined species found everywhere in the fossil record is precisely what you would expect to find if the theory of special creation of the universe and life by God's supernatural action is true. The Bible declares that God created each of the many species "after his kind" which is exactly what the fossil record confirms (Genesis 1:24, 25).

The evolutionists in desperation point to one single fossil, discovered in Austria, which is known as archaeopteryx. They boldly claim that this archaeopteryx fossil provides the absolute evidence of a "missing link" or transitional form between primitive dinosaurs and birds. However, despite the fact that this fossil displays a set of unusual teeth, everything else about the fossil reveals that it is a true bird, complete with fully developed wings, feathers, and warm blood. Although the presence of teeth is unusual, this in no way proves that this fossil was partly a bird and partly a dinosaur as the evolutionary textbooks proudly affirm. God has produced some very strange creatures on this planet, including the duck-billed platapus that has the duck of a bird but the other characteristics of a mammal. There is still no conclusive evidence of a single missing link, let alone the millions that must exist if the theory of evolution was true.

One hundred and fifty years after the death of Charles Darwin most evolutionary scientists are deeply embarrassed by the *total absence* of transitional forms in the fossil record. If evolution truly developed over millions of years, the planet would be filled with missing link fossils that would demonstrate the gradual series of mutations representing a continuum of change in the fossil record. However, biologists know that mutations are random, very small, and almost always harmful to the organism. This reality about the nature of mutations makes it impossible to believe that random mutations could account for the constant improvements in organisms that evolutionary theory demands. Virtually all mutations that have been observed in the laboratory have proven to be harmful, or even fatal, to the organism. Evolutionary scientists admit that more than 999 mutations in a thousand proved to be harmful or fatal.[11]

Despite the fact that tens of thousands of scientists and millions of dedicated amateurs have been searching worldwide for these missing link fossils for a century and a half they have never found a single example. Therefore, the evidence is clear that there is no evolutionary continuum. When the fossil record is carefully examined we find that it reveals both extinct species and existing organisms with clearly defined gaps between them with no transitional forms. This fossil record is precisely what you would expect to find if the Bible's account of special creation is true.

Does the Fossil Record Support the Theory of Evolution?

Dr. Stephen Jay Gold, the Professor of Geology and Paleontology at Harvard University, is a strong and eloquent supporter of evolution but he is honest enough to admit that the evidence from the fossil record does not support evolution. Dr. Gold admits that the number of transitional forms is extremely rare! How rare? The answer is Zero! They have never found one. Dr. Gold actually admits that the illustrations in the evolutionary science textbooks and documentaries are total inventions of creative artists because they do not represent scientific facts. Dr. Stephen Gold wrote the following statement in an article for *Natural History* magazine:

> The extreme rarity of transitional forms in the fossil record persists as the trade secret of paleontology. The evolutionary trees that adorn our textbooks have data only at the

tips and nodes of their branches; the rest is inference, however reasonable, not the evidence of fossils. Yet Darwin was so wedded to gradualism that he wagered his entire theory on a denial of this literal record: The geological record is extremely imperfect and this fact will to a large extent explain why we do not find interminable varieties, connecting together all the extinct and existing forms of life by the finest graduated steps. He who rejects these views on the nature of the geological record, will rightly reject my whole theory.[12]

Incredibly, Professor Gold admits that the claims of science textbooks that the fossil record supports evolution is false. "I wish only to point out that it was never 'seen' in the rocks . . . we view our data as so bad that we never see the very process we profess to study." In other words, he admits that the fossil record does not support the theory of evolution. Since special creation is the only logical alternative to the theory of evolution, the fossil record that only reveals distinct species actually supports the theory of special creation.

The Latest Evolutionary Retreat — Macroevolution or "Punctuated Evolution"

Many evolutionary scientists have admitted that the fossil record provides no evidence whatsoever of the transitional steps or missing links demanded by the evolutionary theory. However, they are now proposing a new theory of evolution called macro-evolution or "punctuated evolution," in which they admit that there is no observed change in a species for millions of years and then, suddenly, these animals change spontaneously to a new species without any gradual or transitional process. This modification of Darwin's theory is, in fact, a total repudiation of his theory of gradual accumulated mutations over millions of years of uniform processes. The real motivation behind their creation of this new theory of "punctuated evolution" is their growing embarrassment that no fossil evidence has been found that shows gradual transitions from simple forms to more complex forms of animals. According to this new theory, this rapid change in one generation accounts for the evolution without any evidence for gradual change remaining in the fossil record. This is not science!

This new theory is a vain attempt to explain the fact that *none* of the data in the fossil record provides evidence for the theory of evolution.

The Fossil Record Does Not Support Evolution

Professor Ronald R. West, Assistant Professor of Paleobiology at Kansas State University confirmed what Dr. Stephen Gold and others have finally admitted — the fossils do not support evolution at all. This fact of course is absolutely the opposite of what virtually every student in the western world was told during his or her science courses. We were constantly told in science and biology courses in high school that the fossil record "proves" the truth of evolution and totally contradicts the Bible's account of special creation. In May 1968 Professor West wrote an article in the scientific journal *Compass* in which he made the following admission:

> Contrary to what most scientists write, the fossil record does not support the Darwinian theory of evolution because it is this theory (there are several) which we use to interpret the fossil record. By doing so we are guilty of circular reasoning if we then say the fossil record supports this theory.[13]

What About the Twelve Fossils of Ape-Men Showing Evolution?

One of the most effective techniques to convince the average person that the evolutionary theory is true is the continual referral to the discovery of a series of twelve hominid fossils that were discovered during the last hundred and fifty years of paleontology. These "missing-link" ape-men creatures supposedly demonstrate the evolution from primitive apes to modern men. The evolutionists have confidently presented each of these discoveries as the promised "missing links," the ape-men which existed as the transition between our ancient ancestors, the apes and the evolution of modern version of homo sapiens. However, a detailed examination of the actual fossil record reveals an astonishing account of fraud, mistaken identification, and outright misrepresentation. Few readers of these "scientific" accounts of evolutionary discoveries of "ape-men" in the popular press know that these so-called hominids often consist of little more than a tooth, a jaw fragment, a portion of an elbow or knee joint. From this sparse material the scientist and their willing accomplices, the evolutionary textbook artists, create an imaginary illustration of a complete human being based on a single bone or tooth!

These evolutionary cavemen illustrations are accepted by the vast majority in our Western culture as overwhelming scientific proof that man developed by gradual transitions through evolutionary processes from an ancient monkey-like ancestor to the introduction of homo sapiens, modern man. However, a careful examination of the actual evidence reveals that this presentation of the evolution of man is a pure fiction based solely upon the underlying evolutionary presuppositions of the scientists. Some of these "discoveries" of small portions of bone and teeth were actually found miles away from the other bone particles that they connect together to form a complete new hominid fossil skeleton.

Other "discoveries" of hominid fossils have proven to be the bones of pigs, donkeys, or apes. Occasionally, these discoveries prove to be a complete hoax, such as the Piltdown Man that was accepted by scientists as legitimate for fifty years. Finally, detailed examination in 1953 proved that someone had placed a modern human skull cap on top of the jaw of an ape in the original site fifty years earlier. Hundreds of researchers and scientists wrote more than 500 treatises about the Piltdown Man as a direct ancestor of modern man during the fifty years that followed the discovery until it was proved that this was a cruel hoax.

Another important hominid fossil discovery is known as Ramapithecus, which was held forth as the primary "missing link" between apes and humans for nearly fifty years. However, few people understood that the whole imaginary skeleton of Ramapithecus was based solely on some teeth. Unfortunately for the evolutionary theory, someone examined the teeth and discovered that they were actually the teeth of a modern orangutan (an ape), not the teeth of an evolutionary ape-man.[14]

The Neanderthal Man convinced many that the scientists had proven the theory of the evolution. However, further research has proved that Neanderthal Man is a fossil of a modern man. The deformed skull was caused by serious damage to his brain. In fact, Neanderthal Man turns out to be a fairly recent human skeleton of a man who suffered from a vitamin D deficiency that produced the disease known as rickets which accounted for the ridges over the eyebrows and his curved leg bones. However, most people who were taught evolution in school still believe that we are descended from cavemen ancestors with heavy ridges on their eyebrows. Not one of the other fossilized skeletons have these raised eyebrows (that resulted from the disease of rickets). "Scientists have concluded that all of the so-called primitive features of Neanderthal people were due to pathological conditions, or diseases."[15]

My personal favorite character in the imaginary evolutionary lineup is the so-called Nebraska Man whose remains were discovered in 1922 in the western portion of the state of Nebraska. The head of the American Museum of History, Dr. Henry F. Osborn, announced that this was evidence of the "missing link" between ancient chimpanzees, Java Man and modern man. Detailed drawings of this illustrious caveman ancestor (and his wife!) with his club were printed in various publications including the *Illustrated London Times* in 1922. However, the artists had to create the entire skeleton, muscles, face, skull, and hair out of their pure imagination because the only thing the scientist actually found was *a single tooth*! The punch line to this sad evolutionary joke is that the single tooth finally turned out to be the tooth of an extinct pig.[16]

The discovery of another missing link, the "Lucy" found in Ethiopia, supposedly provided powerful evidence of another link in the evolution of man. The scientists announced that Lucy was about three and a half feet high, walked erect, and lived over three million years ago. Lucy was described as an early ancestor of modern humans. They catalogued Lucy as *"Australopithecus afaarensis."* However, few people knew that the knee joint used by the scientists to prove that Lucy walked upright as a human rather than an ape was found two miles away from the original discovery of bones. Only a fool would believe that this knee joint was positively related to the rest of her bones which were found two miles away. The scientists wisely refrained from telling the public about this small detail. It is well known in scientific circles that Lucy is another fiction in the ongoing tale of evolution. "Lucy — when they required a knee joint to prove that Lucy walked upright, they used one found more than 200 feet lower in the (earth) and more than two miles away."[17]

Further digging at the "Lucy" site found fossilized bones of extremely ape-like creatures with chimpanzee-sized forearms that made it very likely that these creatures walked on four feet as opposed to the erect walking on two feet by humans (*Nature*, 368:449–451 1994.). One of the most famous of the paleontologists is Richard Leakey, the son of the eminent evolutionary scientists Louis and Mary Leakey. Dr. Richard Leakey identified Lucy as a hominoid, a definite ancestor of mankind. However, Richard Leakey admitted that the paleontologists are often working from their imagination more than from the actual fossil evidence, which is usually so meager. "Our task is not unlike attempting to assemble a 3-dimensional jigsaw puzzle in which most of the pieces are missing, and those few bits which are at hand are broken!" Some of the scientists have candidly admitted that their preconceived opinions in favor of evolution govern to a great degree the conclusions they reach about their fossil evidence. Dr. Gareth Nelson of the American Museum of Natural History admitted this in the following statement. "We've got to have some ancestors. We'll pick those. Why? Because we know they have to be there, and these are the best candidates. That's by and large the way it has worked. I am not exaggerating."[18]

Nine of the Twelve "Missing Links" Have Been Proven to be Apes

An analysis of the so-called "missing link" evidence showing the evolutionary development of man from apes includes twelve supposed hominid fossils presented by evolutionary scientists as evidence of the gradual evolutionary transition from apes to man. However, recent research had proven that nine of these twelve examples of ape-men are actually extinct forms of apes or monkeys and have no relationship to modern humans. Significantly, these nine "missing link" fossil examples that have proven to be extinct apes or monkeys were found in geographic areas where apes and monkeys skeletons are found in abundance. These skeleton fragments are often deformed by the same common diseases experienced by people in past centuries including rickets, starvation, Paget's disease, syphilis, and arthritis. Many of these hominid skulls were believed to be ancient ape-men because the scientists did not know that the normal range of size for modern human skulls included the same small size as found in the skulls of the these so-called ape-men. Scientists have found that modern human skeletons throughout the world differ markedly in the size of the skull and various bones, but they are still modern humans. There is a fairly wide range of skull sizes in modern humans which accounts for the differences discovered in the skull fragments that scientists previously suggested belonged to a previous ape-man.

The nine "missing links" have been found to be fossils of well known representatives of the monkey or ape family of mammals. Each of these fossils were found in areas where monkeys and apes have lived for thousands of years. The nine so-called hominids (as evolutionary scientists call them) are listed as follows: 1. Pliopithecus; 2. Proconsu; 3. Dryopithecus; 4. Oreopithecus; 5. Ramipithecus; 6. Australopithecus Africanus; 7. Australopithecus Robustus; 8. Australopithecus Boisei; 9. Australopithecus Afarensis (Lucy).

The Remaining Three "Missing Links" are Proven to be Modern Humans

The remaining three "missing links" presented by evolutionists have recently been proven to be actual fossil remains of modern humans with no significant differences from our present human skeletons. These three modern human skeletons were found in areas where monkeys and apes never existed. These three fossilized remains that have been proven to belong to modern humans included:

1. *Homo Erectus*: His name refers to the demonstrated fact that he walked erect. The only reason evolutionists suggested he was a sub-human was the fact that this particular specimen had a somewhat smaller brain size than some modern humans. However, it has now been proven that the brain of Homo Erectus was almost the average size of most European men today.

2. *Neanderthal Man*: As mentioned earlier, this fossil was examined by medical experts and found to be a modern human being whose brain was deformed by the disease of arthritis deformans in addition to suffering ridges on the brow plus deformed legs as a result of prolonged vitamin D deficiency or rickets.

3. *Cro Magnon Man*: This fossil is indistinguishable from modern man. The sole reason for supposing that it was that of a

primitive cave man was the fact that it was found near a series of cave drawings that were considered primitive.

The final result of this analysis of the evidence regarding these missing links of evolutionary evidence, for the transition from apes to modern man, is that the evidence for evolution itself is missing. The evolutionary scientists have failed to find a single genuine transitional form between apes and men despite their constant search during the last 150 years.

The Anthropic Principle

In the last few decades scientists have increased their understanding of the known universe through massive additions to our scientific knowledge in a variety of fields including astrophysics, quantum physics, and microbiological genetic research. The sum total of our scientific knowledge is now doubling every twenty-four months — a staggering increase in information unprecedented in human history. We are surely witnessing the fulfillment of the curious prediction of the prophet Daniel made twenty-five centuries ago: "Seal the book, even to the time of the end: many shall run to and fro, and knowledge shall be increased" (Daniel 12:4).

Among the new discoveries made by science recently, one of the most fascinating is called the anthropic principle. This anthropic principle simply concludes that a staggering number of scientific variables such as the composition of our atmosphere, the distance from the sun, the chemical composition of soil are precisely what is necessary for life to exist and prosper.

Recent discoveries in the field of astronomy, for example, prove that human life could not survive if our solar system was even slightly different. An astronomer, Dr. Jastrow, declared that even a small increase in the nuclear forces that hold together all atoms would result in a universe of stars composed primarily of helium instead of the present universe in which stars are made of hydrogen. In a universe with slightly increased nuclear forces the helium stars would have burned up much more quickly than our hydrogen stars. If the nuclear forces were slightly less, the carbon atoms would not have formed. Without carbon atoms, life could not exist.

The same anthropic principle can be seen in the other scientific variables such as the force of gravity which would make life impossible if the force were either much greater or much less. The communication between every one of the trillion cells in our body is based on the earth's magnetic field. Therefore, a reduction of the strength of this magnetic field beyond a certain level would make biological life impossible. Life could not exist if our earth was either too close or too far from the sun which provides the necessities of life through a complete spectrum of radiation including visible light. The twenty-four hour rotation of our planet facilitates life. If the planet did not rotate one half of the globe would be desolate under the constant glare of the sun and the other half would freeze in perpetual darkness. In sum total, the scientists have concluded that there are dozens of these scientific factors that are precisely correct to facilitate life on this planet.

Professor Jastrow suggests that "the universe was constructed within very narrow limits, in such a way that man could dwell in it."[19] In other words, this evidence in support of the anthropic principle strongly argues that our universe and earth were designed for the life of man by an intelligent and supernaturally powerful Creator. The evidence of brilliant design demands that an intelligent Designer must have created that design, namely God. The recent discoveries of science provide overwhelming evidence that the simplistic view of the atheists that our universe and life could have arisen by random chance over billions of years is scientifically false. In summary these scientific discoveries demolish the evolutionary theory of the formation of life by random chance. These discoveries provide incontrovertible evidence that an intelligent Creator purposely designed and created both the universe and life itself.

Dr. Chandra Wickramasinghe suggested that the anthropic principle strongly supported the theory of special creation, as opposed to evolution. When he was asked if his scientific research proved that Charles Darwin's theory of evolution was fatally flawed, he agreed. When asked how he would evaluate the scientific arguments of the Creationists, who suggest that only God could have created the universe and life itself, Dr. Wickramasinghe responded, "You mean the arguments that are justifications of their position? I think they have a very good case by and large."[20]

The Strong Bias of Scientist and Educators
Towards Evolution

In the light of the overwhelming scientific evidence that evolution is not supported by the fossil record and that evolution is mathematically impossible the average reader must wonder why evolution has survived for so long as a universally taught theory. I believe the answer lies in the strong desire by many scientists and educators to escape the consequences of a belief in God and the truth that each of us has an appointment to meet God as our judge following our death. Supporters of evolution understand very clearly that, if evolution is false, then the only possible logical explanation for this universe and the complexity of life is that there is a God who has created us. This alternative conclusion is so unthinkable to many scientists that they will desparately hold onto the faltering theory of evolution to their dying day despite the absence of evidence to support it. Evolutionary scientist Arthur Keith has admitted: "Evolution is unproved and unprovable. We believe it only because the only alternative is special creation which is unthinkable."[21] In reality, these scientists demonstrate a blind faith in their scientific religion of evolution that will ignore all evidence that contradicts their theory. Their realization of the scientific weakness of evolution is the real reason evolutionists are so determined to keep the theory of special creation out of the schools and universites. Evolution can only survive if no one is allowed to challenge it with the facts.

Some evolutionist are honest enough to admit that evolution is a matter of faith as opposed to pure science. Professor G. A. Rerkut of the University of Southampton (London) expressed his conclusion regarding the attitudes of scientists on biogenesis (evolution): "It is therefore a matter of faith on the part of the biologist that biogenesis did occur and he can choose whatever method of biogenesis happens to suit him personally; the evidence for what did happen is not available."[22]

Dr. Henry Morris was a firm believer in evolution until he began to examine the evidence critically for himself. He soon realized that the whole theory was not supported by scientific evidence at all but that evolution had become a new religion for those who wished to escape the consequences of the truth of the Bible about a personal God, salvation, and judgment.

> Many . . . believe in evolution for the simple reason that they think science has proven it to be a 'fact' and, therefore, it must be accepted . . . In recent years, a great many people . . . having finally been persuaded to make a real examination of the problem of evolution, have become convinced of its fallacy and are now convinced anti-evolutionists."

In the last decade numerous evolutionists have admitted that the actual scientific evidence in the fossil record does not support the theory of evolution. Some scientists have acknowledged that they have not found any evidence at all in the fossil record of animals with partially developed organs such as legs, brains or eyes. Yet their theory of evolution, if true, demands that the fossil record must contain millions of such examples.

A strong supporter of the theory of evolution, T. L. Moor, wrote, "The more one studies paleontology, the more certain one becomes that evolution is based on faith alone."[23] Another evolutionist, Dr. Miles Eldredge, has written, "We paleontologists have said that the history of life supports (the story of gradual adaptive change), all the while really knowing that it does not."[24] Another evolutionist scientist, Dr. Solly Zuckerman admitted the truth when she wrote, "(the record of reckless speculation of human origins) is so astonishing that it is legitimate to ask whether much science is yet to be found in this field at all."[25]

Dr. Paul Davies wrote about his personal beliefs and his estimate of the views of other physicists in a fascinating article entitled "The Christian Perspective of a Scientist" in the academic magazine *New Scientist.* Dr. Davies wrote, "The temptation to believe that the Universe is the product of some sort of design, a manifestation of subtle aesthetic and mathematical judgement, is overwhelming. The belief that there is 'something behind it all' is one that I personally share with, I suspect, a majority of physicists" (Paul Davies, *New Scientist*, June 1983, p. 638). Another evolutionist, D. M. S. Watson, admitted: "Evolution itself is accepted by zoologists, not because it has been observed to occur or can be proved by logical coherent evidence, but because the only alternative — special creation — is clearly incredible."[26]

The Biblical Flood of Noah

The Bible's account of a worldwide Flood provides an alternative explanation for much of the geological and fossil evidence that has been produced by scientists in support of their theory of evolution. For those who wish to study the geological evidence for the Flood in depth, I strongly recommend Dr. Henry Morris's excellent study *Scientific Creationism* and Dr. John C. Whitcomb's book *The World That Perished*. Naturally, the evolutionary scientists reject out of hand the theory that the biblical account of the Flood is a true description of an historical geological event. However, a worldwide flood would have produced ideal conditions to create massive numbers of fossils in sedimentary rock.

The Evidence For Noah's Flood in the Ancient Traditions

Obviously, if a worldwide flood actually occurred as the Bible affirms, such a devastating event would leave an indelible mark on the historical memory of various races throughout the world. In addition to the written account in the Bible we would expect to find widespread traditions of a flood in many nations. The Scottish geologist Hugh Miller searched the historical records and found an astonishingly number of Flood accounts among widely dispersed nations and tribal groups throughout the world.[27] Evolutionary critics of the Bible's Flood account often suggest that if there is any truth to the Flood story, then it must have been a local flood. However, the Bible's description of the flood reaching to the heights of the highest mountains proves that Moses was recording a worldwide flood. In addition, a local flood would not have justified the building of the Ark. Why not just instruct Noah's family to migrate to the high mountains to escape a local flood? The area of Mesopotamia is quite flat, which means a flood would inevitably cover a vast area.

Some critics suggest that the Bible's account could not be accurate because Mount Everest and other high mountains now reach to a vast height of several miles above sea level. Does this mean the waters reached many miles in depth? The answer is found in the fact that the Bible suggests that massive geological changes took place as a result of the Flood both during and after that event. Therefore, it is entirely possible that the world before the Flood did not possess the massive mile-high mountains that exist today. Marine scientists have confirmed that there is enough water in the oceans of the world to cover the entire globe to a depth exceeding one mile if the earth was smooth with no deep ocean trenches and no high mountains. Therefore there is ample water to accomplish the Bible's account of a worldwide flood. Furthermore, the explorers and sociologists during the last two centuries discovered that virtually every nation and tribe on earth possesses an ancient tradition of a worldwide flood, the survival of a man and his family with animals in a large boat, as well as stories about the replenishing of the human race following the deluge.

The Babylonian Story of the Noah and the Flood

Beyond doubt the most remarkable flood tradition outside the Bible's own account is found in the ancient tablets of Babylon that were miraculously discovered in the last century during excavations in ancient Mesopotamia. Several years ago I was able to examine the copy of the Deluge Tablet on display at the British Museum in London. Many scholars believe that this four thousand year-old Babylonian clay tablet may be one of the most important inscriptions yet discovered. The Deluge Tablet is the eleventh book of the larger Chaldean *Epic of Gilgamesh*. It has been dated approximately 2200 B.C. Gilgamesh is another name for Nimrod, a name that appears in the biblical Genesis account. This Babylonian account of the Flood is found in the eleventh book of the epic poem because the eleventh month of the ancient Babylonian year was known as the "Month of the Curse of Rain." This month was also known as the "Month of Destruction," and corresponds to the eleventh sign in the Babylonian astrology Zodiac, the sign of Aquarius, the sign associated with fish and water. In this epic poem, the story of the Flood is told to Gilgamesh by his ancestor Nuh-Napishtim, also called Atrahasis, "the very wise or pious" (the Chaldean Noah).

This account of the Flood is of tremendous importance because it contains a number of startling parallels to the biblical account of the Flood as found in the book of Genesis. The Flood, with its destruction of virtually the complete animal kingdom and the death of every human on earth except for Noah's family, would obviously have left its mark on the consciousness of mankind. If such a cataclysmic event actually occurred, you would expect to find a universal race memory of the Flood in the ancient histories and literature of the oldest human cultures. In addition to the detailed biblical account recorded by Moses in the book of Genesis, scholars have discovered a surprising number of Flood accounts in the histories of other peoples that display an astonishing number of parallels with the biblical account. While these nonbiblical accounts naturally contain a number of variations from the Genesis account, the discovery of numerous key points in these stories that parallel the Flood story provide strong evidence that this historical event truly occurred as recorded in the Bible.

Parallels Between the Babylonian Deluge Tablet and the Genesis Flood

In the Deluge Tablet in the *Epic of Gilgamesh* the flood is a punishment of the "gods" for man's sin, exactly as described in the Genesis account. Atrahasis (the Chaldean Noah) and his family were worshippers of Ia, the god of deep waters. The "gods" decreed a flood to punish mankind's sins and overwhelming violence ("the city was full of violence"), as also described in Genesis. Significantly, both accounts record these key events occurring in the same geographical area. Atrahasis (Noah) was commanded to build a ship to protect himself, his family, (and the ship builders), as well as a variety of animals. The ship (ark) was built with a deck house or covering and was covered with bitumen (pitch) both inside and outside exactly as Genesis described ("within and without"). The rainfall lasted only six days and nights in the Babylonian epic as opposed to the Bible's account of "forty days and forty nights."

It is fascinating to note that both accounts record that Atrahasis (Noah) sent forth three birds in succession to ascertain the conditions outside the ark. In both accounts three birds were sent forth from the ark, including a raven and a dove. Both stories record that the last bird failed to return, indicating that it had found a safe home. The two flood accounts record that the ark finally rested on a mountain top at which point the survivors come forth from the ark to offer sacrifice to God. Both histories record that God (or the gods) promised to never again punish mankind with a flood. In the conclusion of the Gilgamesh account, Atrahasis (Noah) and his wife begin to rebuild mankind in a renewed land in what is now known as Iraq-Iran. This is paralleled in the Genesis account as Noah and his family begin to replenish the earth following their departure from the ark. Some of the most important confirmations of the statements found in the Genesis account that are also found in the Babylonian Flood account as noted below in italics.

The Deluge Epic of Gilgamesh

(Key Phrases from the 11th Tablet of the Epic of Nimrod)
(Haupt, Nimrod-Efos, No. 70.)
Nuh-napishtim (the Chaldean Noah) saith to him, even to
    Gilgamesh (Nimrod);
Let me unfold to thee, Gilgamesh, a secret story,
And the decree of the gods let me tell thee
Shurippak, a city thou knowest,
On the bank of Euphrates it lieth;
That city was full of violence, and the gods within it,
To make a flood their heart urged them, even the mighty gods.

Man of Shurippak, son of Ubara-Tutu,
Pull down the house, *build a ship.*
Leave goods, seek life.
Property forsake, and life preserve.
Cause seed of life of every sort to go up into the ship.
The ship which thou shalt build . . .

I will [go] down to the Ocean, [and] with my, [Lord] will I dwell
[Upon] you it will rain heavily . . .

I laid down its form, I figured (or fashioned) it:
    I chose a mast (or rudder-pole), and supplied what was necessary:
Six sars of bitumen I poured over the outside,
Three sars of bitumen [I poured over] the inside . . .

With all that I had of seed of life of every sort [I freighted it] . . .
I put on board all my family and my clan;
Cattle of the field, wild beasts of the field,
all the craftsmen, I put on board . . .

When the Lord of Storm at even tide causeth the heavens to rain
  heavily,
"Enter into the ship, and shut thy door." That time came:
The Lord of Storm at even tide caused the heavens to rain heavily.
I dreaded the appearance of day;
I was afraid of beholding day:
I entered the ship and shut me my door . . .

When the seventh day came, storm (and) flood ceased the battle . . .
The sea lulled, the blast fell, the flood ceased.
I looked for the people, with a cry of lamentation;
But all mankind had turned again to clay:
The tilled land was become like the waste.
I opened the window, and daylight fell upon my cheeks . . .
The mountain of the country of Nizir caught the ship . . .
But when the seventh day was come,
I brought out a dove (and) let it go.
The dove went to and fro, but found no foothold, and returned.
Then I brought out a swallow (and) let it go.
The swallow went to and fro, but found no foothold, and returned.
Then I brought out a raven (and) let it go: The raven went off,
noticed the drying of the water, and feeding, wading, croaking, returned
  not.
Then I brought out (everything) to the four winds, offered victims
  (sacrifices)
Made an offering of incense on the mountain top. . .

Nuh-napishtim shall dwell far away, at the mouth of the rivers
Then they took me, and made me dwell far away, at the mouth
  of the rivers
(the site of Paradise at the mouth of the four rivers including
  Euphrates).

Other Historical Traditions of a Worldwide Flood

Numerous additional historical accounts of the Flood are
found in the traditions of every one of the six inhabited continents.
These independent traditions strongly support the truthfulness of
the Bible's account.

The Phrygian Flood Account

For example, one of the most interesting of the Flood traditions is the Phyrgrian flood tradition that tells us that someone named Nannakos (Enoch), who reached the age of 300, predicted the coming Flood and wept tears in anticipation of the coming deluge. This parallels the biblical account in Genesis where the righteous man Enoch, who walked with God, became the father of a son named Methusalah at the age of 65 and lived for 300 more years. whose His son's name "Methusalah" means "After he goes, it happens." The tradition of the Jewish sages is that Methusalah died on the very day the Flood began. However, the most interesting part of the Phrygian flood account is the fact that a Medal of Apamea (A.D. 201-210) was struck in the mint of Phrygia during the reign of the Roman emperor Septimius Severus which illustrates the Flood account in detail.

The Phrygian Medal of Apamea Showing Noah's Ark

This wonderful Medal of Apamea provides powerful historical confirmation of the Flood from ancient times. Several of these fascinating medals have been found that illustrate a rectangular barge-like ark floating in the water. Through a window of the ark we can see the image of two people, a man and woman. It is fascinating to note that a bird is seen resting on the roof of the ark while another bird is seen flying back to the ark with a branch in its feet exactly as described in the biblical account in Genesis 8:11. Another portion of the medal illustrates the same two people leaving the ark to walk on dry land. Incredibly, several of these Phrygian medals bear an additional inscription containing the Greek letters NΩ or NΩE which means "After the Flood" written on the sides of the ark as illustrated in the medal shown above. This two thousand year-old medal provides powerful historical evidence that the biblical account of the Flood is true.

Other examples of flood traditions are found in Greece where the historian Pindar wrote about their memory of the flood around the fifth century before Christ. The Roman writer Ovid confirmed these ancient flood traditions in which the fountains of the deep were opened to unleash the flood waters that drowned almost the whole race of mankind. Aside from the Greeks and Romans we find few ancient European legends of the Flood for the simple reason that the widespread distribution of the Bible's account of Noah's Flood throughout Europe, as a result of the efforts of Christian missionaries in the early centuries of this era, replaced whatever independent ancient traditions remained about the Flood with the true biblical account from Genesis.

Many of these flood traditions were recorded by the eminent sociologist Professor James George Frazer in his fascinating book *Folk-Lore in the Old Testament* [28]. The North American Athapascan Indian tribes that lived on the West Coast tell about an ancient flood in which the rains continued until the earth was totally covered with water. All animals and birds died in the subsequent flood. Another Indian tribe, the Papago Indians of Arizona, have a tradition that God made man from some clay. When the great flood came, a man named Montezuma and a coyote who predicted the flood survived in a large boat which he built on a mountain. When the flood was over, Montezuma sent the coyote to search the land to verify the water had receded. The Mongolian peoples of northern Asia also have a strong flood tradition.

The Sudanese tribes in East Africa believe there was a massive flood in which a leader named Noh survived. The Hawaiian natives have a tradition that after mankind developed from one man the people became evil and disobeyed God. When the flood came, one righteous man named Nu-u survived with his family by building a huge canoe and filling it with plants and animals. The Mexican natives tell the story that a man named Coxcox saved himself, his family, his animals, and grain from the great flood by building a huge boat. When the waters receded, Coxcox sent out a vulture which did not return because it ate the floating carcasses. Then he sent other birds including a hummingbird that returned with a twig with leaves. The Indian tribes of Alaska relate that their tribal father was warned in a dream of the coming flood. He build a large boat in which he saved his family and all of the animals by floating for many moons on the flood waters.

Sociologists have discovered flood traditions involving boats and animals in the South Sea islands, including Polynesia, Tahiti, New Zealand, and New Guinea. The peoples of India possess strong flood traditions in which a righteous man with the name Manu received a warning that a great flood was coming. He was commanded to build a great ship and fill it with foods of all kinds. When the flood waters came, God commanded Manu to embark upon the ship with seven other people together with ample provisions including all seeds. Manu and his seven companions survived the flood and landed on the highest mountain in the Himalayas. Later Manu became the father of the new race of mankind. The startling parallels to the biblical account include the righteousness of the leader, eight survivors, a large boat, a long flood, the landing on a mountain, together with replenishing the human race.

Professor Hugh Miller added a remarkable detail from this Indian flood tradition in the Sanskrit literature that appeared more than six centuries before the birth of Christ. This righteous Manu became drunk after drinking mead wine and fell asleep naked. Charma, one of his three sons, discovering his naked father, called his brothers to witness his father's drunken shame. The Indian tradition records that the two responsible brothers took some clothes and respectfully covered their father's nakedness. When Manu awakened from his drunkenness, he immediately recognized that Charma had despised him. As a result, Manu cursed his sinful son Charma by declaring, "Thou shall be a servant of servants." This astonishing parallel with the details of the biblical account of Noah's Flood is verified by Hugh Miller's detailed research.

In China they tell the story of a universal flood that destroyed all of mankind with the exception of Fah-he and his family who survived in a boat. Furthermore the Chinese record that Fah-he survived with his wife, his three sons and their wives, precisely eight people as found in the Genesis account. The ancient Egyptian historian Manetho recorded the Egyptian flood tradition in his book written in 250 B.C. A worldwide flood destroyed everyone except Toth and his family. It is fascinating that the Egyptian priest celebrated Toth's survival of this flood by launching a sacred ark onto the sea on the 17th day of Athyr, the same day recorded in the Bible.

The discovery in the last two centuries that virtually every nation and tribe on earth have deeply held traditions of a world-wide flood in the ancient past that destroyed most of humanity save a man and his family who were preserved in a large boat filled with animals and food provides a wonderful confirmation of the truthfulness of the biblical account of Noah's Flood. It is impossible to explain why widely dispersed peoples throughout the globe would simultaneously develop such an astonishing story of a worldwide flood with such agreement in the precise details unless a real historical event actually occurred in the distant past.

Ultimately, when we consider the truthfulness of the biblical account of the Flood we need to examine the evidence from both the Bible and from recent discoveries from the scientists that provide fascinating evidence about the earliest ages of mankind. In this connection we should consider this question carefully: "Why not consider the possibility that life is what it so evidently seems to be, the product of creative intelligence? Science would not come to an end, because the task would remain of deciphering the languages in which genetic information is communicated, and in general finding out how the whole system works. What scientists would lose is not an inspiring research program, but the illusion of total mastery of nature. They would have to face the possibility that beyond the natural world there is a further reality which transcends science."[29]

In conclusion, the inspired Word of God commands us to follow the words of our Lord and Saviour who instructs us as follows:

> If any of you lack wisdom, let him ask of God, that giveth to all men liberally, and upbraideth not; and it shall be given him. But let him ask in faith, nothing wavering. For he that wavereth is like a wave of the sea driven with the wind and tossed. For let not that man think that he shall receive any thing of the Lord. A double minded man is unstable in all his ways (James 1:5–8).

Finally, the Bible tells us in the clearest language that God is the Creator of both our universe and mankind. The Scriptures instruct us to consider the inspired words of the Bible that command us to consider these instructions from the Word of God:

> For the wrath of God is revealed from heaven against all ungodliness and unrighteousness of men, who suppress the truth in unrighteousness; because that which may be known of God is manifest in them; for God hath shewed it unto them. For the invisible things of Him from the creation of the world are clearly seen, being understood by the things that are made, even His eternal power and Godhead; so that they are without excuse: because that, when they knew God, they glorified Him not as God, neither were thankful; but became vain in their imaginations, and their foolish heart was darkened. Professing themselves to be wise, they became fools. (Romans, 1:18–22).

Notes

1. Roy Abraham Varghese, ed., *The Intellectuals Speak Out About God* (Chicago: Regnery Gateway, 1984) 100–103.

2. Chandra Wickramasinghe, *The Intellectuals Speak Out About God* (Chicago: Regnery Gateway, 1984) 25–26.

3. B. G. Ranganathan, *Origins?* (Carlisle: The Banner of Truth Trust, 1988) 11.

4. David Humphreys, speech, "Evidence for a Creator," University of Waterloo, Canada, July 12. 1997.

5. Chandra Wickramasinghe, *The Intellectuals Speak Out About God* (Chicago: Regnery Gateway, 1984) 25–29.

6. Chandra Wickramasinghe, The *Intellectuals Speak Out About God* (Chicago: Regnery Gateway, 1984) 29.

7. A. E. Wilder-Smith, *The Illustrated Origins Answer Book* (Gilbert, AZ: Eden Communications, 1995) 25.

8. Fred Hoyle, "Hoyle on Evolution," *Nature*, vol. 294 (12 November 1981) 105.

9. Wendt, Herbert, *From Ape to Man* (New York: The Bubbs Merril Co., 1972) 59.

10. Charles Darwin, *The Origin of Species* (London: J. M. Dent & Sons Ltd., 1971) 292–293.

11. Henry, M. Morris, *Evolution and the Modern Christian* (Phillipsburg, NJ: Presbyterian and Reformed Publishing Co., 1988).

12. Jay Gold Stephen, *Natural History* (May 1977) 14.

13. Ronald R. West, *Compass*, vol. 45 (1968) 216.

14. Duane T. Gish, *Evolution: The Fossils still say No!* (El Cajon, CA.: Institute For Creation Research, 1995) 326.

15. Duane T. Gish, *The Amazing Story of Creation from Science and the Bible* (El Cajon, CA: Institute for Creation Research, 1990) 81.

16. Duane T. Gish, *Evolution: The Fossils still say No!* (El Cajon, CA.: Institute For Creation Research, 1995) 326.

17. Duane T. Gish, *The Amazing Story of Creation from Science and the Bible* (El Cajon, CA: Institute for Creation Research, 1990) 83.

18. Garth Nelson, *Lucy's Child* (New York: William Morrow and Co., 1989) 74.

19. Robert Jastrow, *The Intellectuals Speak Out About God* (Chicago: Regnery Gateway, 1984) 100–103.

20. Chandra Wickramasinghe, *The Intellectuals Speak Out About God* (Chicago: Regnery Gateway, 1984) 36.

21. B. G. Ranganathan, *Origins?* (Carlisle: The Banner of Truth Trust, 1988) 22.

22. G. A. Rerkut, *Implications of Evolution* (London: Pergamon Press, 1960) 150.

23. B. G. Ranganathan, *Origins?* (Carlisle, PA: The Banner of Truth Trust, 1988) 22.

24. Philip Johnson, *Darwin on Trial* (Washington, D.C.: Regnery Gateway, 1991) 59.

25. Philip Johnson, *Darwin on Trial* (Washington, D.C.: Regnery Gateway, 1991) 82.

26. D. M. S. Watson, B. G. Ranganathan, *Origins?* (Carlisle: The Banner of Truth Trust, 1988) 22.

27. Hugh Miller, *The Footprints of the Creator* (New York: Robert Carter and Brothers, 1881).

28. James George Frazer, *Folk-Lore in the Old Testament* (London: MacMillan and Co., Ltd., 1919).

29. Phillip Johnson, *Darwin on Trial* (Washington, D.C.: Regnery Gateway, 1991) 110.

15

Who Do You Say That I Am?

When Jesus came into the coasts of Caesarea Philippi, he asked his disciples, saying, Whom do men say that I the Son of man am? And they said, Some say that thou art John the Baptist: some, Elias; and others, Jeremias, or one of the prophets. He saith unto them, But whom say ye that I am? And Simon Peter answered and said, Thou art the Christ, the Son of the living God.   (Matthew 16:13–16)

"Whom say you that I am?" This question by Jesus Christ is the most fundamental and important question you and I will ever answer. Upon our answer to that question lies our present happiness, the forgiveness for our sins, and our eternal reconciliation with God in heaven. If we reject the claims of Jesus as the true Son of God, we will have, in effect, chosen to be our own God — our own supreme being in our life. The eternal consequences of such a choice are beyond the scope of human language to express. If we reject the only salvation that God offers to us, then we will end our lives as unrepentant sinners, and will have chosen to go to our deaths in permanent rebellion against God.

Throughout the pages of the Scriptures, we read the claim that Jesus is the Messiah, the Son of God. Furthermore, the Bible declares that His death on the Cross is the only acceptable sacrifice that will pay the full price of our sins. The apostle Paul warns mankind of this in his epistle to the church at Rome, "For the wages of sin is death; but the gift of God is eternal life through Jesus Christ our Lord" (Romans 6:23). As a result of our sins, each of us has walked away from God in disobedience. The problem is this: How can we ever be reconciled to a holy God when we have been rebelling against God all our lives? Every person who has lived on earth has rebelled against God and lived their life as a sinner. The apostle Paul declared, "For all have sinned, and come short of the glory of God" (Romans 3:23).

There is nothing in our sinful nature that would make it possible for us to totally reform and stop sinning. Even if the impossible occurred, we would still be barred from the gates of heaven because of our past sins. The only way to live with God in heaven after this sinful life is to somehow become holy. But it is impossible for us to accomplish this on our own. Paul declared that the only way we would "see the Lord" was to walk in "holiness." "Follow peace with all men, and holiness, without which no man shall see the Lord" (Hebrews 12:14).

God knew that the only way we could ever be reconciled to Him and become capable of entering heaven forever was to transform those of us willing to repent of our sins. Paul explained God's purpose in bringing salvation to those who would confess their sins in this passage: "To the end he may stablish your hearts unblameable in holiness before God, even our Father, at the coming of our Lord Jesus Christ with all his saints" (1 Thessalonians 3:13).

One of the most important decisions a person must make is what you will do with the written revelation of God found in the Bible. Your decision as to whether or not the Bible is truly the inspired Word of God will profoundly affect every other area of your life. If the Bible is true, then we are accountable to Jesus Christ, and He will judge each of us at the end of our life. However, if the Bible is not the inspired Word of God, one could ignore its commands and warnings about heaven and hell. In the absence of the written revelation found in the Word of God, those who search for ultimate truth are lost and without any hope of finding it.

In light of the overwhelming evidence presented in *The Handwriting of God* regarding the inspiration and authority of the Bible, any unbiased person can conclude that only God could have produced the Bible. The evidence in this book proves that the

Scriptures contain scientific, archeological, and historical information that only God could produce. However, there are many people who will still state that they don't believe the claims of the Bible. The problem with those readers who still refuse to acknowledge the evidence for inspiration is not one of conviction; rather it is their lack of willingness to accept information that challenges their long-held positions. It is extremely difficult for most people to abandon their previously held agnostic positions. After years of defending such a liberal position, it is very hard to admit fallibility and submit to the truth. The problem is not an alternative explanation for creation; rather, it is a fear of how the acceptance of this information will mandate a change in their daily life.

Those who have previously rejected God and the Bible have made a huge emotional and intellectual investment in their declared position of agnosticism or rejection of the Scriptures. When they are faced with the evidence that proves the Bible is inspired by God, they naturally feel threatened because they must think seriously about God and their responsibility to Him. Many people have never seriously considered the claims of the Gospels about Jesus Christ. They have never even thought about the matter. Their denial of the authority of the Bible has shielded them against asking questions such as: What if the Bible is true? What if there truly is a heaven and hell? However, in light of the evidence presented in this book, we need to carefully consider the implications. If the Bible is truly the Word of God, then every one of us will stand before Jesus Christ at the end of our life to answer the question: Who do you say that I am?

On that day, those who have accepted Christ's salvation through His sacrifice on the cross will bow their knees willingly to Jesus knowing that their sins are forgiven by God. Their destiny will be to live joyfully with Christ forever in heaven. However, those who have chosen to reject the Bible and Christ's salvation will be forced by their irrevocable decision to bear punishment in hell forever. Many in our modern society are offended by the fact that the Bible says that there is only one possible way to be saved. However, the apostle Paul spoke about the absolute necessity of faith in Jesus Christ: "Neither is there salvation in any other: for there is none other name under heaven given among men, whereby we must be saved" (Acts 4:12). This declaration of Paul runs counter to the natural inclination of mankind to believe that all religions are equally true and that "all roads lead to Rome."

Many suggest that, as long as one is sincere, they will make it to heaven. This is a lie from the pit of hell. The Word of God declares that sincerity is not enough. If you are sincere in your faith, but have chosen to place your faith in a false religion, then you are sincerely wrong and lost for eternity. Why would Jesus Christ have willingly gone to the Cross for your sins if there were other equally valid ways to be reconciled to God?

One of the religious leaders of Israel named Nicodemus came to Jesus secretly one night to ask Him how he could be assured of salvation. The gospel of John records the answers Jesus gave to Nicodemus. Jesus told him, "Ye must be born again" (John 3:7). He explained to Nicodemus, "Whosoever believeth in him should not perish, but have eternal life. For God so loved the world, that he gave his only begotten Son, that whosoever believeth in him should not perish, but have everlasting life" (John 3:15–16). Every one of us is a sinner who therefore stands condemned by God. Jesus said, "He that believeth on him is not condemned: but he that believeth not is condemned already, because he hath not believed in the name of the only begotten Son of God" (John 3:18).

Your decision to accept Jesus Christ as your personal Savior is the most important decision you will ever make. This commitment will lift the guilt of sin from your heart and give you an abundant new life in Jesus. However, the Lord Jesus Christ asks His disciples to "follow Me." That decision and commitment will change your life forever. Your commitment to Christ will transform your life into one of joy, peace, and spiritual purpose beyond anything you have ever known. Jesus challenges each of us to consider the choices of life in terms of eternity, "For what shall it profit a man, if he shall gain the whole world, and lose his own soul?" (Mark 8:36).

If you are already a follower of Jesus Christ, I would like to encourage you to share this book with your friends and family. It is an effective way to share your faith in Christ. However, we need to remember that the evidence that the Bible is inspired by a supernatural God will not, of itself, lead anyone to a personal faith in Christ. That decision to follow Christ is a fundamental choice of each person to choose spiritual life over spiritual death by responding to Christ's offer of salvation. However, the evidence supporting the supernatural origin of the Bible presented in this book may assist someone in taking the Scriptures seriously and considering the claims of Jesus Christ for the first time.

If you have never accepted Jesus Christ as your personal Savior, I pray that the evidence in *The Handwriting of God* persuades you that God has inspired the writers of the Bible to record His message to mankind. Someday you will meet Jesus Christ. Will you accept Him as your personal Savior and meet Him with open arms? Or will you reject Him and be forced to meet him as your final judge? The decision is yours.

Selected Bibliography

Anderson, Christopher. *The Annals of The English Bible.* vol. 1 & 2. London: William Pickering, 1845.

Anderson, Sir Robert. *Human Destiny.* London: Pickering & Inglis. 1913.

Aviezer, Nathan. *In The Beginning...Biblical Creation and Science.* Hoboken: KTAV Publishing House, Inc., 1990.

Ball, Rev. C. J. *Light From The East.* London: Eyre and Spottiswoode, 1899.

Blomberg, Craig. *The Historical Reliability of the Gospels.* Leicester: Inter-Varsity Press. 1987.

Blunt, Rev. J. J. *Undesigned Coincidences in the Old and New Testament.* London: John Murray, 1876.

Bready, J. Wesley. *England: Before and After Wesley.* London: Hodder and Stoughton Ltd., 1939.

Bright, John. *The Authority of the Old Testament.* Grand Rapids: Baker Book House, 1967.

Burrows, Millar. *The Dead Sea Scrolls of St. Marks Monastery.* New Haven: The American Schools of Oriental Research, 1950.

Canton, William. *The Bible and the Anglo-Saxon People.* London: J. M. Dent & Sons, Ltd., 1914.

Cobern, Camden M. *The New Archeological Discoveries.* London: Funk & Wagnalls Co., 1929.

Duncan, J. Garrow. *Digging Up Biblical History*, Vol. I & II. London: Society For Promoting Christian Knowledge, 1931.

De Haan, M. R. *The Chemistry of the Blood*. Grand Rapids: Zondervan Publishing House, 1943.

Finegan, Jack. *Light From the Ancient Past*. Princeton: Princeton University Press, 1946.

Finegan, Jack. *Archeological History of the Ancient Middle East*. New York: Dorsett Press, 1979.

Flavius, Josephus. *Antiquities of the Jews*. Grand Rapids: Kregal Publications, 1960.

Frazer, Sir James George. *Folk-Lore in the Old Testament*. London: Macmillan and Co., Limited., 1919.

Gaussen, L. *The Divine Inspiration of the Bible*. Grand Rapids: Kregel Publications, 1971.

Greenblatt, Robert B. *Search The Scriptures*. Toronto: J. B. Lippincott Co., 1968.

Jeffrey, Grant R. *The Signature of God*. Toronto: Frontier Research Publications, Inc. 1996.

Keith, Alexander. *Evidence of the Truth of the Christian Religion*. London: T. Nelson and Sons, 1846.

Kenyon, Sir Frederic. *The Bible and Archeology*. London: George G. Harrap & Co. Ltd., 1940.

Kenyon, Sir Frederic. *The Story of the Bible*. London: John Murray, 1936.

Kenyon, Sir Frederic. *Our Bible and the Ancient Manuscripts*. London: Eyre & Spottiswoode, 1948.

Layard, Austen H. *Discoveries Among the Ruins of Nineveh and Babylon*. New York: Harper & Brothers, 1853.

Little, Paul. *Know Why You Believe*. Downers Grove: Inter-Varsity Press, 1988.

McDowell, Josh. *Evidence That Demands a Verdict*. Arrowhead Springs: Campus Crusade For Christ, 1972.

Mercer, S. A. B., ed. *The Tell El-Amarna Tablets*, vol. 1&2. Toronto: The Macmillan Company of Canada Limited, 1939.

Morris, Henry M. *Many Infallible Proofs*. El Cajun: Master Books, 1974.

Morris, Henry M. *The Bible and Modern Science*. Chicago: Moody Press, 1968.

Morris, Henry M. *The Biblical Basis for Modern Science*. Grand Rapids: Baker Book House, 1984.

Morris, Henry M. *Scientific Creationism*. El Cajun: Master Books, 1985.

Morris, Herbert W. *Testimony of the Ages*. St. Louis: William Garretson & Co., 1884.

Panin, Ivan. *The Writings of Ivan Panin*. Agincourt: The Book Society of Canada, Ltd., 1972.

Rambsel, Yacov A. *Yeshua - The Name of Jesus in the Old Testament*. Toronto: Frontier Research Publications, Inc., 1996.

Rambsel, Yacov A. *His Name is Jesus*. Toronto: Frontier Research Publications, Inc. 1997.

Rawlinson, George. *History of Herodutus*, 4 vol. London: John Murray, 1875.

Richards, Lawrence O. *It Couldn't Just Happen*. Fort Worth: Word, Inc., 1989.

Robertson, A. T. *Luke the Historian in the Light of Research*. New York: Charles Scribner's Sons, 1923.

Robinson, John A. T. *Redating the New Testament*. Philadelphia: The Westminster Press, 1976.

Robinson, Gershon. *The Obvious Proof*. London: CIS Publishers, 1993.

Rule, William Harris. *Biblical Monuments*. Croydon: Werteimer, Lea and Co., 1873.

Sayce, A. H. *Records of the Past*, 5 vol. London: Samuel Bagster & Sons, Ltd., 1889.

Sheppard, Lancelot C. *Prophecy Fulfilled - The Old Testament Realized in the New*. New York: David McKay Co. Inc., 1958.

Siculus, Diodorus. *Library of History*. Cambridge: Harvard University Press, 1989.

Smith, William. *A Dictionary of the Bible*. Boston: D. Lothrop & Co., 1878.

Stoner, Peter W. *Science Speaks*. Chicago: Moody Books, 1963.

Thompson, J. A. *The Bible and Archeology*. Grand Rapids: Eerdmans Publishing Co., 1972.

Tiffany, Osmond. *Sacred Biography and History*. Chicago: Hugh Heron, 1874.

Unger, Merrill F. *Archeology and the Old Testament*. Grand Rapids: Zondervan Publishing Co., 1954.

Varghese, Roy Abraham. *The Intellectuals Speak Out About God*. Chicago: Regnery Gateway, 1984.

Vermes, Geza. *The Dead Sea Scrolls In English*. London: Penguin Books, 1988.

Vermes, Geza. *Discovery in the Judean Desert*. New York: Desclee Co., 1956.

Vincent, Rev. J. H. *Curiosities of the Bible*. Chicago: R. C. Treat, 1885.

Vos, Howard. *Can I Trust The Bible?* Chicago: Moody Press, 1963.

Warfield, Benjamin Breckinridge. *The Inspiration and Authority of the Bible*. Philadelphia: The Presbyterian and Reformed Publishing Company, 1970.

Wilson, Bill. *A Ready Defense - The Best of Josh McDowell*. San Bernardino: Here's Life Publishers, Inc., 1990.

Speaking Engagements
or
Teaching Seminars

Mr. Grant Jeffrey is available for seminars or other speaking engagements throughout the year for churches, conferences, and colleges.

Subjects included are Prophecy, Apologetics, Evangelism Training, and General Bible Teaching.

Please contact:
Grant Jeffrey Ministries
P.O. Box 129, Station "U"
Toronto, Ontario M8Z 5M4
Canada

ORDER FORM

Quantity	Code	Description	Price	Total
		Softback Books		
	BK-3	Messiah – War in the Middle East & The Road to Armageddon	$12.99	
	BK-4	Apocalypse – The Coming Judgment of the Nations	$12.99	
	BK-5	Prince of Darkness – Antichrist and the New World Order	$13.99	
	BK-6	Final Warning – Economic Collapse and Coming World Government	$13.99	
	BK-7	Heaven – The Mystery of Angels	$12.95	
	BK-8	The Signature of God – Astonishing Biblical Discoveries	$13.95	
	BK-9	Yeshua – The Name of Jesus Revealed in the Old Testament	$11.95	
	BK-10	Armageddon – Appointment With Destiny	$12.99	
	BK-11	His Name is Jesus – The Mysterious Yeshua Codes	$12.99	
	BK-12	The Handwriting of God – Sacred Mysteries of the Bible	$13.99	
		ANY THREE BOOKS OR MORE **EACH**	**$11.00**	
		Videos		
	V-1	Rebuilding the Temple and Its Treasures	$19.99	
	V-2	The Ark of the Covenant and The Red Heifer	$19.99	
	V-3	The Coming Russian Invasion and Armageddon	$19.99	
	V-4	Russia's Secret Agenda	$19.99	
	V-5	The Rebirth of Israel and The Messiah	$19.99	
	V-6	The Antichrist and The Mark of The Beast	$19.99	
	V-7	The Rapture and Heaven's Glory	$19.99	
	V-8	The Coming Millennial Kingdom	$19.99	
	V-9	The Search for The Messiah	$19.99	
	V-10	The European Superstate and The Tribulation	$19.99	
	V-12	Financial Strategies and Assault on Our Freedom	$19.99	
	V-13	Archeological Discoveries: Exploring Beneath the Temple Mount	$19.99	
	V-14	Prince of Darkness and The Final Inquisition	$19.99	
	V-15	Agenda of The New World Order and The Tribulation	$19.99	
	V-16	Rush to Armageddon	$19.99	
		ANY TWO VIDEOS OR MORE **EACH**	**$17.00**	
	ORDER THE ENTIRE FRONTIER RESEARCH LIBRARY	(All of the above items)	**$339.99**	
		Total this page (to be carried forward)		

continued overleaf

ORDER FORM

Quantity	Code	Description	Price	Total
		Total from previous page		
		Hardcover Books		
	HC-H	Heaven – The Mystery of Angels	$19.95	
	HC-S/G	The Signature of God – Astonishing Biblical Discoveries	$19.95	
		Double-length Videos		
	V-17	The Signature of God – Astonishing Biblical Discoveries	$34.95	
	V-18	Mysterious Bible Codes	$29.99	
	VP-1	Final Warning, Big Brother Government	$29.99	
		Audio Cassettes		
	AB-14	The Signature of God (2 tapes)	$15.99	
	AB-15	Mysterious Bible Codes (2 tapes)	$15.99	
	AP-01	Super Money Management for Christians (6 tapes)	$39.99	
		Computer Programs		
	PC-1	Torah Codes (educational software for IBM-compatible computers)	$call	
	MAC-1	Torah Codes (educational software for Macintosh computers)	$call	
	PC-2	Bible Scholar (educational software in Hebrew and English)	$call	
	MAC-2	Bible Scholar (educational software in Hebrew and English)	$call	
	PIB	**Product Brochure**	No charge	
		Monthly News Updates		
		Destiny Dateline Tape of the Month (12 tapes)	$89.99	
		Oklahoma residents add 7.5% sales tax		
		Canadian residents add 7% G.S.T.		
		One low shipping and handling fee (per order) for U.S. and Canada	$4.95	$4.95

*Additional shipping charges will apply to orders
outside North America*   **Grand Total** [   ]

U.S. orders: mail along with your check or money order to:
Frontier Research Publications • P.O. Box 470470 • Tulsa, OK 74147-0470

U.S. credit card orders: call 1-800-883-1812

Canadian orders: remit payment to:
Frontier Research Publications • P.O. Box 129, Station "U" • Toronto, Ontario M8Z 5M4

Canadian VISA card orders: call 1-800-853-1423

Prices effective July 1, 1997